AFTERIMAGE

A BROKENHEARTED MEMOIR
OF A CHARMED LIFE

Carla Malden

GUILFORD, CONNECTICUT

An imprint of Globe Pequot Press

skirt!® is an attitude . . . spirited, independent, outspoken, serious, playful and irreverent, sometimes controversial, always passionate.

Text permissions appear on pages 312–13.

Text design: Sheryl Kober
Layout: Kirsten Livingston

Library of Congress Cataloging-in-Publication Data is available on file.

ISBN 978-0-7627-6382-5

Printed in the United States of America

10 9 8 7 6 5 4 3 2 1

PREFACE

What the heart has once owned and had,
it shall never lose.

—Henry Ward Beecher

This book is not like me. I am guarded. I am careful. I am circumspect. I am private. I am, above all else, in control. But pain took over. This story, or whatever it is, was more than I could hold in. Besides, I needed to write a love letter, no matter what shape it took.

Lao Tzu says the Tao that can be told is not the eternal Tao. So, too, the life that can be articulated, charted, is probably not the essential life. The true life. I suppose I have tried to capture here, in the smallest measure, who my husband was. Who he very much still is. But that endeavor was strictly for me, not for anything he would have wanted. It was born of an impulse to attempt a sort of alchemy, a transmutation from words back to life.

Like Tolstoy's unhappy family, every grief is surely unique. It must find its own course. This is one, or more correctly, the beginning of one—the story of a last year and a first year. Nothing more.

CHAPTER ONE

Dear Mr. Fantasy, play us a tune,
Something to make us all happy.
Do anything, take us out of this blue.
Sing a song, play guitar, make it snappy.
                    —"DEAR MR. FANTASY"

"Mrs. Starkman," said the doctor, "sit down."

Ten months, three weeks later, my husband was dead.

Cancer is an awesome opponent. Sometimes it wins. Even when it most should not. Even when all goodness is on the other side.

This was not the ending this book was supposed to have. This was not the end my husband was meant to meet. This was a cosmic mistake. I know that for certain and I will never believe otherwise. This ending—his ending—was not written by some omniscient hand, and if it was, it was a misprint. Some might call it plain, dumb bad luck. And bad luck is part of it; bad luck contributed mightily. But it's more than that. It's something gone drastically wrong. It's a mistake.

This should have been a book about overcoming life's obstacles, about getting up in the morning and making the climb no matter how relentless and uphill, about the rewards of never giving up. Imagining that book, a triumphant tale of love conquering all, kept me going through what I continually tried to convince myself was destined to be a finite nightmare, our *annus horribilis*.

As I typed random notes into my computer, midnight after midnight, in an attempt to purge the terror, I fantasized that maybe other people treading similar waters would read my words and find some small meaning, perhaps even faith in the inevitability of steadfast perseverance earning a happy ending.

The struggle to keep on top of the medical minutiae was supposed to provide a lesson in the triumph of organization and persistence. The task of coordinating all the players in white coats was supposed to remind us that you cannot scream too loudly or cause too big a nuisance when you're saving someone's life. Descriptions of the waves of panic that washed over me when Laurence was first diagnosed—and then, for the next three hundred twenty-nine days—were supposed to transform into passages reflecting a profound and abiding sense of accomplishment, a testimony to the power of hope. Words would blossom like my husband's renewed health.

But no matter how hard I tried to pretend otherwise, no matter how I strived to mold the events of the past year into something that made some sense, this was not art. This was life.

As a screenwriter, I have been in the business of creating plots imbued with cause and effect. But there was none to be found here. No cause and effect. No setup and payoff. And, as it would happen, no happy ending. Because in life, unlike art, senselessness often prevails no matter how hard you try. And we did try. But cancer was the villain in our story, and while I emerged from this year with no glimpse of God, I began to wonder toward the end if, in fact, the devil does indeed exist, and if we were not battling him mano a mano.

There will be no revelations in these pages. No blinding insights. Just flashes of clarity about pain and fight and love that, on a good day, make this point in my life almost bearable. It is a weird, through-the-looking-glass starting point—dismally unwelcome—where hopes and dreams and the whole concept of the future are distorted at best, obliterated at worst.

I will say it right now, from the start, that the most I will be able to offer is this: for some inexplicable reason—at once miraculous and diabolical—the heart keeps beating even when it is irreparably broken.

⁓   ⁓

Laurence had a history of ulcerative colitis. We were already "going together" when he was first diagnosed. He must have been about twenty or twenty-one. I remember his annoyance at being hospitalized, hardly something on the weekend agenda of a college kid. I remember this incident particularly well because it served as my introduction to the dynamic of his family.

As fate would have it, it was a Friday afternoon when he had the misfortune of being diagnosed with the colitis—a chronic inflammation of the lining of the colon—and immediately admitted into the hospital. His father, Max, maintained a strict routine that included spending weekends in Palm Springs in order to recover from the stress of his work week as the head of a prominent, eponymous architectural firm in Los Angeles. It fell to Laurence's mother, Gloria, to chauffeur Max to "The Springs." He was simply that worn out by Friday at five. Unnegotiably worn out. He not only required the getaway, but demanded to be driven as well.

It was the 1970s, and that was the way things were in the Starkman household.

So, when Laurence ended up at Cedars-Sinai on a Friday at four o'clock, Max took it as a personal affront. I recall much high drama as Gloria, normally a larger-than-life character with a minimal brain-to-mouth censor, went through the motions of defying her husband. Even Laurence, ever the self-proclaimed outsider in his own family, dug deep and uncharacteristically urged his father to please, just this once, stay in town.

Max replied, "It's not like you're dying."

Gloria screamed briefly, then gave in and slid behind the wheel of her shiny black Lincoln Continental so that Max could nap in the backseat for the duration of the two-hour drive.

Laurence navigated the emergency hospital stay without his parents.

And I thought, *Wow, this is a different kind of family.*

There was a course of IV steroids, as I recall, and scopes and scans, no doubt. I don't remember the medical side of things all that well. I was the girlfriend. I sat and watched TV with Laurence and rolled my eyes when he instructed a friend to fetch his movie camera from home. That was so Laurence, to want to turn his weird little hospital stay into a weird little movie.

In one of the boxes high in the rafters of our catchall closet still remains stashed the Super-8 footage of him wheeling his IV down the halls, his hospital gown precariously flapping in the rear. Cut to his dinner tray arriving. Insert shot of him lifting the chrome lid to reveal a pasty mass masquerading as seafood Newburg, just the kind of thing you want to be served when you're having gastrointestinal distress. He mimed a wide-eyed, if ironic, "Mmmm" of anticipation for his reverse close-up.

After a time, Laurence's symptoms abated.

His colitis flared up on occasion, sometimes worse than others, predictably following bouts of extreme stress or after a round of antibiotics. But over the years, the flare-ups grew fewer and farther between. By the time we were married, and certainly by the time our daughter was born, the condition was more than controlled, largely a thing of the past, just a pesky detail to be explained on health insurance questionnaires.

Over the next thirty years, Laurence did as he was told. Colonoscopies every two to three years. Little snips of the colon to make sure everything was clean. They never revealed anything of concern.

I sat in many waiting rooms while Laurence lay, half-drugged, being scoped on a table. I made fun of him. Only Laurence, I often joked, having spent the previous day complaining his way through gulp after gulp of god-awful Go Lightly, the foul stuff that cleaned you out pre-procedure, sits there waiting for his colonoscopy while reading *Gourmet* magazine. Only Laurence would get up out of his recovery-room bed after said colonoscopy, discussing where we should go for lunch on the way home. (Years later, when we were all fashionably taking to the gym, and businessmen watched ESPN or the stock-market crawl while jogging on their treadmills, there would be Laurence passing his treadmill time watching Food Network.)

Only Laurence.

There had been only Laurence in my life since I was sixteen years old. For many years, I found that fact sufficiently embarrassing that whenever it came up, I sidestepped the question. Yes, we met during our senior year of high school, I would say, quickly adding that we then went off to different colleges. I went away to college in Northern California for my freshman year. Then I transferred to UCLA while Laurence went to California Institute of the Arts . . . only miles up the freeway. He then transferred to USC, only miles down the freeway in the opposite direction. We were both in L.A. We were together. So the truth is that we met our senior year of high school and had, for the most part, been together ever since. Whatever misspending of our youth we did, we mostly did together. So, during an era that put a premium on debauchery of all kinds, neither of us managed a particularly respectable job of misspending.

Only in the last several years, as I have watched so many friends get divorced or just listened to them complain, have I begun to allow myself to be proud of the longevity of our relationship. There is something to be said for having history with someone. Without it, life must lack a certain texture, I imagine, and it must be so exhausting—all those fresh starts and laborious explanations, no in-jokes or shared disappointments. Sitting across the table from someone who, when handed the dessert menu, doesn't already know whether you would rather split the flourless chocolate cake or the poached pear.

There were times, though just a few, that approached being deal breakers, but we turned them into near deal breakers, and we went on. The truth is, we (especially me) were both highly critical of other people, and when push came to shove, neither of us could imagine that there could possibly be anyone out there who would put up with us, let alone understand us, or, perhaps most preciously, make us laugh. We were one another's best friend. We got each other in a way that we both knew no one else ever would or could. Soul mates, they call it. But ultimately, the thing is, we loved each other. Always had. Always would. We were stuck with each other for what would certainly be the rest of our long lives.

Until February 28, 2006. And then the clock started ticking.

— —

Anyone who has been married for any length of time knows that conversations tend to repeat themselves. Dialogue scats through versions on a theme. You circle an exchange, refine it a bit, and settle in, until the same words, the same lines, the same speeches, are delivered over and over again. It becomes a routine.

Some are funny. Some are angry. Some are profound. Most are none of the above. They are just words that you say because that's what you've come to say in a given situation. Verbal security blankets. In-jokes. Shared history.

They say that the secret to a happy marriage is to be married for better, for worse, but not for lunch. Laurence and I were the exception that proved the rule.

Laurence had multiple professional lives—sometimes sequential, often simultaneous. Before there were hyphenates, there were filmmakers. Inspired by the often rebellious, cutting-edge independent filmmaking of his teenage years—"underground film"—Laurence considered himself a filmmaker. Happily hired to be a one-man band.

When he was very young, right out of college, he specialized in what used to be called kinestasis. *Kine* for movement, *stasis* for still. It was a form of animation popular in the 1970s and '80s that involved camera moves on still images. Laurence spent countless all-nighters filling out exposure sheets—arm-length papers divided into slots onto which the animator had to account for every single frame of film. These were the days of film rather than video. That's twenty-four frames per second. There were just as many jobs for which, due to their last-minute nature, Laurence showed up at the camera house carting a bundle of art and a soundtrack and proceeded to call out shots over the cameraman's shoulder, flying by the seat of his pants. The result—opening title sequence, montage, early music video—was usually stunning either way. Trafficking in the manipulation of images came naturally to him because he saw things differently from most people; no visual nuance was lost on him.

He edited. He directed. He was a cinematic Renaissance man.

But, either in the background or the foreground of his other careers, we were always writing screenplays together. Often, in pitch meetings, we would be asked what it was like to write with your spouse. Who did what? Who wrote the dialogue? Who choreographed the action? We developed a stock answer: she's more verbal, he's more visual. Our writing partnership may have started out that way (although never with quite such precise delineation), but over the years, any line that may have once existed blurred. We learned from each other. We absorbed each other's strengths and made them our own, just as we buffered each other's weaknesses. We quipped that we had one brain between us—on a good day—which did not, however, mean that we always agreed.

Hammering out a new screenplay involved a fair amount of "negotiating" at varying decibel levels. (I screamed, Laurence argued). But we always knew that if we disagreed about something vehemently, it meant there was a better answer out there, waiting—the perfect solution. We had come to this realization after years of writing together. If one of us believed that something didn't work—a plot point, a line of dialogue, an entire scene—then it didn't work. It really was that simple. Invariably, a better idea would present itself. We perfected our method of writing together into an intimate dance that bespoke our commitment to each other as much as any other facet of our life.

When we belonged to a writers' group briefly years ago, we were mind-boggled to meet another male/female writing team married not to each other, but to other people, committing what struck us both as a sort of creative and deeply personal adultery.

Often, we would reread something we had written and have no idea which one of us had written it. That's when we knew it was good. We'd each claim it, of course, especially if it made us laugh. One of us would be reading silently through a scene and chuckle.

"What's so funny?"

"This bit here."

"I wrote that."

The truth was, no matter which one of us had said the words, we wrote it together.

So, many days—probably most—we were married for better, for worse, *and* for lunch.

Laurence and I had one of those long-married routines at lunchtime. If we had hit a stumbling block in our writing—if the second half of Act II needed higher stakes, or a secondary character had lost his idiosyncratic way of speaking—we'd start mentioning lunch around eleven o'clock. Shame usually prevailed; no self-respecting adult can eat lunch at that hour. But by eleven forty-five or so, respectability held little sway, and we'd adjourn to the kitchen.

I could eat tuna from the can over the kitchen sink. Not Laurence. So we made ourselves a real lunch, even if it was just turning that tuna into sandwiches. And then the routine went like this. As we carried our plates to the kitchen table, Laurence would say, "We forgot the chips."

Laurence claimed that when I got pregnant, he gained weight. The middle-age ten pounds around his middle made me keep vigil over his chip intake, or at least pretend to. So I would say, "No chips for you."

"But you know," Laurence said, "chips make every day a party."

He was only partially right. Chips just added to the party in our house.

Of course, I know that every day was not a party, though the inclination now is to dip all memories in hyper-saturated early Technicolor. Friends and associates generally saw in Laurence a sunny disposition and upbeat outlook. He was, naturally, far more complex than those impressions would imply. He knew moods as overcast as the sunny days most people saw, many downright bleak.

"*Ungeblusen*," he would say, invoking his grandmother's Yiddish for the blues.

Whenever we vacationed in San Francisco, he always insisted we stop in at a little club called Biscuits and Blues. It was not my favorite place, but we made repeat visits because the whole gestalt of the joint spoke to Laurence. He liked to say that "Everyday I Got the Blues" was his theme song.

"You know why I . . .?" He would finish the sentence in various ways.

"Because everyday you've got the blues?"

"That's right," he would say.

A year after Laurence died, I went to see John Mayer in concert. "You'll never guess what song he did," I said to our daughter, Cami, when I was telling her about the show.

"What?"

"Everyday I Got the Blues."

"I didn't know that was a real song," she said. She thought her daddy had made it up.

The truth was that even when he had the blues, even when he felt morosely *ungeblusen*, you knew that Laurence felt grateful and blessed and fundamentally present. All the things that are supposed to earn you good luck with the universe. That's what people responded to in him.

And that's why it is difficult to imagine one good reason why, instead of just living my life, I didn't spend every day reveling in the party. Chips or no chips.

⌐   ⌐

The play is Thorton Wilder's "Our Town."

During the intermission between Act II and Act III, the stage has been set to signify a cemetery, the dead taking their seats in the three rows of chairs facing the audience. The Stage Manager, our narrator, informs us of time passed, changes made, and so many changes not made. Things stay pretty much the same in Grover's Corners. He tells us, too, about the dead. This is New England; the dead in this particular cemetery date way back and, of course, not so far back at all.

He remarks on the sorrow that this place has known. How the seasons come and go. How we move through them, folding grief into our everyday lives, transforming it from something wild into something we can get our arms around.

He tells us that the stuff of this life is not where the eternal resides, suggesting that even the stuff of the cosmos—the earth and the stars—is not where the eternal resides. He reminds us of what we already know: that deep in every human being, there is something eternal. That the eternal resides in the human heart.

A procession of mourners crosses the stage holding umbrellas. It is only fitting that it should be raining. Emily Webb is dead. Lovely Emily, young and full of life. Until now. Until Act III.

She converses with those longer dead, her mother-in-law and other townspeople, as she struggles with the feeling of having newly arrived here, of still being "one of *them.*" Somehow, she senses that one can go back and rejoin the living. The Stage Manager and her fellow dead warn her against doing so, but she cannot resist. She begs for one day. Just one day.

Her mother-in-law advises her that it is not wise, but Emily cannot break her attachment to life, to the living.

EMILY: But it's a thing I must know for myself. I'll choose a happy day, anyway.

MRS. GIBBS: *No!*—At least, choose an unimportant day. Choose the least important day in your life. It will be important enough.

Emily chooses her twelfth birthday.

Non-momentous birthdays. School-night dinners at the kitchen table. Playing Santa's elf at midnight. They are important enough.

Moments.

Ordinary days.

Snapshots.

SNAPSHOT

Laurence was four or five, a skinny kid with deep-set green eyes and a '50s haircut, when he saw the thing flying overhead. Huge and silent and menacing. He ran inside the house, adrenaline pumping, to warn his family: "There's a bomb! There's a bomb!"

I don't know how, at that young age, he knew what a bomb looked like, but he was right. The thing was conical, metallic, ribbed.

As it turns out, however, bombs didn't cruise over Shenandoah Avenue in Los Angeles all that much in the late '50s. The thing was a blimp. The blimp, as we are prone to say in L.A. As in "There's the blimp," or "Did you see the blimp?" as though there were only one, which, until far more recent years, there was.

Thus began Laurence's lifelong fascination with the blimp and all things blimpy.

Twenty years later, Laurence and I, already living together, were taking classes at Sherwood Oaks Experimental College, a short-lived exercise in creative education for postgraduate film-maker types, which offered a hodgepodge curriculum. Laurence was down the hall studying screenplay structure with Syd Field, the maven of the day, while I studied the fine art of screenplay coverage in a story analysis workshop.

A young woman in my class—a rather large and sturdy young woman—mentioned that she happened to be the first female blimp catcher, one of the crew who grabs hold of the tethers extending from the airship and moors it to the ground.

It was a small class, and over the weeks, most of us became friendly enough. By the end of the session, I sprung the question. "What do you have to do to get a ride on the blimp?" She explained that you had to pull a lot of strings, pun intended. There were waiting lists and VIPs and corporate mucky-mucks. It helped if you were one of those. Or you could know a blimp catcher who nodded with simpatico when you explained that your boyfriend had a thing for blimps.

I set a date for several months in the future. Nonetheless, it was a confirmed date. (I believe that flying is a means, not an end, so I would not be joining Laurence on this particular adventure.)

We waited. And we waited. When we spotted the blimp during those intervening months, Laurence eyed it with a sly smile. They had an upcoming rendezvous, this airship and he.

Laurence may not have slept the night before his ride on the thing. He was little-kid, night-before-Christmas excited.

When he came home, he was—you might say—flying high. He talked about how the passenger compartment of the blimp felt no bigger than the interior of a station wagon. What a different view it provided from any he'd ever seen. How quiet it was. And mostly, how the thing wanted to go up. Planes, he explained, feel like they have to work to stay up by comparison. The blimp wanted to drift upward. It wanted to be in the sky. It fought being returned to Earth.

At a family event some time earlier, Laurence's mother had held court as she often did. She may have been dipping into her repertoire of favorite stories: being awarded a pair of roller skates as a teenage beauty-contest winner, the circumstances of her proposal from her husband, the births of her children. She went on to talk about her four kids, summing each of them up in a single word. When she came to Laurence, her second-born, she said, "Laurence—he's my dreamer."

It took some effort for Laurence to remain earthbound. He was inclined toward the clouds.

CHAPTER TWO

For at least a month before that last day in February, 2006, I had found myself studying Laurence's face at odd moments.

"You don't look good."

"You look kind of pale."

"Do you feel all right?"

I later realized that when we would go out to dinner with another couple, I'd compare Laurence's pallor to the other man's. I'd glance back and forth between the friend and Laurence, Laurence and the friend, more than once during the course of a dinner, trying to discern whether all middle-aged men begin to look a bit ashen and lose the pink in their lips. I would check out the lighting to see whether Laurence was sitting under a yellowish bulb or in the heaviest shadow at the table.

Every time, Laurence paled in comparison. Literally.

I rationalized that we had had a stressful year. Our only child, Cami, had gone off to college, two thousand miles across the country to a small liberal arts school in eastern Ohio. That alone was enough to drain the color from her father's face, I figured. For those first few months there, it was as though we were living in a cartoon where the sun shone everywhere but over our house; we missed her that much.

Professionally, we had lost the option on a book we had been trying to set up as a movie for the past four years. Just when it looked like a deal was within reach, our option expired and we lost the rights to the project. The piece had been unusually dear to us. We had written several drafts of the screenplay. It had taken considerable work to get it right, but we were finally pleased, and Laurence took the loss of the option very hard. He grew a little greener around the gills.

But by February we were more accustomed to Cami being out of the house—indeed, out of the state, across the country—and we had turned to another project, sliding an idea from back burner to front and enjoying the writing. We began to talk about this new phase as empty nesters with unexpected enthusiasm. The desolation was waning, and we realized that this time in our life actually held enormous promise.

We got excited. We talked about traveling more. We talked, amusingly enough, about taking ballroom dancing lessons (if I, a long-ago dancer, promised not to lead). We signed up to be mentors in the Young Storytellers program with the Los Angeles City schools. We were fingerprinted (as the law requires for work with schoolchildren) and trained. We even harbored a secret plan to consider the program as a subject for a documentary, a field that Laurence had worked in as a young filmmaker and for which he had been hankering once again. We couldn't wait for our first session with the kids, set for Wednesday.

Laurence's routine colonoscopy was on Tuesday.

Too long in the waiting room. At first, it just felt like a little too long. I checked my watch. I walked next door to a bagel shop and bought a cup of tea. I eavesdropped on a doctor telling a woman, older than I, that her ninety-year-old mother was fine. No polyps, no nothing. That's when I started to worry. It flashed across my brain: *that's not going to be us.* I did everything possible to tamp down the thought, but my heart was pounding. Weirdly, it had been pounding for some time for no good reason.

A strange feeling of dread had, in fact, hung over me for the previous several months—half fear, half butterflies—as though something seismic were about to happen. My sixth sense just couldn't decipher what it was. Sitting there in the waiting room, I suddenly knew it was going to be horrible. I pushed the feeling down farther.

In another fifteen minutes, I'll be thinking how stupid I was. Why do I do this to myself?

Then . . . *After the next fifteen minutes go by.* And . . . *the next fifteen.* I revised my thinking. *It will all be fine. It's always fine.* Soon I realized that I had been staring at the same page in my book for forty-five minutes. I gave up and closed the book. Then I opened the book and stared some more.

If I pretend I don't have this feeling that the bottom is about to drop out of my life, it will go away.

A nurse finally came out and led me into the back of the endoscopy center. Laurence lay there, just like he had after all his past colonoscopies. He said that the doctor had told him nothing. My heart pounded a little harder.

The nurse didn't look me in the eye. The room—not even a room, but a curtained-off section of the recovery holding tank—began to shrink into a tunnel.

Finally, I spotted the doctor approaching. I had never met him before. Laurence's longtime doctor, the one who had done all the previous exams, had retired seven years before. Because Laurence's colitis had been such a nonissue for so long, a thing of the past, he had let a few extra years pass before settling on another doctor.

Although I had never met this new G.I. specialist, I knew he was our doctor. I could tell by the look on his face.

He stepped into our cubicle and said, "Mrs. Starkman, sit down."

"No," I said. "I won't." *If I don't sit down, you won't say it. And if you don't say it, it won't be real. Let me salvage a few more seconds of normal.*

But he said it anyway.

Cancer.

The end of our life as we knew it.

I'm not sure of what happened next.

Laurence swore. "I fucked up. Goddammit. I'm so stupid. I fucked up."

I cried and held his face. "You're going to be all right. You're going to be fine. It's all going to be okay."

I can't remember now if I believed that or not. I know that I wanted to, so desperately that I verged on a metaphysical commitment to creating matter out of energy. Or, in this case, dissolving matter—about nine centimeters of matter, we would come to find out—with the sheer force of my will. But undeniably, the look on the doctor's face told me this was not good, not good at all, and that look haunted me with every rise and fall of the roller coaster onto which we had just unwillingly been strapped.

Time and space did a funny telescoping thing for several minutes.

Laurence kept saying, "Call the Young Storytellers people. You have to tell them we can't come tomorrow." He repeated the request over and over, and I kept saying, "Don't worry about it. It's not important."

But he was adamant. It must have been his way of hanging on to the present instead of propelling himself into the future— suddenly, in a heartbeat, such a horrible place.

In an obvious case of shooting the messenger, we would replace that doctor within several days. But right then, this guy was calling the shots. He ordered an immediate CAT scan.

I phoned my sister and her husband to pick us up because I didn't think I should drive—or even could drive the few blocks to the scanning facility. What I really needed was a friendly face to tell us it was going to be all right.

My brother-in-law is a cardiologist, but surely he must see people cured of cancer all the time. Healed like magic. Just a blip in their lives. Survivors, they call them. If other people can be survivors, we can be survivors. We work in Hollywood, after all. If that isn't the very definition of surviving a continuous barrage of blows to the spirit, then what is?

By the time Mila and Tom arrived, I was swirling in the realization that our life would never be the same. I knew that even the best-case scenario would mean tests and scans, sleepless nights of waiting for results, constant worry. At that point, I could not see a way clear to coping with worry so constant, so present, so intense. I am not a person who does well when something is hanging over me, regardless of the magnitude. I was the kid who always got her homework done the minute I got home from school, for no other reason than the fact I hated knowing it was waiting for me. No leaving dinner dishes in the sink until the next morning. No dental cleanings past the six-month due date. Anal, compulsive, neurotic, efficient. Whatever you want to call it, that is who I am. Surely this degree of worry would be too much for me.

As I stood there next to Laurence's bed, I kept thinking, *I am going to lose my mind. Even if this turns out to be a blip in our life, I will lose my mind anyway, knowing that every few months, bad news could be dropped again. Like this. Like this bad news. This bad news which is actually happening.*

Now, these many months later and Laurence dead, it seems absurd that I was so terrified of the worry, such a two-bit stalker compared to grief.

But in that moment, the concept of a lifetime clouded by worry consumed me. I remember being confused about what was real. *Surreal* literally means "on top of the real." And there was indeed a new overlay on reality, born of panic and terror, that warped every moment for the next few weeks. Maybe it was the adrenaline. Everything pulsated. Each minute moved, simultaneously, at hyper-speed and molasses-crawl. For that prolonged period in the waiting room I had been imagining the worst. Now, I began to wonder if I had just talked myself into the worst, thought myself into a nightmare. Rod Serling must be lurking in the corner, smoking a cigarette. Maybe I was having some sort of hallucination. I kept thinking what everyone who ever lives that moment must think. *This is not what happens to us. This is what happens to other people.*

I am still thinking that.

I presume I will think that every day for the rest of my life. And I will shake my head every single day as I try to process the fact that I am now other people's other people. We all do it: stretch our brains for reasons why—why the horror that happened to someone else will not befall us. Especially with cancer. Excuses. Reasons. Folly. She smoked; he drank; she only went to the doctor when she was having a baby. The list goes on and on. Proof positive why it won't happen to us. Without the explanations, without enumerating the ways in which foolish other people magic-markered a bull's-eye onto themselves, we could not sleep at night.

So, I am providing a reason to hang on to. Laurence became complacent and missed a colonoscopy. He went six years between tests rather than the prescribed three for someone with his medical history. He forgot about that history. He was living life. He slipped up.

But the truth is, we will never know if that made a difference. February 28, 2006, might have unfolded in exactly the same way whether he had had the test precisely on time or not. I will never know if those extra years made a difference in our outcome— never. But, for the rest of my life, I will feel guilty for having been oblivious, for letting them pass. Orbiting that uncertainty describes one of the circles of my personal hell.

Either way, fate dealt us what it did that day, and all the days thereafter, and there was no going back to February 27 and all the days before. I like my truth served up in Fred Astaire movies. In *The Gay Divorcee*, Rodolfo Tonetti, the buffoonish Italian gigolo, mangles the aphorism, "Chance is the fool's name for fate." It comes out, "Fate is a foolish thing to take chances with." He got that right. It's a random universe, capricious and nihilistic. But even so, test taken or test missed, fate surely is a foolish thing to take chances with.

Fate booted us down the rabbit hole and there was no clawing our way out. If I had known at that moment that I was taking up permanent residence there, deep down that hole, I might have actually lost my mind just as I feared I already had, right there within the curtained-off cubicle where my husband lay on a narrow recovery bed, his face contorted with fear and disbelief and rage.

And something else hung between those curtains, too. The cancer. This new thing that would always be in the room with us from then on. It was an illusion to believe that the doctor was calling the shots. He may have maneuvered the scope and studied the mass it encountered. He may have ordered the CAT scan, and then the PET scan, but it was the cancer that had already begun to call the shots. And it would for the next year.

In many ways, I suppose, my challenge now is to say, *Okay, you won. But that means you cannot call the shots anymore.* That's the struggle, because even now, with my husband dead, the cancer flaunts its monstrous victory and continues to call the shots twenty-four hours a day. When it wins, it wins big. One person may stop breathing, but it never takes just one life.

My sister, Mila, drove me the few blocks down Wilshire Boulevard to where Laurence would have a CAT scan, while her husband, Tom, drove Laurence. I never asked what they talked about in the other car—if Tom offered words of reassurance or if Laurence elicited a promise to take care of Cami and me if the day were to come when he wouldn't be here to do that himself. I am ashamed to admit that I didn't think, *Don't let him be in pain.*

I'd had no experience with life-threatening illness. It didn't occur to me what kind of suffering might lie ahead.

Instead I said to my sister, "I'm going to be alone. I'm going to be all alone."

Maybe if I said it out loud, I could wrap my mind around the fact that suddenly, this was a very real possibility. Or maybe if I said it, it would sound so impossible that it simply couldn't be true. Strangely, it had never occurred to me, in all our years together, that there was ever a possibility that someday I might be alone. That I might grow old alone.

By the time we arrived at the radiation clinic, I knew the possibility would hover around me for the rest of our life. I just didn't know how soon it would morph from possibility into probability into certainty.

Laurence sat silent in the waiting room. I cannot remember if I held his hand. I hope I did.

When they called him in, I stepped outside. It was one of those midwinter L.A. days that prompt people to move to Southern California. Blue skies, sun shining. How could it be that all was not well with the world? I knew that I had to call Cami, our daughter. The only reason she happened to know in advance that Laurence was going for his colonoscopy was because an opportunity had arisen for us to attend the Academy Awards the following week. This coincided with Cami's spring break, which meant she could join us at the awards.

The night before, she and I had been discussing the invitation. I had said, "Let's wait till after Daddy's test to say yes." I don't know why I said that. I normally would have launched into a conversation about what to wear. I should have assumed that everything would be fine, just like all those times in the past. But there were those pesky butterflies, so much so that when we lay in bed that night—the night before the test—watching TV, I put my head on Laurence's chest and said, "Promise me this test is going to be fine." He did, of course. As far as I know, that was the first promise to me he ever broke.

I knew that Cami would be waiting to hear, eager to find out if she was going to the Oscars. I knew, too, that she would be starting to worry by now. Too much time had gone by. It's strange how there is always too much time to worry when suddenly the clock starts ticking for time to run out. I pulled out my phone and called Cami. In the back of my mind, the thought was already forming. No matter what happened—if this disease took Laurence's life, if it punched a hole in the rest of mine and let the air hiss out—it was not going to ruin hers.

"Hi, sweetie. I have some bad news. Everything's going to be fine, but . . ."

—   —

Everything that happened in the next few hours amounted to a good news/bad news tug-of-war. Lymph node involvement—yes. Liver involvement—no. I cried either way, whatever the news. All you can do is cry at first. And, uncharacteristically, beg for Xanax. Not to take the terror away; nothing could do that. Just to take enough of the edge off so that I could function, if just minimally. Functioning seemed critical.

I found myself sitting across from our internist to get the prescription. He had been our family doctor for ten years. Sorrow and disbelief washed across his face, but there was something else, too. Guilt.

"Is there anything you want to ask me?" he said.

I shook my head.

"Anything you want to say to me?"

I shook my head.

I could not formulate anything to say to anyone. He may have wanted me to accuse him, to rail, *How could you have let this happen?* Maybe if I had said it, it would have lessened his own guilt, but even at that moment, I knew this was not his fault. What difference did it make now, anyway? That's what I would think over the next many months, but right then, I could only shake my head no. *I have nothing to ask. I have nothing to say. I am in a foreign land and I do not speak the language.*

Family Doc handed me the prescription for Xanax. Me, who doesn't even drink socially simply because I don't like the taste or the headache. That's how deep I had already trekked into this foreign land.

He called later that evening to tell us he had gotten Laurence an appointment with a top oncologist for eight o'clock the next morning. But once he'd recited name, address, and suite number, he said what was really on his mind.

"I've got Laurence's file in front of me. Three years ago we discussed his finding a new G.I. guy."

"It's not your fault," I told him.

But I knew he was sitting there, after hours, with Laurence's file sprawled in front of him, berating himself for not being more insistent.

And so was I, trying to blame him, wanting to serve him up all the blame. *Here, take it.* But I couldn't. I was too busy blaming myself.

And, most agonizingly, so was Laurence. Blaming himself with a vengeance. In the ten months that lay ahead, Laurence's guilt about those extra years between exams was so excruciating that it frequently dwarfed everything else—the fear, the anger, the pain.

It was with guilt and shame that he called his siblings and a few friends. His mother had died thirteen years earlier, his father just a very few. Shortly after his father died, Laurence announced quite matter-of-factly one day, "Well, I'm an orphan." It was, of course, not a happy announcement. But on this day in February, I think he was glad he did not have to also phone his parents with this news—the news no parent should have to hear.

Including mine. In the whirlwind panic of the day, it fell to my sister to inform my parents. Laurence and I were spared their faces—my mother's involuntary gasp, my father's summoning of steeled determination. Several days later when a gap in doctors' appointments afforded me a few minutes to stop in at their house, just eight minutes down Sunset Boulevard, my father wrapped me in his arms and promised me it would be okay. "This is a tough one," he said, "but it's going to be okay. I just know it." In that moment, I believed him, because I wanted to. And because my father never lied to me.

But that night, that first night, we lay in bed, Laurence and I, nowhere near sleep, Xanax notwithstanding. (I was lucky if it brought me down to somewhere approaching a normal adrenaline flow.) We repeated this conversation all night.

"I'm so stupid."

"You're going to be okay."

"Fuck. I'm so fucking stupid."

"You're going to be okay. It's going to be fine."

We invoked the name of a celebrity or a friend or the friend of a friend who had become a "survivor."

But mostly we cried.

— —

The next morning while Laurence showered and dressed, I warmed my hands around a mug of tea downstairs in the kitchen. It had not even been twenty-four hours, yet this kitchen was a strange place; the world was a different place. I remember realizing that a long day lay ahead, going from doctor's office to doctor's office, and that perhaps I should try eating something. I swallowed two bites of yogurt. Then vomited them into the kitchen sink.

How could we—Laurence-and-Carla, Carla-and-Laurence— be sitting in an oncologist's examining room? We had heard this doctor's name before. It seemed as though he had miraculously saved the life of a friend of ours just a year earlier, a friend who had a much rarer breed of malignancy than Laurence's garden-variety colon cancer. If this doctor could accomplish that—could send our friend to the electronics convention in Las Vegas, to which he and Laurence made an annual pilgrimage—then surely this brilliant mind could fix Laurence. That's all we needed.

Just fix this, I pleaded silently. *Just fix him. Just get us back to normal. I don't need better than normal. I'll never need better than normal.* It had been less than twenty-four hours since our diagnosis, and already normal seemed like a lifetime away. And it looked so beautiful, like a mirage shimmering in the distance. Ordinary quotidian life. It doesn't get much better than that. *I already knew that,* I thought. *I'm not someone who needed to be taught that lesson. No fair.*

Surely this doctor could get us there. It couldn't be that far back to everyday life.

I listened to him talking on the phone outside the door.

"How big is this thing?" he was asking.

Laurence started to say something to me, but I shushed him. "He's talking about you."

And thus began my obsession with every little detail that any doctor would ever say. And every nuance in the way he said it.

Then Oncology Man entered the room—that's how I wanted to picture him, with a giant "O" on his shirt. He opened with, "This isn't incurable."

That became our mantra for the next many months. But in my own brain, I parsed that sentence often. *Why did he put it that way? Why didn't he say, "This is curable?"* Something about the double negative left me uneasy. Uncertainty hung in the semantic difference between the two statements. It gnawed at me, even as I repeated the sentence the doctor had actually spoken, over and over, to Laurence, and, more constantly, to myself. "Remember, this isn't incurable." But there were moments when my mind fell deep into the gap between the two phraseologies, the one used and the one not used.

Oncology Man told us he would always give it to us straight. We could count on him for that, he promised. There would never be any sugarcoating.

When someone tells you that, you have to respond by saying, "That sounds great. We wouldn't have it any other way." Anything else would constitute the medical version of political incorrectness. But part of you wants to say, "I'll take as many spoonfuls of sugar as you've got, thank you very much."

I envied Laurence's characteristic lack of interest in all things medical. Talking himself into the most positive scenario possible, he chose to assume that if they removed his colon, there could be no more colon cancer. Oncology Man explained otherwise.

"Where would it come back?" Laurence asked him.

I almost interrupted. *Don't say it. The words will make it come true*. But I kept my mouth shut.

"Liver, lungs, abdominal cavity, and bone."

Shit. You can't go around taking out all those body parts one by one.

We told Oncology Man that we would go anywhere, do anything. He nodded, but that wouldn't be necessary, he was quite sure.

We came out of our first meeting with Oncology Man ready to do whatever needed to be done. Remarkably, he had already consulted with the guru of gastrointestinal cancers at the University of Southern California's Norris Cancer Center. I didn't know if he had done so as a special favor to our family doctor, if it was standard procedure, or if there was something extraordinary about our case. I knew this was a time when you didn't want to be extraordinary.

That night he would be presenting Laurence's case to the "tumor board" there. It was hard not to picture, for just an instant, a room full of tumors, all shapes and sizes, gathered around a conference table. Tim Burton meets Pixar.

There would be surgery followed by chemotherapy. Oncology Man assured Laurence that the chemo specific to his disease would be "relatively manageable." By the time we left his office, we had stepped onto a moving sidewalk that would deposit us at doctor after doctor after doctor.

We felt good about the oncologist. He had a rumpled, sort of absentminded-professor demeanor. He dressed almost exclusively in khaki pants and blue oxford shirts. No necktie or white coat. On one visit, I noticed a good-sized rip in the sleeve of his blue shirt. I took that to mean he had no time for such mundane cares. He was in the business of saving lives. In fact, he made a point of telling us a few of his life-saving tales. We knew from the grapevine that he was the son of a well-respected rabbi, and that he had the reputation of being really smart. Better yet, he was always on the phone, picking the brains of other really smart doctors.

Laurence played an unconscious game of telephone with this word-of-mouth reputation and began telling people his oncologist was "some sort of genius." I was never exactly sure of what prompted the leap from smarts to genius, except that Laurence needed to rocket himself there wholeheartedly, to a place where a genius was in charge. He was also the kind of doctor with whom you could feel a connection. He was a person, and he knew that you were a person.

The next few days were like a game of dodgeball forming in a schoolyard. We were building the best possible team. We pick you. And you. But not you. The surgeon came on board next. She was . . . well, she was blunt. She cuts people open, after all. She drew diagrams of the gut and talked about bags and pouches, terms I assumed she was using interchangeably but, it took me a week to realize, turned out to be two completely different things.

As we sat in her office, we began to negotiate precisely how much of Laurence's colon would go and how much would stay. (Had he not had his particular history, that discussion would have been more straightforward, but the colitis lurking, although long dormant, in his background—or, more specifically, in his interior—made the conversation much trickier.)

We weighed the options, balancing subtle and not-so-subtle quality-of-life issues against the odds for life, period.

Interspersed with the medical pros and cons, I inquired about the picture of the surgeon's children behind her desk. What are their names? How old are they? Where do they go to school? I was trying to say, *We're both women here, we're both mothers . . . help me.* She answered perfunctorily. This was not a coffee klatsch.

At one point, Laurence said, "My wife's afraid that—"

Scary Surgeon Lady interrupted, "I know what your wife's afraid of. She's afraid you're going to die."

That about said it all.

She still scared me, but now I respected her. She got it. And she was going to save my husband's life.

We interviewed other surgeons, but Scary Surgeon Lady was the one. She returned our calls after hours from her home. She talked about the two-year marker and the five-year marker. If he's clean that long, we might get to feel out of the woods. I thought, *It won't matter if we're out of the woods or at the beach, I will have taken up residence in a padded cell.*

We tracked down Laurence's longtime G.I. doctor, now retired in Laguna or La Jolla, one of those beachy towns to which people retire. Scary Surgeon Lady talked to him at length in order to glean any pertinent information.

She also pushed for the most radical surgical option. Laurence questioned that advice repeatedly. He wanted to keep as much of his body intact as possible. She argued for taking the maximum, invoking "the gold standard of care." But then, when

Laurence stepped out of her office to have blood drawn by a nurse, Scary Surgeon Lady leaned in close to me and whispered, "Don't tell him I said this, but if it were me, I'd be thinking the same thing."

What does that mean? I wondered. And then I thought, *Surely she doesn't think I'm not going to tell him she said that.* Is that doctor-speak for "off the record, but pass it on"?

When Laurence reentered the room, she returned to her party line. I told him her secret the minute we left her office.

Next on board was a new G.I. guy.

The son of friends of my parents phoned me one night during that first week. I didn't know him, had never met him, but I was aware that this older couple had two sons: one an architect, the other a gastroenterologist. I assumed he had somehow heard of Laurence's diagnosis and was calling to offer assistance. In fact, it turned out that he wanted to pick my brain about schools for his son, a soon-to-be kindergartner. I answered all his questions, singing the praises of the school Cami had attended from kindergarten through twelfth grade. I offered to write a reference letter for the little boy, asking about his interests and temperament, and then I asked the really important question, the one that had been burning since I'd answered the phone: "Are you the architect or the doctor?"

He was the doctor. *Jackpot.* Someone with a family connection, albeit oblique. Laurence was in his office the next day.

And so Sweetheart G.I. Guy joined the team. That's exactly what he was from start to finish. Here's the thing. He always told me we could do this, that beating this thing was doable. You need someone like that on your team, and I thank him for that. I am not suing him for giving us false hope, as many physicians fear will befall them. Without hope, false or otherwise, the last months of Laurence's life would have been too bleak to envision. I believed that Sweetheart G.I. Guy believed, and that was good enough for me. That was a gift.

SNAPSHOT

"In-A-Gadda-Da-Vida" is almost a joke now. If you want to compose a mental image of '60s psychedelia—undulating amorphous light-show amoebae—you play "In-A-Gadda-Da-Vida" on the stereo of your mind to accompany those visuals. It's heavy. In 1968, it blew your mind. All seventeen minutes, five seconds of it. From the opening organ riff to the final explosion of guitar.

But for Laurence, it was all about the drums.

He'd been playing drums for a few years by then. He had asked his father for a drum kit and a deal had been struck. Drum kit on the condition of drum lessons. No problem. Laurence got the drum kit. He breezed through the lessons, never really learning to read drum notation properly, but finding himself in possession of a fairly remarkable ear that enabled him to play what he heard. Nothing fancy, no complicated jazz rhythms, but everything you'd ever need to get by playing rock-and-roll. It was the '60s. Was there anything but rock-and-roll? So he faked his way through the lessons, wowing his teacher despite his secret inability to read music.

And then he joined a band—many bands as the years went on. The Impulses in junior high. The White Cadillacs in high school. (And in recent years, his midlife-crisis band, The Lower Companions. That meant a new set of drums and a renewed passion for drumming, which, as it turned out, he had missed more than he had known.)

Rock-and-roll. A string of girlfriends. Back then there was only one other element Laurence needed to feel like he owned the world. In Southern California, it had to be a car.

Laurence's first car was a heap. A metallic-blue Chevy Impala, christened the Blue Jew because of its broken nose. (Political correctness was not even a gleam in a sociologist's eye back then. It was all about what was funny to a bunch of teenaged boys, themselves mostly Jewish by birth, but worshipping at the altar of irreverence more than anything else.)

Whenever "In-A-Gadda-Da-Vida" came on (usually the abbreviated AM version), Laurence would crank up the radio. He would reach over the wheel, steering with his forearms, and pound out the drum part on the dashboard. Alone or with a friend riding shotgun, freeway or surface streets, coming home from school or from a party at two in the morning.

The '60s. It was a good time to be a teenager.

CHAPTER THREE

The thirteen days between diagnosis and surgery provided their own kind of torture. It wasn't just the waiting, but also the ongoing process of decision-making as to how extensive the surgery should be. Even though we felt good about our team, we consulted with, I think, two more surgeons and two more G.I. guys. There was more than one phone conversation with Laurence's old doctor. We lived the old joke: "Ask three doctors; get four opinions." Take it all—the entire colon and the rectum. Take just the colon. Take the left side, or the left side and part of the right side.

Many days were spent discussing every millimeter of my husband's gut. One doctor said there was no guarantee that Laurence's history of colitis had anything whatsoever to do with his current condition. Another proposed that his history made him "a cancer-making machine." Laurence sided with the former. I wanted to do whatever the latter recommended if it meant it would give us the best odds. But no one really mentioned odds or percentages or success rates. At that point, we were all focused on getting that fucker out of there. After that, we would do whatever was necessary to make sure it never came back.

Ultimately, we negotiated to save the rectum. I told friends that this was a sentence I had never expected to say in my life, but it was the truth. Apparently, my sweet husband's rectum was remarkably pristine—so much so that upon reviewing the results of his colonoscopy and examining him personally, Scary Surgeon Lady wondered if he was sure his decades-old diagnosis of colitis had been accurate. Except for that pesky cancer, his colon appeared remarkably dandy.

The second and equally confounding component of the surgery decision involved reattaching or not reattaching—in other words, living with a bag for the anticipated six months of chemotherapy, and then reattaching afterward in a second surgery. Naturally, Laurence wanted the reattachment done right there on the table. But Oncology Man suggested the side effects of the chemo might include such ferocious diarrhea that the six-month course of chemo might have to be interrupted or even halted altogether, a major oncology no-no. That's what you don't want. You want to forge ahead, machete-ing your way through treatment, until you come out the other side.

Laurence acquiesced. The bag, while anyone's nightmare, would only be temporary, and would allow him to soldier through the chemo. Just six months. You can do anything for six months. Then there would be a second surgery, not terrifying like this upcoming one, but wondrous and exciting and downright celebratory. We would get there, we were sure. How could we not? We were people who had done everything right, and, more important, we were people who had never been anything but grateful for all of our good fortune. People like that are rewarded. This would be our bump in the road that we would look back on. In just six months. Over and done with.

We shopped for new sweats for Laurence to wear while lounging about the house post-surgery. He chose several pair of his favorite brand, soft and cozy. I piled them onto the counter at Frontrunners to pay for them. As I handed over my Master-Card, my eye fell on a basket of yellow rubber Livestrong brace-lets. I held one up, showing it to Laurence—partly acknowledging Lance Armstrong, the name that springs to the lips of every newly diagnosed cancer patient, and partly asking if we should buy one. He shook his head no. That wasn't him. He wasn't a real cancer patient. He wasn't taking up residence in the world of cancer; he was just passing through. In a perverse twist of the old Groucho Marx joke that came to us via Woody Allen, we were not going to be members of a club that had just recruited us so rudely.

I joked that the whole episode would one day be relegated to an anecdote of how we came to own a La-Z-Boy. Amid all the researching and interviewing and hand-wringing about the extent of the surgery, Laurence had declared, "I'm getting a La-Z-Boy." Though this went against the grain of the design aesthetic that permeated every aspect of his life, he plainly had a mental picture of himself—feet up, head back at just the right angle—that constituted what recovery should look like. I was not about to argue.

We bought a forest-green leather floor sample and moved it into our bedroom in place of one of a pair of floral easy chairs, which was promptly relocated to Cami's room.

"It's not really so ugly," we said.

"It's kind of kitsch," we said.

"It doesn't matter. It will just be for a while," we said.

We could not have predicted that within the year, the revolving furnishings in our bedroom would tell a different tale.

— —

The surgery happening in the OR scheduled for Laurence's surgery was running long. St. John's Hospital in Santa Monica is a busy place, and, strangely, Laurence was not their only patient. My obsessive-compulsive disorder was in full throttle. For several days, I had been thinking, *All I have to do is get to five o'clock on Monday.* With every minute that ticked by, I had to amend my personal deadline.

Cami had returned home three days before, having begun her spring break a few days early. She and I sat in the prep room—an antiseptic study in beige—while Laurence lay there, still whole. A friend had given Laurence a book of Sudoku, the kind of thing that would never hold any interest for him, but which I began to work, one puzzle after the other. Seven here, four there, no eight possible in that square, can't put a six or a three in this one. The little puzzles required concentration of precisely the level I could muster—just enough brain occupation to focus my anxiety on rows of numbers rather than the reality of the day. When I neared the end of a puzzle, filling in the final squares faster and faster until the last one completed the grid, it gave me a momentary boost. It buoyed me enough to cling to the illusion that the world could be as orderly as the subdivided three-inch squares on the page.

It was impossible to reconcile the reality in that prep room with the fact that so recently, we three had been merrily obsessed with finding the perfect college for Cami.

— ~

Stoma.

You learn a lot of new words when you find yourself talking to doctors and nurses. They throw them at you as though you've been trained to catch them.

A stoma is a piece of the intestine brought to the outside of the body through a surgical opening in the abdominal wall in order to bypass the normal intestine, or what's left of it. Why would anyone ever want to know that? And who knew there were special nurses dedicated to stoma care?

While we were waiting in the pre-surgery room, our stoma nurse arrived, a brittle woman with bleached-blonde hair. A mask of black-and-blue bruising butterflied across her nose and under her eyes. I assumed she was recovering from a nose job. Over the course of the next several days, during which she would become a regular visitor to Laurence's room, I learned that she had, in fact, taken a fall. But her initial battered appearance just added to the bizarreness of the day. Despite her raccoon eyes, she was friendly and forthright, and acted like we knew exactly what would happen next. We didn't.

She was there to mark Laurence's abdomen—a little "X" marks the spot with magic marker—for where his ileostomy should exit the body and meet the bag. She fiddled with the waistband of his khaki cargo pants and we joked about the ten pounds, all right there around his middle, that he'd been promising to lose for the last twenty years. Those few pounds were making the placement tricky. What if he lost them all post-op? What if he didn't? You want the bag to hit in just the right spot, preferably below the waistband of your pants, so that your pants don't interfere with comfort, and no one ever knows it's there. Except you, of course, when you have to change it five or six times a day. As the stoma nurse measured and marked, I knew what Laurence was thinking. *I should be going for the reattachment on the table. I've made a mistake.* But he said nothing.

And so he found himself with a good-sized dot of ink on his lower-right abdomen where there soon would be a hole. And a stoma. We would look forward to it being closed up again. When that day came, we would celebrate. Like there was no tomorrow.

When Scary Surgeon Lady popped in, she was wearing her street clothes. And purple suede pumps. I figured someone who wore purple shoes would understand how important it was that she fix my husband.

"Great shoes," I said.

"Thanks." Who was I kidding? If she hadn't been interested in talking about the daughters in the photographs, she wasn't going to waste time on pumps. She informed us they'd be getting a late start. We had figured that out already.

But she was chomping at the bit, and that was good. She wanted to get in there and do her thing. She was ready to show that cancer who was boss.

She was just about to walk out the door of the little pre-op room, when, for some reason, she felt the need to editorialize. "I told my partner what you finally decided." We knew exactly what she meant. Every conversation we'd had with her—many of them well after office hours—had been about the extent of the surgery. She knew how we'd agonized. She went on: "When I told my colleague, she said, 'What?!'"

The decision as to exactly how much to surgically remove was precarious; whatever confidence I'd had shook like a BB rolling out of its tiny hole in one of those miniature handheld mazes. Now I felt like I'd never be able to finesse it back in. Though it didn't seem to bother Laurence—that kind of thing wouldn't—I couldn't figure out why she'd felt compelled to drop this bomb at just that moment. *That's why she's a surgeon,* I thought, I hoped. *That's why she must be an especially brilliant surgeon. People are just body parts to her.*

Yet this was the same woman who had whispered to me, "I'd be thinking the same thing." If it were her, she had confided, she'd want to keep as much of her body as possible. No kidding.

Finally, two hours late, the orderlies arrived to wheel Laurence down the hall. The anesthesiologist had already shot him with something delightful to take more than a bit of the edge off. He would remember nothing of the thirty minutes before the surgery. He was downright loopy. Cami and I kissed him and kissed him again, then followed behind. We burst into laughter when we heard his voice receding down the hallway. "I could really go for a hamburger."

— —

Forget the misty gloom of the ancient Greek Hades. Forget the frozen, blizzard-swept plain of the Buddhist Arbuda. Never mind the thorny tree whose bitter fruit intensifies the torment of the Islamic damned. Or the good old fiery pit. Not to mention gonzo chef Gordon Ramsay's kitchen.

Hell is a surgical waiting room.

I sat between Cami and my sister. Our old friend, Larry, sat across. I stared at the television mounted high on the wall, channel fixed. I stared at my book. I crossed to the coffee stand at the other side of the room, passing the volunteers manning the desk—older women with badges clipped to the pockets of their blue smocks. We had checked in with them when we entered the waiting room, their domain. Starkman. We're here for Starkman. We're the ones you want when the phone on your desk rings and the person on the other end says, "Is there anyone there waiting for news on Starkman? The surgery's finished. He's fine. He's cured." We're the ones waiting for the good news.

I'm the one over there, staring at the television, staring at my book, staring into space.

I should never have asked Scary Surgeon Lady how long the operation would take. It ran over by two hours plus. By the end of that time, the rest of the assembled personnel—Mila, Tom, and Larry—were growing as distracted with dread as I. Only Cami seemed somewhat calm, due in part to a congenital inability to measure the passage of time (definitely not inherited from her mother), and, more significantly, to the fact that the frame of reference afforded her by her entire life up to this moment did not encompass the possibility that anything could go wrong.

It's true that there had been a remarkable absence of life-and-death bad news in my own life story—the most significant instance of loss being the death of a dear friend in his thirties. But my imagination more than made up for what personal experience had spared me. Besides, even though you may not believe you now actually find yourself in this situation, in this waiting room filled with the ashen loved ones of strangers anesthetized on tables down the hall, part of you knows your number has to be called sooner or later.

My brother-in-law, Tom, and I peered through the glass in the door that led down that hall to the operating rooms. I was worried that Tom was so worried. He's a doctor, after all. But he had also lost his father to cancer, and his sister. He studied the faces of the doctors emerging from their ORs.

"Is that her?" he asked.

I shook my head no.

"Is that her?"

No.

He had stood in a waiting room like this when his father was on the table and when the doctors had appeared—too soon—they said what you never want to hear. "We just closed him back up." Nothing to be done.

We couldn't hear that now. It wouldn't be taking so long if that were the case . . . right? Not Laurence. Not Cami's daddy. *Forget about me,* I thought. *This can't be happening to my little girl's father.*

In the days when I was the mother of a small child and my fear-of-flying nerves grew more jagged, as new parents' phobias often do, I would fasten my seat belt and then help Cami with hers as we prepared for takeoff. I calmed myself by thinking, *We're completely safe because nothing can happen to this child.* I enlisted that thinking now. *Laurence is more than my husband. He is Cami's daddy. Nothing can happen to her, so nothing can happen to him.*

And suddenly, there she was, walking down the hall, talking on her cell phone. Scary Surgeon Lady.

"That's her," I said to Tom.

By the time she had passed through the door, we—the people who had endured the waiting—were all standing there, sick with fear. Tom put his arm around me. I might have looked like I was going to faint.

"There was omental involvement," she said.

I had no idea what that meant, though I knew, obviously, that involvement of any kind was not good. It was the opposite of all good things. Contained, confined, encapsulated—those were the words we wanted to hear. Not involvement.

Mila stood directly across from me in our little circle around the surgeon. I saw my sister's face grow white and her eyes dart upward in the universal expression of *Oh no*.

My head slumped against my brother-in-law's chest.

The surgeon remarked that Laurence appeared "very well nourished." That should have been funny, but not today. She explained that the omentum is the "watchdog of the abdomen," a layer of fat and tissue that protects the vital organs.

"It did its job," she said. It had taken the hit for the liver and the stomach and everything else in there that we really need. And she thought she had gotten it all. No more cancer.

But the subtext was unmistakable. *There had been a lot to get, more than she had hoped.*

Here's the deal with cancer. It's sneaky. You never know when a rogue cell will go floating away, undetected, to take up residence in an unsuspecting place. You just never know. Even if you wear a white coat for a living.

The surgeon finished the briefing, leaving us, the gathered huddle, to stare at one another, trying to determine how much relief she had actually afforded us.

Our Family Doc passed through the glass door to check on Laurence in the recovery room. He reported back that Laurence was in a lot of pain. I was not surprised; he had just had a body part removed. We could deal with pain as long as it would buy us a happy ending. We'd pay absolutely any price for that happy ending. *Sign us up for pain. If that's the bargaining chip, give me a heaping helping, too.*

There is a fine art to not asking questions you do not want to know the answers to. It is not an easy thing to do, especially for our generation—a generation who came of age drunk on our own power, the generation who chanted "No rain!" at Woodstock, believing that communal energy could control the elements and stop a biblical downpour. When magic did not do the trick, we became a generation trained to believe that knowledge is power. Give me a term to Google. If I know enough, I can fix it. So when Family Doc and I were standing alone in the hallway of the hospital, positioned between the surgical waiting room and the restrooms, I asked, even though part of me did not want to know.

"What does this mean? Omental involvement?"

"It means there's a greater risk of recurrence."

Maybe knowledge isn't power. Maybe it's torture.

I nodded. Of course that's what it meant. But that wasn't going to happen. I wasn't going to let it. Even after the previous two weeks, I still believed we had some control over the situation. Even as our life was spinning out of control, I thought that I could affect the outcome of where it would stick to the wall of the centrifuge when it stopped spinning. I just had to remember not to look down, like in one of those old-fashioned amusement park rides where the bottom drops out and you spin and spin and spin, plastered against the side of the giant barrel by centrifugal force. If I had looked down, then I would have seen that the bottom had already dropped out.

Laurence spent hours in the recovery room. His brothers joined us. We loitered in the hallways and in the "Family Room," where pamphlets promised help in LIVING WITH CANCER. I dismissed them as unnecessary. In my naiveté, in my arrogance, in my desperation, I thought, *We will not be living with cancer. We are here so that we can live* without *cancer. Normal. We're here to resume normal.* That word—cancer. It fixated me so completely. I did not know how soon I would have thrilled to the mere suggestion of "living." At that moment, I just wanted to see my husband.

It was midnight by the time he was wheeled into his room. Only Cami and I went in. Laurence had specifically told me in advance that we were the only people he wanted there. "Just you and Cami. Nobody else."

We watched as the orderlies transferred him from the gurney to the bed. The anesthetic was wearing off, and he was in agony the like of which I had never witnessed. I couldn't bear watching Cami watch her daddy's pain. But I'd stick to the bargain—trading this pain for life.

As the nurse checked IVs and tried to make Laurence comfortable, Laurence looked up at him and asked, "Do you mind if I swear?"

The nurse didn't mind.

Laurence let loose.

Then he looked over at Cami and me and said to the nurse, "These are my two pretty girls."

A strange sound came out of Cami—strangled, primal, percussive. For a moment, I thought she was laughing, but no, she was sobbing.

"Was she smiling?" Laurence wanted to know. "Was she happy?"

He was talking about the surgeon.

"Yes," I said. "She was really pleased. She got it all. She was smiling."

Laurence smiled.

Cami told him, "She was smiling, Daddy. She had a big smile."

Laurence nodded. He could do this. It was going to be okay.

I wasn't sure if Cami actually believed the surgeon had been smiling. She was like her father; sometimes she saw what she wanted to see. Sometimes she believed so hard she actually saw an altered reality.

I leaned in close to him. "The worst part's over. The waiting's over."

With the surgery, the opening salvo had been fired, and we were now ready to do battle. From here on out, it was all about recovering and returning to blessed normal.

Nothing in my life had prepared me for the possibility that the known could be more daunting than the unknown.

CHAPTER FOUR

In the following days, I worked Sudoku after Sudoku at Laurence's bedside. There was something so reassuring about the puzzles' intrinsic order: the lines within the grids, the boxes within the squares, the process of elimination that yields the disproportionately satisfying act of filling in columns, one number at a time. Sudoku make sense. Sudoku are sublimely manageable. Sudoku imply an ordered universe where enough study and stick-to-itiveness create a gratifying finished product—a whole.

Between puzzles, I wandered into the corridor or into an unoccupied room nearby to return phone calls. Laurence's room was so cold. The hall was cold. The empty rooms were cold. I bundled myself in sweaters, heavier each day. And I cried. I cried in the corridor and I cried in the vacant rooms. And I really cried in the car on the way home to catch a few hours' sleep. I cried until I could only scream to make myself stop, and I screamed until I could only cry to stop the screaming. I turned on the radio, but when you have been with someone your entire life, every song holds a memory.

My CD changer happened to contain an eclectic mix just then. Five of the six CDs were too painful to listen to, but the sixth, oddly, was *The Best of the Rat Pack*. I discovered that the only track that got me home without producing hysterics was Dean Martin singing "Volare." When he sang, everything was right with the world.

Dino on the "Repeat" button night after night for the ten-minute drive home.

Let's fly way up to the clouds
Away from the maddening crowds.
We can sing in the glow of a star that I know of
Where lovers enjoy peace of mind . . .

Once home, I stormed through mail and e-mail, phone messages and lists. So many lists—items Laurence wanted from home (books, headphones, beanbag neck pillow, cozy socks, See's butterscotch lollipops); a growing catalog of nearest and dearest whose calls of well-wishing I'd yet to return; small household chores too many days neglected. I rampaged through the house, then flung myself into a hot bath, trying to warm a chill too deep to be thawed. Yet too antsy to lie there in the tub. Just in and out. Nightgown on and into bed. Crumb of a Xanax and Letterman, the TV on sleep timer in a vain hope that the combination of chemistry and cathode ray would put me out before the TV flickered off. Usually not.

Then up at dawn or before, ticking off the items on the to-bring-to-the-hospital list as I gathered them up from around the house and tossed them into a tote bag.

At the hospital, the days blended one into the next. Nurses rotated in and out of our room, checking the numbers that flashed on all the machines to which Laurence was attached. I brought different pillows from home nearly every morning, trying to find the right combination to make this bed—this ten-thousand-dollar bed, we'd been informed—comfortable. It could raise and lower you millimeter by millimeter, isolated body part by body part—head, back, feet. On the panel along the side of the bed were buttons: FOOT ADJUST, HEEL SUSPENSION, an icon that looked like a key, and diagrams depicting straight lines at various angles. It boasted a panel dedicated to elevation, another to the mattress, and one to alarms, including an "exit alarm." Alert Security—Laurence Starkman making a break for it! The bed inflated section by section at intervals. It did all these things as though it had a brain, but the one thing it could not seem to do was offer a comfortable position. So Laurence engineered a construction of pillows behind his head and neck, under his arms, wedged between his knees.

I smoothed and readjusted, then admonished him not to get too comfortable. After all, he was coming home soon.

The verdict to be delivered by the biopsy results still hung over us, but Laurence didn't seem to think about it, so I tried not to either. It felt like it was easier for him. Coping with pain demanded all his energy. Coping with fear was demanding all of mine.

The curse of the screenwriter molded my imagination. I envisioned how I would handle whatever kind of news the biopsy would bring. I pictured myself seated at Laurence's bedside, Scary Surgeon Lady and Oncology Man entering together, a duo of superheroes, to dispense the news. I tried to write a scene that would end with, "And so, since this was the easy kind of cancer you had there, we're home-free." That's the scene I was rehearsing.

When the moment came, I was standing in the hall with a nurse, Laurence undergoing some procedure on the other side of the door. The nurse was talking to the surgeon on her cell phone. (What did nurses do before cell phones? Strapped to their waists like six-guns, they now seem as critical to their arsenal as a stethoscope or thermometer.) Then, with none of the ceremony I'd anticipated as buildup to the dissemination of this information, the nurse handed me her phone.

"We got the pathology back," said Scary Surgeon Lady.

I don't remember her exact words, but they didn't sound anything like the ones I had scripted, the ones that were supposed to nudge me back closer to normal. They sounded bad. Bad enough so that when I heard them, I slid down the wall just like a scene in a different kind of movie, the kind of scene that makes you think, *People don't really do that.* It even felt like a movie. Just not the movie I'd been writing in my head.

Later that evening, Oncology Man stood by Laurence's bedside to elaborate on the findings. The particular type of cancer cell, he explained, was very aggressive. And there were what he called "a number of lymph nodes involved."

In an exercise of character building that nearly pulled a muscle, I bit my tongue and did not ask precisely how many. I knew, even in that split second, that whatever the number, I would obsess about it. I would see it flying toward me as I lay in bed at night. I would see it swirling as I stirred the milk into my tea. It would be a huge, chiseled mountain of a number, positively unscalable. It would be everywhere, like a *Sesame Street* number of the day. No reason to know. And if I didn't know, I could still pretend that a "number of lymph nodes" referred to three or four or five, even if the pit of my stomach was believing twenty or thirty or one hundred. So I didn't ask. I adopted a don't-ask, don't-tell policy that went against all my instincts, except for the most fundamental one of self-preservation.

Laurence didn't ask either. But then again, he wouldn't. *What's the difference?* he would say. Three or thirty, he was sure he was going to be okay.

From the moment he came to after the surgery, he told everyone, "They got it all. I'm just doing the chemo so it won't come back." And he believed that absolutely. He believed it so strongly and so completely that there were moments when I believed it, too. But it was harder for me temperamentally.

A friend who visited shortly after Laurence got home from the hospital remarked that if one of us had to get sick, it was a good thing it was Laurence. "You," she said, nodding toward Laurence, "are a glass half-full kind of person. Whereas you, Carla, are a there's-something-wrong-with-this-glass kind of person."

We laughed when she said it. We laughed because we knew she'd nailed us.

The part that she didn't have to say was that whichever one of us had gotten sick, it was happening to both of us. We were both swimming in that half-full, half-empty, cracked glass, no matter what.

⚊   ⚊

Stoma Nurse reappeared a day or two after the surgery. The bruises from her fall were healing, though her face was still discolored. When I asked her, she conceded that she was still in a good deal of pain. I made it a point to inquire about her progress every time I saw her. My goal, fluctuating between conscious and subconscious, was easy to analyze. Make these people our friends. Make them see that we two, Laurence and I, are people who love each other, that we're people who have a daughter, so they'll try as hard as they've ever tried for anyone. Of course, I knew that they try equally hard for everyone. They're professionals. But something gnaws at you, wondering if there is an extra half-percent to be had, and, just in case there is, tap-dancing in every way you can think of to tip it your way.

Basically, she had come to introduce Laurence to his stoma.

"It's red like the inside of your mouth," she said.

He was normally the more squeamish of the two of us, but when she unbandaged his lower abdomen and revealed the bulge of intestine—a protrusion of insides now out—he didn't flinch.

To me, however, when Stoma Nurse first unveiled the fifty-cent size stub of intestine, it was as though she had flipped the switch on a neon sign declaring my husband a cancer patient. She handed him a folder full of information on caring for the stoma, and lists of contacts for ordering supplies as though they were party favors.

She experimented with various templates to find a fit for the opening of the disc that would sit over his stoma and attach to the colostomy bag. Laurence's stoma seemed to be a little less than uniform in size. I knew that if he had to be shaving tiny slivers of plastic with an X-Acto knife in order to make the pre-cut saucer fit perfectly, he would do that. A slightly imperfect stoma would have a happy home with Laurence Starkman.

I left the room, barely making it out the door before dissolving into tears.

Sweetheart G.I. Guy happened to be coming down the hall.

"I'm sorry," I said. "The stoma nurse is in there."

"Is this the first time you've seen it?"

I nodded.

He understood. That's why he's the Sweetheart G.I. Guy.

—　—

Originally, the surgeon had estimated that Laurence's postsurgical hospital stay would last five days. As with the duration of the surgery, she had underestimated. This meant that seven days after the surgery, Laurence was still in the hospital, and Cami's spring break was ending. She bummed a ride to the airport with a friend returning to the same school in Ohio.

We held each other for a long moment before I ushered her into the car.

"It's going to be all right," I assured her. "Everything's going to be fine."

"I know."

We both meant it, too. She was going to return two months later, her freshman year completed, and her father two months closer to perfect health.

In our old life, our normal life, I could never have imagined being relieved to have Cami gone, back east to college. But that morning I was. The task ahead seemed easier if there were no world beyond the hospital. I could focus my attention like a laser, with no distractions. I needed for no one else to inhabit our world.

Gradually, that world inside the hospital was beginning to expand. Laurence moved from the bed to a chair, to a few steps down the hall. Then to the nurses' desk. To the picture window at the end of the corridor, where a statue of Jesus greeted us, arms open. And then, to making laps around the entire floor. Around and around, trying to figure out why anyone would select such dizzying swirls of teal and khaki for the carpet.

Laurence didn't peek into other rooms. He didn't want to see wizened old people, the hollows of their cheeks sunken with world-weariness, straining to sit up, shuffling from bed to bathroom with elastic socks stretched tight around their bony calves, or sleeping, slack-jawed and mouth agape. Instead, we made puns about the signs outside their doors: DAILY WEIGHT. FALLS RISK. MEASURE OUTPUT. We had no signs next to our door. We weren't like them.

One afternoon, Laurence became nauseated. Violently. They suspected an intestinal obstruction. Nurses and techs invaded the room and snaked a nasal-gastric tube up Laurence's nose and down his throat into his stomach. He sat on the edge of the bed and swallowed that tube, gulp after gulp, while I stood behind him on the other side of the bed. The private nurse we had hired clamped a beefy arm around my shoulder and shook her head *No*, admonishing me, *Don't cry*. Or, more specifically, nodding toward Laurence, his back toward us as he swallowed and swallowed and swallowed some more, *Don't let him hear you cry.* The nurses praised him, telling him they had never seen a patient swallow one of those tubes so unflinchingly.

"It wasn't so bad," he said.

But they continued to marvel. It was impossible to know if they were telling the truth or just offering the verbal equivalent of a lollipop after a shot, but even our private nurse confirmed to me how remarkably he had accomplished the miserable task.

It worked for me. *Great,* I thought, *he's the best patient that ever was.* He was certainly among the kindest and most appreciative to the nurses. I didn't care how—I just wanted him to continue racking up brownie points. They had to be worth something karmically. When it would come time to redeem them, like so many Skee-Ball tickets, I wanted the biggest prize on the top shelf: absolute health and exquisite normal life.

After the procedure, Laurence lay back down. They hooked the tube up to a suction pump. They suspected the obstruction was preventing the downward motion of everything that should have been heading in that direction, so that it had begun backing up instead. The pump would do the work of peristalsis, the work that his post-op sluggish digestive system was not up to doing. It whooshed, a constant white noise, for the next several days, until they decided to try disconnecting him. No more nausea.

At which point, everything seemed fine. We had made it over that hurdle. We picked up speed toward recovery. Day by day, we walked the halls, lap after lap around the floor, trying to keep ahead of the acrid odor which wafted in the wake of the cleaning crew. We admired the surprisingly decent art as though we were strolling through a gallery. Within the week, I had become one of those people who know all the nurses by name.

"Good morning, Lisa."

"Are you feeling better, Barbara?"

"Seven o'clock so soon, Nico?"

I shoved See's suckers and bags of cookies at them, a plea for special care in the form of sugar. But I didn't really want to become their best friend. I just wanted to get out.

We made it out on day ten. Two private nurses were scheduled to return home with us, one for day and one for night. Laurence had only been home for a few hours when the nausea returned, that ferocious nausea which had necessitated the pump.

By two in the morning we were in the emergency room, accompanied by our home night nurse. She was meant to be downstairs on the couch in our den, at the ready, while we slept upstairs. Why wasn't anything going as written? She and I sat in the little ER cubicle as Laurence lay there, struggling to get comfortable.

"Are they going to have to operate again?" I whispered to her. She didn't know.

I knew these questions were unfair, out of her purview, but I couldn't help myself.

"What do you think is wrong?"

She didn't know. She was scared, too. It was obvious.

During the past several days at the hospital, we had forged one of those foxhole bonds, she and I, screaming at the contestants on *Deal or No Deal* along with Laurence. "Don't be so greedy, you fool; be happy with what the banker is offering you!"

Then, each night around eleven, she ushered me out the door, insisting that everything was under control and that I should go home and get some sleep. She always promised that she would call at any time of the night if I were needed. I would leave, conflicted—exhausted and eager to wash off the smell of disinfectant, to try to eat something that did not come from the cafeteria—and feeling guilty for wanting to get out, for wanting to slide between my own sheets, even though I knew I'd be too engulfed by the loneliness of my own bed to sleep. But I would go, driving home with Dino, then phoning to say good-night, often two or three times.

But now at four in the morning, after having been home for only a matter of hours before returning to the emergency room, our night nurse was not so confident. When morning came and her shift ended, we still were not sure exactly what was going on in Laurence's gut. Whereas she was usually the one sending me home from the hospital to get some sleep, this time I insisted she do the same.

By the time she returned the next night, Laurence had been checked back into the hospital. Over the course of the day, the crisis had subsided. The nausea had passed. All scans indicated that if there had been an obstruction of some kind, it had resolved itself. Scary Surgeon Lady explained it away as a phenomenon not unlike a kink occurring in a garden hose. When I asked her what we should do if this happened again, she suggested, "He could spin on his head." She wasn't really kidding. The kink just had to unwind itself.

Gun-shy, our A-team of doctors kept Laurence in the hospital for another four days to make sure his intestines didn't coil or kink or do anything untoward. This time his intestines cooperated. He started to look better. He felt better. Our laps around his floor of the hospital got faster and faster. When they released him the second time, day fourteen after the surgery, we felt convinced it would be for good.

Our private-duty nurses came home with us just as they had four days earlier, one for day and one for night, but thankfully, they didn't have much to do. After just a few days home, Laurence dragged the day nurse into the study to play the drums for her, and she realized there was no more reason for her to stay. After a few more shifts, the night nurse said good-bye as well, assuring us that, "Someday I'll just be a distant memory." I was ready to remember her, to hurl her into the past. Remember it all as if it were a dream.

The 'round-the-clock nurses were replaced by a visiting nurse who dropped by every few days. Every time she rang the doorbell, I was reminded that we were still a household requiring medical attention. On cue, at the sound of the bell, I became a bitch. In spite of my snippiness, she was always friendly and cheerful. A slightly pudgy redhead who chattered about her grandchildren, she took Laurence's vital signs, charted them earnestly, and helped with the care of his stoma. This involved shaving the area around the stoma so that the adhesive for the bag could best stick to the skin, then fitting the sticky disc, and replacing the bag. The bags used and recommended in the hospital were reusable. They required flushing out and were, in general, a nuisance. One of the first things Laurence did when he got home from the hospital was hit the Internet. He found a supplier of disposable bags that would make life easier and more pleasant, and ordered a few cases for immediate delivery.

As the days went by, the protrusion of gut began to cooperate as well. It evened itself out so that, within a few weeks, the nurse declared that she was no longer necessary. Laurence told me that he did a better job than she did anyway. He was able to slap a standard-issue disc on there, attach the bag, and go on his merry way. He did this with enormous aplomb, no fuss, as though he were performing just one more step in anyone's daily ablutions, like brushing your teeth.

Friends dropped by. I was reminded of a teacher of one of the prenatal classes we took before Cami was born—Lamaze or infant CPR—who admonished the husbands (or significant others) that a crucial part of their job was to run interference when friends came calling. It was my turn to be the policeman now, keeping the visits short, not caring if I bruised a guest's feelings.

I ended up alone in the kitchen with one friend who was duly impressed by Laurence's appearance and energy, not to mention his credo: "It's all gone. I'm just going to do the chemo to make sure it never comes back."

Encouraged by this party line, our friend asked me, "Not so worried anymore?"

I couldn't answer. I just raised my eyebrows as if to say, "I wish." By nature, I always have a decent reserve of worry on board. Much as I would have liked to, I hadn't yet come close to running out.

Laurence continued to recuperate at home for another three weeks before beginning chemo. He was to have a port-a-cath inserted under the skin through which the chemo would be infused. This way, he would not have to have a new line opened into a vein for each treatment. This procedure was to have been piggybacked onto the big surgery of a few weeks earlier, but after three attempts, Scary Surgeon Lady had been unsuccessful in doing so due to an anomalous twist of Laurence's artery. She had determined that it would be best to have a radiologist insert the port with the help of a fluoroscope for better imaging. A few days before Laurence's first scheduled chemo treatment, we returned to St. John's for the procedure.

I watched again as they wheeled Laurence down the hall. With undue optimism, I had brought a book to read. But I couldn't concentrate. Instead, I flipped through magazines and returned a few phone calls. One friend provided me with a blow-by-blow of the previous night's *Grey's Anatomy*. I couldn't concentrate on that either. I felt like a kid with ADD lost in algebra class. I endeavored to follow who was sleeping with whom at Seattle Grace, but soon gave up. I didn't care. *Grey's Anatomy* was irrelevant. Laurence's anatomy was all I could think about.

He lay on a table a few doors away as a radiologist snaked a catheter into an artery. This time, all went smoothly. Laurence emerged with his port in place, a silver-dollar-sized bulge under the skin just below his left collarbone. Its removal, post-chemo, would be another great day, a day to look forward to.

We all smiled when the radiologist said, "See you in six months."

"See you in six months," we replied.

Oncology Man had assured Laurence once again that this particular protocol of chemo was fairly well tolerated. Hair loss would be minimal; nausea, mild and treatable with medication; fatigue a factor, but generally manageable. All that said, Laurence was terrified the night before his first scheduled treatment. It was one thing to know you were sick but to still feel fine; it was another to feel rotten. Well tolerated, manageable, minimal—these were promising words, but it was still chemo—a drug cocktail designed to target the evil cells as specifically as possible, but inevitably wiping out healthy cells along with them. Laurence was scared of the chemo in a way he had not been afraid even of the surgery. I could say nothing to make it better. There are certain things that cannot be made better; you only hope that your being there, that not going through it alone, makes it a little better. Waiting for chemo was one of those things.

We arrived at Oncology Man's office early on a Wednesday morning and were introduced to the routine. Laurence's blood was drawn in the lab across the hall, as would become the drill before each treatment. Then we toured the chemo suite, an entire side of the office building in which our oncologist had his clinic. Rows of recliners ringed each section of the room. Although we were there by eight a.m., several patients were already hooked up, individualized killer cocktails dripping into their bodies through IV lines. Plastic bags of clear liquid hung from IV poles at every recliner.

Some patients wore headscarves to cover their chemo baldness. Others looked frail and peaked. Still others appeared quite robust. Though Laurence was only three and a half weeks post-op and had lost that ubiquitous ten pounds and then some, he fell into the latter category. Proudly, I might add. He looked pretty damn good.

Chemo nurses are a special brand of angel. They run these rooms, administering life in a slow drip. With grace and good humor, they smile and assure the frightened and apprehensive into their chairs, then ease the needles into their patients' arms, or, as in Laurence's case, into their ports. They permit you to bond with them, never fearing their own anguish if a fight is lost.

In the beginning, two particular nurses tended to Laurence. One had survived breast cancer twenty years ago. This was her way of giving back. The other had eight children of her own. I guess this was her way of getting out of the house.

They kept us looking forward. If we just kept doing that, we knew, soon enough we'd be looking back on all of this. "A distant memory," our nurse had promised. That's the way time works, after all. You wait and you wait, and then the thing you've been

waiting for has come and gone. Laurence promised me repeatedly that life would be "better, sweeter," but I begged him not to
ask for anything more than what we'd always had.

Normal was as good and as sweet as we needed, and more
than most people got. Cruising the supermarket aisles in search
of new food. Sneaking onto a construction site during a neighborhood stroll to check out the progress. Sitting across from each
other at our partners' desk, navigating a plotline. We were lucky
and we knew it. Weird, eccentric maybe—not living a life that
looked like most other people's—but lucky. Sometimes when I
met girlfriends for dinner, I enjoyed myself, but driving home, I
usually thought, *Aren't I lucky? I have such good friends, but I get
to go home to my* best *friend.*

Now, as I sat in the chemo room watching my husband get
hooked up to the first of several bags that would drip, drip, drip
into him for the next six hours—poisoning him to make him
well—I wondered how I'd come to assume that mere gratitude
would protect us. How foolish I had been. I didn't want Laurence to be so presumptuous as to ask for more. Our normal
was already better, sweeter, I told him. That's all we need. And
surely we'll have it again after the chemo, after the port-a-cath is
removed, after the reattachment surgery. After.

On that first day of chemo, it seemed unthinkable that normal would never return. At the same time, it was a struggle
to remember how cozy normal had felt when we had been all
wrapped up in it like a childhood blanket.

Laurence had packed a survival kit to see him through the
hours there. Snacks and gum and Pregger Pops (nausea-quelling
lollipops I'd spotted in the pharmacy); his iPod; and his portable
DVD player with an assortment of DVDs: *Don't Look Back* and

various documentaries about the British invasion. Since our trip to England several months earlier, including a magical day in Liverpool, Laurence had spent hours surfing the Net for books and videos about the Mersey Beat and the early British pop scene. Little did he know when they had started arriving in the mail under what circumstances he would find the time to watch them.

The chemo nurse talked us through what would happen, zipping through the order in which the various chemo drugs would be administered: Decadron (a steroid for good measure), Oxaliplatin, and Avastin. Avastin was a relatively new drug of the anti-angiogenesis type. *Anti* as in "against," *angio* as in "blood," *genesis* as in "beginning." It aims to cut off the blood supply to the vessels that feed the cancer cells. Sounded like a plan. Finally, Laurence would be hooked up to the more-traditional colon cancer chemo drug, the aptly named 5-FU—a drug with attitude.

Becoming acquainted with the routine of drug delivery was only part of it, however. Welcome to the world of side effects. The nurse handed us drug company pamphlets and a royal blue tote bag. Inside were fleece gloves intended to bring relief from the neuropathy threatened by the Oxaliplatin. I had no idea what that meant. *Neuropathy.* She explained the condition—numbness, tingling, iciness of the extremities—but we didn't really understand the potential severity. How bad could it be if a pair of plush gloves in this lovely swag bag could make it better? She cautioned Laurence against reaching into the refrigerator and to avoid icy drinks, warning that the nerve damage could become permanent. Still, I thought, *No nerve damage for us. We're on our way back to normal.*

Thankfully, not every chemotherapy comes with nausea. If Laurence experienced any, it was mild and handily eased by an oral medication called Kytril. The chemo nurse stuffed several sample boxes into our goodie bag, explaining that Laurence should take the pills preventively, not to wait for a wave to turn him green.

A few recliners over, a chatty woman wearing a head wrap was laughing with her nurse about her "chemo brain." I had never heard the term before, but a ripple of acknowledgment spread through the room. Patients nodded, nurses chuckled, as if to concur almost wistfully, "Ah yes, the old chemo brain . . ." I made a mental note of something more to fret about, to be on the lookout for.

Here's the odd thing about a chemo suite—well, one of the odd things. There's a lot of banter. People tend to introduce themselves to the patient in the next recliner before they busy themselves working on their computers or knitting or reading.

It's an ongoing joke in my family that my sister knows everyone west of the 405 freeway, a main north-south artery that cuts through Southern California. Sure enough, within the first few minutes of chatting with the patient opposite Laurence, I discovered that he and his wife knew my sister. Friends of a friend. The husband was the patient, a distinguished gentleman with gray hair and a close-cropped beard. He looked up from his laptop on which he was updating the website he had already established to keep his friends and family abreast of his condition: a rare lymphoma. Within minutes, he had vowed we would all be there to support one another, no matter what. *We've just got ordinary colon cancer,* I thought. *This poor guy thinks maybe he's not going to make it.*

Laurence's nurse stuck a needle into his port. So began the drip down the tubing from the plastic bag hanging on the IV pole into his body. A healthy hit of Benadryl came first to preempt any potential allergic reaction. The chemo suite was divided into several pods, each with four to six recliners. A dozen nurses flew from patient to patient, disconnecting empty medication bags, hanging new ones, adjusting drips. Laurence put on his headphones, turned on his iPod, closed his eyes, and checked out. He was sitting there, in the middle of the busy chemo room, but, like Elvis, Laurence Starkman had left the building.

Throughout the months ahead, when people asked if it drove him crazy to sit there for those long hours, he always told them, "I have no trouble doing nothing." But he was never really doing nothing. Something fascinating was always going on in his head, especially if he was listening to music. Never in my life did I hear him complain that he was bored.

I, however, remained acutely aware of our surroundings. As any number of radio shrinks would say, that room was not a healthy place for me to be. So we developed a routine. Every other Wednesday, I dropped Laurence off in the morning, watched him enter the building carrying his tote bag stocked with food and distractions, and then he called me when it was time to pick him up some five or six hours later.

I rationalized that it did Laurence no good for me to flit around him, growing so anxious and distraught that it took me days to recover—the very days when he himself was at his physical low in the chemo cycle, often preternaturally fatigued. He didn't seem to mind if I didn't hold watch, chair-side, while the plastic bags of chemicals were switched and the drip speed adjusted. In fact, he claimed to prefer it. I'm sure he did. I wouldn't have wanted to look at my face either.

So every other Wednesday I dropped him off and picked him up. He emerged from the building a little paler than he'd entered and wearing the "pack," a pump about the size of an old-fashioned transistor radio. It delivered the 5-FU extremely slowly into his port over the next forty-six hours. When everything was quiet, you could hear its little burst of mechanical energy every ninety seconds or so. Its cord was long enough so that Laurence could place it on the floor under a pillow to muffle the noise while he slept, and out the door of the shower with the rest of the pack wrapped in Saran. Occasionally, the line would crimp, causing the alarm to beep. But in general, it was just another cancer accoutrement—part weapon, part reminder.

Laurence wore it until Friday, at which time I dropped him off at the office again, this time just for fifteen minutes, to get disconnected. The thing began to beep when it was nearly empty, then more rapidly when it was completely empty. The beeping usually began on our ride to the office. Our timing was impeccable—just another indication of how we were doing this curing cancer thing just right.

These every-other-Friday disconnect appointments were usually in the late morning, so I would wait for Laurence at the IHOP across the street. We got the routine down so well that he would phone me when he was leaving the doctor's office, happily unencumbered once again, and I would order for him. Cheese blintzes or Swedish pancakes, well done. We weren't worrying about cholesterol just then, though when the waitress set down his plate, I always said, "When this is all over, you can't eat that anymore." I was banking on the fact that there would be a time when saturated fat would matter again.

We would smile over our pancakes in a leatherette booth at the crummy IHOP and tick off another treatment, a mini victory, a step closer to normal.

"One down, twelve to go."

"Two down, eleven to go."

The course was to be six months long, May through September. That's what Oncology Man had told us at the outset. I had counted thirteen treatments in that period of time. I flipped the pages of the calendar repeatedly, counting them out one after another, checking and double-checking, hedging my bets against any surprises due to miscalculation. We were ecstatic after treatment number six when Oncology Man clarified that he had been figuring a standard two treatments per month. Six months was meant to be synonymous with twelve treatments. We celebrated, able to scratch off one treatment without actually having to go through it. And that put us fully on the other side of the halfway mark.

"We're doing it," I would say. "We can do this. This is doable."

In a perverse way, the task was energizing. We were on a mission. Unambiguous, defined, calendared.

Even though I was preoccupied with charting the ups and downs of the chemo cycle, I look back on those first few rounds, oddly, as a sort of honeymoon period. Laurence was still recovering from the surgery, so neither of us expected much of him. We stayed home and received guests who told him—truthfully—how great he looked. I offered snacks every two to three hours as though my husband were a toddler. We watched a lot of TV, vicariously globetrotting with chef Anthony Bourdain, smiling at each other to acknowledge the hard-boiled brilliance of his narration. We got caught up in shows like *Big Love* when we otherwise might not have made the commitment required by an ongoing soap opera of a series. I perused the daily television schedule with a new enthusiasm, becoming familiar with obscure programs and giving other pop favorites a chance. So involved in the escape offered there, I actually voted online for the next Food Network Star. We watched movies as they arrived from Netflix instead of letting them pile up. We got through the day together, and that was enough. That was plenty. We nested. If we kept our world small, the outside world could not attack.

Even so, we knocked on wood a lot.

Laurence kept telling friends, "They got it all. I'm just doing the chemo so it won't come back." And then we knocked wood.

My knuckles should have been black and blue.

At one point during this period at home I stopped wearing my watch for days on end. Why bother? I realized the only purpose my watch served was to remind me of how many hours to go before I could put my nightgown on again. I began climbing into bed earlier and earlier, partly because scratching off another day meant moving one day closer to normal. But also, to be candid, because I couldn't wait to pop that baby dose of Xanax on my bedside table. Years before, I had secured a prescription for the anti-anxiety medication before flying, using one or two from a bottle of fifteen that had then expired on the top shelf of the medicine cabinet. Now, I felt like a drinker waiting for the cocktail hour. I joked that I was going to drive straight from Laurence's second surgery—the happy one—to the Betty Ford Clinic. Maybe it wasn't really a joke, not entirely, but I didn't care. I thought, *Whatever gets you through the night.* And this was one helluva long night.

Oddly, I may have stopped wearing my watch, but I didn't stop wearing makeup. When a dear friend lay dying in a hospital bed twenty years earlier, I found a room in the hospital where his wife could sneak away for a two-minute shower. After she had washed and put on clean clothes, she gazed blankly into the foggy hospital mirror and put on her eyeliner. It struck me as odd at the time, yet I instinctively understood. Or at least I thought I did. Now, I completely understood.

I stared at myself in the mirror every morning and wondered who that person was, so weary yet strangely blank for all the inner turmoil, for all the terror and panic. I put on my makeup to make me look like me. As I smudged a gray pencil along my lash line or swiped some gloss across my lips, I remembered our friend in the hospital shower room. She was asserting, *I am still myself. This is one tiny thing I can still do no matter if my world is crumbling around me. I need to be able to recognize myself.*

Around this time, early in the chemo, people began to tell me how well I was doing, how strong I was. They commented that I was doing so many things right. It made me crazy. And, now all this time later, it still does. The disconnect between how I seemed—how I appeared, how I behaved, how I functioned—and how I felt began to widen in that post-surgery, early-chemo time. At the very beginning, the onslaught of the diagnosis and my instinct for immediate action left no room for behaving like anything but the raw nerve I had become. But as the weeks passed, I found that the appearance of normalcy was worth something. Fake it till you make it, they say. I clung to the corollary: if you fake it convincingly enough, you will definitely make it.

One friend said she couldn't believe my hair was clean.

Washing my hair is the easy part, I wanted to scream. Just like putting on mascara and all the rest. But look at my eyes: *I'm not here.*

You start to go a little nuts when the way people perceive you doesn't match your insides. You feel like a fraud. You question the way in which you have related to people all your life. How did you become so expert at deception, at feeling one way and behaving another? Surely you don't just wake up one morning when your husband has cancer and find yourself so skilled at pretending.

One day another friend said that I was sounding much better; she was glad that I had managed to detach. I didn't know how to process that comment. I could not have been less detached. She might as well have said, "It's so great that you have trampolined right out of your life."

In all fairness, no one could say anything right.

Another friend asked, "Trying to stay optimistic?" I wanted to slit his throat. What I wanted to hear was, "Everything's going to be perfectly fine." If "staying optimistic" required an effort, maybe we were fighting a battle that could actually be lost. I had no tolerance for hearing that. While I sought every single moment to maintain a fingerhold on optimism, I wanted everyone else around us to assume, to believe our happy ending was a sure thing. Having to *try* to stay optimistic—it was that word "try" that bristled—meant that what was wrong was so big that optimism might be misguided.

Despite friends' well-meaning comments, despite my overanalysis of what were intended as encouraging words, despite my exhaustion, sometime around week six, something strange happened. Were I a believer, I might have presumed I found myself in the grace of God. My obsessive thoughts about the future subsided.

A friend I've known since childhood who had undergone successful cancer treatment a few years earlier suggested a trick.

"Ask yourself," she said, "what's so bad about today?" Often, she promised, the answer would be, "Nothing." And, lo and behold, as Laurence recovered from the surgery and acclimated to the chemo routine, there came a string of days that turned out to be manageable, even better than manageable. During those weeks, I discovered contentment, even pleasure, in the smallness of our life. Newsy phone chats with Cami, visiting with the oldest of friends, meals at home. It was not the life we were used to living, but it had a simpleness to it, a confinement, that was curiously comforting, as though we were swaddling ourselves in what was really important and letting the excess fall away.

SNAPSHOT

Laurence spent his sophomore year of high school at Dunn School—he always called it Dunn School, never simply Dunn—in the Santa Ynez Valley, twenty-eight miles northeast of Santa Barbara. It was a boarding school, but unlike most kids, he was there of his own accord. Since his older brother had enjoyed being away from home for his high school years, Laurence thought he'd give it a try. However, the hard-core, chop-your-own-wood program of his brother's school did not appeal, so Laurence ended up at Dunn School.

Once he got there, however, he hated it. For him, its only saving grace lay in its proximity to Solvang, a Disneylandesque version of a Danish town, known for its pastries. Laurence rode his bike there every chance he got for a cream puff or an éclair or some of those little Danish pancakes called ebelskiver. More likely, all of the above. The baked goods beckoning from nearby Solvang seemed to comprise the most, nearly the only, pleasant memory of that year.

But there was this one night. Laurence always intended to write it into a movie. Apparently, one of his schoolmates was the son of a Thai businessman, or a diplomat perhaps. After Christmas break at home in Thailand, the young man returned with a pack of Thai playing cards, whose interest lay not in their spades or diamonds, but in the naked women pictured in lewd poses on the other side. A pack of cards that made this kid pretty popular at an all-boys' school in sleepy Los Olivos, California.

He also brought with him a box of porno slides.

As legend had it, some of the boys—explosive with testosterone— wrangled the slides from him and began projecting them onto an exterior wall of a massive, barn-like structure. Within minutes, every boy in the school was out on the field in front of the barn, whooping and shrieking louder each time a new slide flashed onto the wall, pumping their fists high above their heads in what Laurence always described as the closest thing to a tribal ritual he had ever witnessed.

I'm not sure, but I believe Laurence manned the projector.

That night was the highlight of an otherwise-dismal year, and it was now just a question of which school to transfer to for his junior year.

A friend of his was driving down to L.A. to take the entrance exam and have an interview at a relatively new school called Oakwood. He wondered if Laurence would drive with him. For lack of anything better to do, Laurence decided to take the test, too. And have an interview. His friend didn't get in.

Laurence did.

Oakwood inhabited a converted church that was in a less-than-fashionable area of the San Fernando Valley. Although in the intervening years it has transformed itself into a highly respected prep school, at that time, it had a reputation for being what used to be called "progressive." A hippie school. Freewheeling, iconoclastic, downright subversive. The ideal place to see out the last few years of the '60s and welcome the '70s.

It was the first school that Laurence ever liked, where his creativity was both encouraged and appreciated. It was the anti–Dunn School.

It was also the first school that I ever liked, when I arrived there for my senior year the following September. For me it was the anti–Westlake School, the prestigious girls' school I had attended since first grade, where we wore uniforms, learned to curtsy, and saluted the flag with full regalia every Friday.

Though we weren't in any classes together, Laurence and I must have had the same free period that September. I remember our sitting on the Spanish tiles of the courtyard that was the heart of the school while most other kids were in class. I think he may have been killing time between English and his senior elective, the Buckminster Fuller–inspired Comprehensive Anticipatory World Design Science. We talked about movies. There may have been earlier meetings, but that is my first image of a conversation between us. Just getting to know each other, becoming friends.

I was the new girl. The only new girl in a senior class of only forty-five students. It was a heady time. Boys—actual boys—were asking me out. No cell-phone calls, wondering if you wanted to meet right then, ten minutes from now. But dates—deliciously planned days ahead. I had no clue what was expected—what to talk about, how to behave. Half the time, the night was as much about getting to the postmortem with a girlfriend as it was about enjoying the evening.

"Dating" Laurence (if you could call it that) was somehow different, almost from the start. Whenever I've described our first date to Cami, I always joked, "On our first date . . . our only date . . ." That's the way it was, because very quickly, it didn't feel like dating. It just felt like the way life was supposed to be.

I like to think that maybe, when it came to high school memories, talking about movies with the new girl during free period ranked right up there with Thai porn and cream puffs from Solvang.

CHAPTER FIVE

From the minute Laurence was diagnosed, one thought plagued me. I wondered if we had used up our allotted time, like so many heartbeats in a life, finite and irrevocable. So much togetherness. Together so many years. Together so many days, all day. If Laurence had gone to a nine-to-five job, would this not have happened? Was cancer pointing its bony finger at a tally kept by the universe and punishing us for our greed?

I was still greedy. I wanted more time.

Greedy and angry.

Angry, obviously, at that same universe and its horrible accounting of all those moments, years, a lifetime together. Angry at Laurence, for what he had let his body do when he dropped his vigilance, for dropping his vigilance. But if I were going to play that game I had to be equally—if not more—angry with myself for not also keeping better guard. And then the counter-thought would ping-pong back. No one could (or, at any rate, would) say with any certainty that a cancer this vicious could not have appeared even if Laurence had not delayed his test.

But then there was that other anger—an anger I actually cultivated. I mentally scrolled through the list of things Laurence had ever done that infuriated me—from the kind of tiny behavioral tic that spouses find annoying to the very few times he had really wounded me. I can't say exactly why I did this, but it quelled the mania. It reminded me that he wasn't perfect. It may have been a psycho game I played that allowed me to pretend the thought of living without him might be tolerable. At that point, early on, I honestly didn't believe there was any reason to entertain that thought, but you think it anyway. When you hear the "C" word, it's as though a giant hourglass has been turned upside down. Everyone reassures you, and rationally you know it's not the death sentence it once was—medical science has come so far and all that—but still, each grain of trickling sand abrades your psyche.

The antidote is hope. As screenwriters in Los Angeles, our professional lives were nourished largely on a diet of hope, frequently false hope springing eternal. But hope depends on time. It requires a seemingly limitless stretch of time, like so much highway snaking out before you. If you follow the white line long enough, if you keep a steady hand on the wheel and crank up the radio loud enough to stay awake, you'll get there in one piece.

Suddenly, with one sentence—"Mrs. Starkman, sit down"— the highway had abruptly dead-ended. Time telescoped in. I plunged headlong into bargaining, bypassing denial. A small dose of denial would have been a comfort, but there was none to be had. Our whole life had felt like a blessing; that was the problem. This thud was the dropping of the cosmic other shoe.

Nonetheless, bargaining came naturally. It's hard to feel like you're bargaining effectively when you don't believe in God. You don't have a lot of leverage. But that didn't stop me. If you, O

Universe, make him well, I will be such a better person. The list of my flaws was endless, more than enough chips to lay on the table. I will do more volunteer work. I will not lose my temper so easily. I will never gossip again.

I could and would do or not do all those things. What I wasn't sure I could do was live without hope. At that point, so early on, I was wishing for normal life, but there were moments when the best I could hope for was for hope to return. Somehow, there were moments when I managed to be truly hopeful. How could I look at Laurence and be anything but?

First of all, he looked so damn good. This was of enormous reassurance to him as well. I can't count the number of times he stood in front of the bathroom mirror and said, "I look pretty good, don't I?"

It had nothing to do with vanity. (Well, maybe a little. We're all entitled, even men.) It had so much more to do with the fact that, just like me putting on my makeup, his reflection in the mirror reaffirmed that he was the same person he had always been. And that gave him the confidence to go out into the world and behave like the same person, like himself. The world never reacted to him as though he were sick or, more specifically, and God forbid, a cancer patient. The only thing worse than having a disease is being pitied because you have the disease.

When Oncology Man first gave us the initial rundown on the chemo protocol, Laurence had asked, "Will I lose my hair?" I was momentarily surprised. Who cares? What we don't want you to lose is your life. But Laurence understood that his perception of himself could hinge on others' perceptions of him. He was pleased when the doctor said hair loss would be minimal. Indeed, it was. There were mornings when a few more strands than usual littered the shower floor, but I was looking hard. Laurence gained back most of the weight he had lost right after the surgery, and except for the three days immediately following each chemo treatment, his color was excellent. He looked well-nourished, rosy, and well-coiffed.

He was absolutely right; he did look pretty good. Actually, he looked better than pretty good. Of course we know that at the best of times, looks aren't everything. But, as it turns out, at the worst of times, they mean more than you'd think.

The truth is, when you look good, it's easier to feel good. It's even easier to feel young. Certainly, children are stricken with cancer (possibly making the best case for nihilism imaginable), but if you're middle-aged when cancer finds you, it sneaks in an extra indignity: you can no longer pretend to be young. For baby boomers, that's a really low blow. That furrow between your brows is one thing, the marionette lines etching themselves from the corners of your mouth to your jaw another, but cancer is really insulting. Good-bye endless summer, hello back to school.

SNAPSHOT

There was a joke going around during our senior year of high school. They used to call them shaggy dog stories. Does anyone tell them anymore? Do kids still have the requisite attention span? Can they listen without checking e-mail, "poking" a Facebook friend, or texting? We had the time to listen. Laurence had the time to tell it. He loved the joke and told it often.

Little did he know then that we would come to find it emblematic of our generation, that he and I would often use the punch line as code to comment on a variety of situations in the years ahead. Back then it was just funny.

When I first met Laurence, he talked fast. Really fast, with an almost manic energy. It suited this joke. He told it well.

There's this explorer flying in the Himalayas, and this big storm comes up and his plane crashes. He's lost for weeks. Living on nothing but snow. He's close to death, crawling along on his hands and knees, when suddenly, his head bumps into something. He looks up and sees this big neon sign: HIMALAYA RESTAURANT. SPECIALTY OF THE HOUSE—SHLEMMA PIE.

He stumbles in and grabs a seat. The waiter rushes over and asks him what he wants.

"Anything! Bring me anything!"

And the waiter says, "How about Shlemma Pie? It's the specialty of the house."

"Sure, sure. Shlemma Pie."

Well, it's the best thing the guy's ever tasted. It's incredible. So the guy's there a couple of weeks eating nothing but Shlemma Pie. Little by little he gets his strength back. After a while, he figures he better get back to the wife and kids. He grabs an armload of delicious Shlemma Pies and heads down the mountain.

But it's all blizzardy, so he gets completely lost. He's eaten his last Shlemma Pie when miraculously, he finds civilization. He hops a steamer for home and everything's cool for about a year. But he just can't seem to forget about Shlemma Pie. He's desperate for Shlemma Pie. He's just got to get more.

He puts himself in hock to get money for another expedition, says good-bye to the family, and heads back to the Himalayas. Finally, he's climbing back up the mountain. But wouldn't you know it? Another blizzard. All the Sherpas turn back, but not our guy. He's got to get that Shlemma Pie.

The guy's breathing his last breath, crawling on his hands and knees, when . . . *Boom*! His head bumps into something. He looks up. Himalaya Restaurant! Specialty of the house—Shlemma Pie.

He has a sudden burst of strength. He gets up and walks in. But he wants to keep cool, you know? So he sits down and orders a whole meal. Then, the moment he's been waiting for.

The waiter comes over and says, "Would you care for some dessert?"

The guy looks up and says, "Yeah. I'll have some Shlemma Pie."

But the waiter says, "I'm sorry, sir. We're out of Shlemma Pie."

". . . Okay, I'll take apple."

CHAPTER SIX

"I'm not having grandchildren without you."

I said that a lot.

When you find yourself waging a life-and-death battle, the dialogue starts to sound like a Douglas Sirk movie. But I meant it. It was unimaginable that Laurence would never know Cami's husband, or that he would not stand over her child's bassinet beaming beside me. Occasionally, when we were new parents, sleep-deprived and ragged, we would say to one another, "Won't it be great when we're grandparents?"

How could it be possible that something so far beyond our control would stop him from sticking to his end of the bargain? I took it as a personal dare. I wasn't going to let that happen.

Despite the insular honeymoon period of the chemo, bizarre as it was, a watchfulness continued to grow in me. I refused to be caught off guard again. When Oncology Man requested that Laurence appear in his office on an "off" week, a week between chemo treatments, I panicked. Rationally, I knew there had been no new battery of tests, nothing that could have yielded new results, new bad news, but I fell victim to Seen Too Many Movies Syndrome. I envisioned the doctor calling us in, sitting us down, talking about the matter of time. Once you have heard bad news, really bad news, from a doctor, you cannot help but picture more bad news tumbling down on you. The avalanche had been set in motion. I was determined to steel myself against it.

As it turned out, Oncology Man had been out of town when Laurence had gone for the previous week's session. The doctor just wanted to eyeball him, ask how he was doing.

Certain things change your life. Others change who you are. I knew from the moment we heard the word that the cancer had changed our life forever. But when the doctor sent us on our way that "off-week" day, all systems go, I felt my muscles relax with relief. I hadn't realized how much I had tensed against the wallop. I knew that the cancer had not just changed our life; it had changed who I was as well. I was now someone on the lookout, in the bell tower, rifle poised.

There would be no easy breathing.

I have never breathed easy when there was something amiss with someone in my little family. When Cami was school-aged and had a cold, a mental countdown began with the first sniffle. Seven days minimum, a full ten before the last remnants would disappear—the stray cough from her bed at night, the stuffy twang, the liquid eyes. I was calculating my own anxiety as much as her discomfort.

What would be the timetable for cancer? Six months of chemo, two more before the second surgery. I was betting on the presumption that the anxiety, in all its deranged intensity, would abate around then, surely after a couple of clean scans. There would be longer and longer stretches of easier breathing between them. But I knew there would never be a full sigh of relief. How many years of clean scans would equal the last sound of a child's stuffy nose?

Relief did come in strange places . . . but not without shame. Whenever I read of a famous person undergoing treatment for cancer, my first reaction was a sick horror, eerily intimate. But then, and I am loath to confess this, I enjoyed an undercurrent of relief that was as deep as my empathy for their suffering. I have never been a team player, but it was comforting to be on their team. High-five to that actor, that sports figure, that rock star. It was partly because of the obvious: a bad thing is not only happening to us.

I have a friend who is the mother of autistic twins. She is also a social worker in a hospital among the disenfranchised and downtrodden. I asked her once why she did this. Didn't her profession add to her emotional burden? But now I understood. She did it so that she would have daily reminders that life assails us all indiscriminately. Surely that was part of what I found consoling in the misfortunes of others, if disgracefully.

But there was more to it even than that. Many of these celebrities have made a career out of youth. If cancer could catch up with them, then how could we possibly outrun it? If they were not exempt, how could we presume to be?

So, if we couldn't escape it, we were at least going to do it well. Laurence was the poster boy of how to go through chemotherapy. He did it with grace and equanimity. If attitude were half the battle, then we were halfway there. There were small stretches of time, occasionally a few days in a row, when life felt almost normal.

The strangest things would remind me it was not. Often the smallest things.

One Sunday in May, I brought in the newspaper to find the annual list of movies scheduled for summer release, a list so comprehensive that it requires its own section. Los Angeles is a company town, after all. My usual reaction would have been a combination of excitement and anticipation, along with a touch of anxiety. So many movies, so little time, not unlike laying eyes on the syllabus for an English class in college, thinking: all these books look great, but how am I going to digest one every four days? This year, I scanned the list with peculiar detachment. The old me—someone with a different life, someone whose husband didn't have cancer—would try to fit seeing all these movies into the next three months. The new me would choose one or two here and there for a late-afternoon showing when the theaters were empty and a stranger three rows behind us would not be likely to sneeze.

Before beginning the chemo, I had asked Oncology Man how paranoid we should be about germs now that Laurence's immune system would be compromised. "I wouldn't go to a bar mitzvah," he said.

Okay, stay away from children and slobbery kisses.

But I decided he meant: be as paranoid as you want. Children. Slobbery kisses. Crowds. People in general.

"Don't kiss Laurence," I told friends.

"Sorry, we're not hugging these days."

I washed my hands with the hottest water I could tolerate. I kept a supply of Purell wipes in my purse and in the glove compartment of my car. When we made grocery-store runs, midday, at its least crowded, I never let Laurence push the cart.

I stood guard against minute cold germs because, ultimately, I could do nothing but rail ineffectually against the giant ogre which had already laid siege. You pretend it's about being safe. But it's really about control—or, more precisely, the illusion of control. *Let me control these tiny things because the big picture is so out of control, there's no grabbing hold.*

— ⁓

More about neuropathy.

The first day of chemo, Laurence's nurse explained the side effects. She mentioned something called neuropathy, which could be brought on by the Oxaliplatin. Would be brought on by the Oxaliplatin. Definitely. Medical personnel assume you know these words, that you bandy them about in everyday conversation. Even the most empathetic among them don't fully realize how frightening the words sound, because they themselves do, in fact, bandy them about in everyday conversation.

When I first heard the word—neuropathy—it sounded like it meant nerve damage. It did. Laurence's nurse told him that he would almost definitely experience some neuropathy (specifically "peripheral neuropathy" of the hands and feet) from the Oxaliplatin, one of the cursed marvels dripping into him. Apparently, everyone on the drug ends up affected to some degree. She reiterated the standard warning: No refrigerator. No chilled beverages. Each time we heard the drill I was terrified into cockiness. I thought, *We'll do precisely what she says, and then some. We will avoid all cold. No permanent neuropathy for my husband. No neuropathy at all.*

I don't remember how many treatments Laurence had undergone when the first signs of neuropathy appeared. A little tingling. A little numbness in his fingers and toes. He did not reach into the refrigerator. He asked for water without ice in restaurants, but I always touched the glass, testing, before letting him pick it up. He started wearing fleece gloves when we took walks around the neighborhood.

"How do people do this in really cold places?" we wondered, grateful that his treatment would be over well before the advent of our own Southern California–style winter. We tried to feel lucky in every way we could. *Still grateful,* you try to emit. You want to feel like you're still in the running for honorable mention in the luck department, even though you'll never again have a shot at the blue ribbon.

— ⌒

Cami came home from her first year of college in early May. We were not the same family who had sent her off the previous August. Laurence had already undergone three rounds of chemo. He was feeling remarkably well, but we weren't about to chance an airport run—so many people, so many germs—so I picked her up alone. She and I wrangled her oversized duffel off the luggage carousel. We managed to heave it onto a cart and maneuver it into the trunk of the car. Daddy tasks.

We talked enthusiastically, Cami and I, about her upcoming job teaching art at the summer camp held at her old elementary school. We didn't talk much about Daddy. She had left him in his hospital bed less than a week after surgery. I thought she'd be amazed at how hale he looked now, how nearly back to his old self, but I didn't want to oversell. Better to be pleasantly surprised than disappointed.

She was indeed amazed, confiding later that she had

envisioned a bedridden version of her father for the duration of the chemo, not this upright, vital Daddy asking where we should all go for dinner on her first night home. I could tell she was relieved, relieved enough to cry.

As we both lay on my bed crying, I managed to say what I had been wanting to say to my daughter since Laurence had been diagnosed. "I don't ever want you to feel responsible for me. No matter what happens—and nothing's going to happen—but no matter what happens, please don't ever feel responsible for me."

She nodded, unable to speak. There was nothing to say anyway.

It was too scary to think about what was absolutely not going to happen.

— ~

All things considered—and there were many things to be considered—it ended up being an ironically uneventful summer. I just didn't know it at the time.

There were moments when we actually felt empowered. When one of the pre–treatment blood tests came back revealing a low potassium level, Laurence made a deal with Oncology Man. He promised to down the dreadful syrup as prescribed if, by the next test, he had not been able to raise the level through other means. He began eating bananas, one or two a day, and I hit the Internet for further, less-common-knowledge sources of potassium. We were in luck. Watermelon turned out to be rich in potassium, and it was summertime.

We bought a shiny new juicer. The thing sounded like an airplane taking off, and it shot out juice like a nuclear reactor. We juiced and we juiced and we juiced some more, adding ingredient after ingredient to our concoctions, each for its unique anti-this, pro-that properties. Colorful berries, leafy greens, ginger. We fed them all into the chrome cylinder and rammed them down with the plunger. Laurence drank what poured out—sometimes murky and mud-colored, other times cheery and vibrant.

By his next blood test, Laurence's potassium level was smack in the middle of normal range. It was a sweet victory. Surely this suggested a larger progression toward perfect health. If a daily banana and a few glasses of juice could win a battle, the heavy-hitting chemo surely must be winning the war.

I trained Laurence well. He handed me a copy of his blood work the second he got into the car after each chemo treatment. I scanned the pages, looking for any number in bold type, indicating an element of his blood chemistry even slightly out of whack. (Only one or two ever were, and if they were, they were so minimally out of normal range that my brother-in-law-the-doctor advised us they meant nothing. He assured us that Laurence's blood work was better than a lot of his "healthy" patients'.) What I was really looking for each time I studied the sheet was the value of the so-called "cancer marker." It consistently fell well within normal range, generally, in fact, at the lower end. Hope in the form of a laboratory printout.

I filed the blood work results away week after week, but sometimes, in the middle of the night, I padded downstairs and removed the folder from the file drawer. I slid the most recent sheet out of the file folder and stared at that encouraging number next to the cancer marker, so then, maybe, I could get some sleep.

Reminders that our life wasn't normal happened at the strangest times. After a while, our chemo drop-off and pickup routine didn't faze me. It was just the way we spent every other Wednesday and Friday. Until one day in July.

Cami had been teaching art to elementary school campers and invited us to the end-of-session exhibition of their work. The festivities were set for a particular half-hour on a Friday. It happened to be one of those every-other Fridays, a chemo week, when I circled the block while Laurence popped in to the doctor's office to get disconnected from the slow-drip pump. The whole procedure usually took no more than fifteen minutes.

But on this particular Friday, the office was understaffed and overrun with patients. (There's a lot of cancer going around these days; when it hits you, you discover this. Everyone has a relative, a friend, a beloved.) I drove around the block and around the block and around the block again. And again. And again. As I sometimes did, I pulled over and parked, waiting for Laurence to phone to tell me he was ready. Then I waited and waited and waited.

I knew I was overreacting. My child was not one of the eight-year-olds whose artwork would be on display. She was their teacher. She wasn't going to get a lump in her throat, choking back tears, if we didn't show up, as she might have when she was their age. But the lump was growing in my own throat. Nothing ever kept us from celebrating anything our daughter ever did. I couldn't have imagined anything that would. Except maybe cancer.

By the time Laurence emerged from the medical tower, I had worked myself up into what can only be called a tizzy. Normally, I can go from zero to sixty in any tizzy race, but these days there was another component. Panic.

"You were in there for forty minutes."

"I'm sorry. The place was packed today."

"You know I was looking forward to this thing all week." As if it were his fault.

"I knew you'd be going crazy," he said. Of course he knew.

I may have started to cry. And then I lost my temper, full out. It wasn't his fault, of course, but when the cancer panic washed over me, it morphed into rage. Often. I'm not proud of that. It was easier to explode out than in. But my husband knew me well. Although I have no doubt he would have much preferred I not lose my temper, I try to believe that he knew where the outbursts came from, and that he understood. I was furious that they'd kept him waiting. I was furious that we had missed the art show.

I was furious that he had cancer.

— —

We may have missed a few events that summer, but we celebrated a lot, too. My birthday in July. Our anniversary in September. Family dinners out. Gallery openings. If they fell on a good week, non-chemo or post-chemo days, we were there. A run of blank spaces on the calendar followed by engagements. It was almost like our normal social life. It was our social life . . . lite.

I began to pick and choose who we spent our time with, although sometimes encounters were unpredictable. In June, Laurence's cousin and her husband visited from out of town and threw a dinner party at a nearby restaurant. It was a "good" (non-chemo) week.

I ended up sitting between Laurence and our host. Across from us sat a couple we'd never met. I passed the appetizer and pasta courses making small talk with the woman across from me—books, travel, our children. We had almost finished the entrees when I got caught up in a conversation with a different cluster at the table. Out of the corner of my eye, I saw our host lean in toward the woman with whom I'd been chatting and whisper something in her ear. The woman, this stranger, stared at Laurence, stunned, unaware that I was watching her. And because she was unaware that I was watching her, she didn't even try to mask her horror.

As far as I was concerned, dinner was over.

I whispered to Laurence, "We've got to get out of here."

We were out of there in minutes. No doubt, Laurence's cousin, our hostess, assumed tears were welling in my eyes because she had suggested we come for a visit in the spring. Surely the notion of all this being behind us had moved me so. But that had nothing to do with my tears. It was the look on that stranger's face. The shock, the horror, the pity. It was the pity most of all. I cried all the way home. I shouldn't have.

"People don't know what to do," Laurence said.

I wouldn't let it go. "He shouldn't have said anything to that woman."

"Just forget about it."

I made Laurence comfort me. How crazy. Of course, if I had suddenly become someone who managed her tears more efficiently, he would have thought I'd been replaced by the pod version of myself.

Sometimes it was easier to stay home, I decided, cocooned in the new normal we had created.

I kept at the Sudoku, the puzzles' initial seduction having evolved into something of an addiction. If a two goes there, then another two has to go there, which means this box has to hold an eight or a three. I have no special fondness for numbers. And I'm not great with patterns. My palms always got a little clammy whenever I was confronted with one of those tests that require you to figure out which way gear #3 turns if gears #1 and #7 rotate clockwise. But Sudoku was something else. A kind of Zen. When I picked up a pencil and opened a puzzle book, it was as close to meditation as I could get, with the added plus that you don't have to focus on your breathing.

So I worked a lot of Sudoku. And I shopped.

My first time shopping, post-diagnosis, was early in the summer. We had heard about a Rolf massage therapist purported to help chemo patients stay strong and side effect-free. I hadn't heard the term "Rolfing" for at least a decade, probably two. Even all those years ago, when one could still conjure a cultural hippie afterglow, it sounded like so much hocus-pocus. But now, even though the times had a-changed and a-changed some more, the benign laying on of hands in the name of staying as robust as possible did not seem so foolhardy.

Though she was middle-aged, the Rolf practitioner worked out of the pool house behind her parents' home in the heart of Beverly Hills. What else does one do with an hour to kill mere blocks from Rodeo Drive?

It was a spectacular Southern California morning with marine-blue skies. I dropped Laurence off in front of the pink Monterey-style house and drove the few blocks to the Stuart Weitzman boutique.

Shoes. I admit it. Buying shoes gives me a boost in the best of times. But what that pastime could do for me in the worst of times proved to be a revelation. My half-hour with Stuart offered distraction, to be sure, but it was more than that. I discovered a sort of retail *Field of Dreams*. Underlying the process—the meandering through the shop, the trying on, the actual buying—lay a tacit mantra: if I buy it, life will come.

In the months that followed, I shopped for more than shoes, never leaving Laurence alone at home, but often when he was at chemo or lunching with a friend. I hit all the favorites, any mall in a storm. Shopping took on an electric charge. Every time I tried on a pair of ballet flats or slid a sweater over my head, the message to myself was clear. We have a future where I will need to wear this.

And I felt potent. There was something gratifying in the actual transaction itself. I handed the salesperson my credit card; she handed me my item. Cause and effect—that's all I was after. If I could find a little of that in Bloomie's, maybe we could earn some in the chemo room.

— —

But as the close of the chemo portion of the program drew near, I found myself feeling anything but celebratory. Laurence's increasing neuropathy had become so severe that Oncology Man had omitted the Oxaliplatin from the last two treatments. We all feared that the nerve damage would become even more incapacitating—and permanent—if the drug were continued. Already, Laurence had extreme difficulty tying his shoes and buttoning his shirt.

"Help me with this, would you?" he'd ask casually. I knew it had to be bad for him to ask.

The neuropathy continued despite the withdrawal of the culprit drug.

There were hiccups, too. These were not a mere annoyance; they were persistent and violent. Long bouts came and went, echoing through the house—spasms that would be enervating even without the chemo exhaustion.

And there was the "chemo brain" I'd heard mentioned that first day in the chemo room. Had I never heard the term that day, I probably would have thought, *He's tired. He's preoccupied. All his energy is going toward getting well instead of following some irrelevant conversation.* But from the moment I'd heard the term—"chemo brain"—I suppose I was looking for it. If Laurence momentarily forgot why he'd entered a room, I'd think "chemo brain." If he repeated something he'd said an hour earlier, I'd think "chemo brain." If he didn't pay attention to what I was saying, I'd think "chemo brain." When I did any of those things, I never bothered to wonder, *What's my excuse?* Or to realize that everyone I know does the exact same things, too.

We continued to work on our new screenplay, logging time at the computer in spurts during Laurence's good-energy, non-chemo weeks. And a friend had hired us to write trivia questions for a DVD game he was producing. It offered the perfect kind of busywork. It occupied us, but didn't demand too much concentration or creative thought. We worked mostly from home, but sometimes joined in the writers' meetings at the office in Hollywood. Occasionally, I would notice Laurence repeating what someone else had just said, or having trouble following a train of thought. The room was something of a free-for-all, like most writers' rooms, and no one else noticed. But I did. *Chemo brain,* I thought.

And then I would be reminded: *we're in the middle of chemo because we've got cancer.*

But, finally, the chemo was over. Friends clapped Laurence on the back; he still looked so damn good, after all. Some phoned to schedule congratulatory dinners at special-occasion restaurants. Others suggested vacation spots where the two of us could catch our breath while ocean breezes blew, places where we could enjoy doing nothing, as opposed to this day-counting version of so much nothing that had consumed our past six months.

I told myself that I would feel more like celebrating when the scans came back clean three weeks after the last treatment. When we could say, like a toddler over an empty plate, "All gone!" Normal should have seemed within sight, but instead it just seemed less distinct, paler, as though it were fading the closer we got.

SNAPSHOT

Laurence's birthday was December 24th. Christmas Eve. No fair.

I overcompensated over the years, throwing him more than his share of surprise parties. Four, to be exact. That's a lot of surprise parties—months of planning, months of secret-keeping for, possibly, several minutes of shock, all totaled. Each party has its own story, naturally, but the story of the limousine surprise party has the best punch line.

Laurence and I were living together, not yet married, in a condo in Westwood, what was then the movie-theater mecca of Los Angeles. (This figures in the scheme.) We were hanging around the house, watching TV, I guess, when the phone rang. Laurence answered. (Also part of the plot.) It was our friend, Ron. Apparently he was on a date and they had just come out of the movies to find that his car wouldn't start. Since we lived so close by, he wondered if we could pick them up. Sure.

We pulled up in front of the spired Fox Village Theater to find Ron standing there alone. He told us that his date had gone from bad to worse. Now the girl was sick and had retreated to the ladies' room in the theater. Would I go in and check on her? Sure. I hopped out of the car while Laurence drove off to park.

As soon as Laurence was out of sight, Ron and I ran to a limo waiting a block away—a dozen of Laurence's friends inside—so that when Laurence returned, on foot, neither of us was anywhere in sight.

We sent the limo driver to summon Laurence to he-had-no-idea-what. We watched from behind the blackout windows as the driver exchanged a few words with him. Then the chauffeur led him back to the stretch-out. The driver opened the door for Laurence to great huzzahs from all of us inside.

That was the extent of the surprise, and all that our budgets could support at the time. We drove around town for an hour or so, just cruising L.A., and ended the evening by driving through a Jack in the Box.

Laurence would tell me later, and whenever he relayed the story thereafter, that when he was standing there alone in front of the movie theater in Westwood Village and was approached by the chauffeur, he didn't find it one bit odd. Not for a second. He always believed destiny held something marvelous.

The elegant gentleman in black uniform and cap had asked, "Mr. Starkman?"

And Laurence had thought, "This makes sense. This seems right. It's only been a matter of time."

CHAPTER SEVEN

The second go-round blindsided us almost as much as the first, if that is possible.

On September 29, Laurence went for his scans, both CAT and PET (such friendly acronyms). It was a Friday. We waited and we waited. No doctor called. I knew I couldn't make it through the weekend without the results. Why is it that tests always seem to fall on Fridays? I begged Laurence to call one of the doctors, any one of them. He was more nervous than he let on; it didn't take much pleading.

He phoned Family Doc.

The nurse answered the phone. Just when she was about to put Laurence on hold to buzz the doctor, she added nonchalantly, "Congratulations."

"What?"

"Your scans are good."

Our internist came on the line with confirmation. The news was indeed good.

I cried, hard enough to make up for the past six months when I tried so often not to. And we held each other for dear life.

I couldn't believe it. We'd made it through the rain, as though we were living a bona fide Barry Manilow moment.

Laurence believed it. In the middle of the night, in the chemo room, in his deepest heart, he had no doubt been bargaining, too. This was the outcome he had ordered.

We scheduled the reattachment surgery for early in November. Now all we had to do was keep him well and strong until then. No problem. He was feeling well enough to take a drumming gig.

But there was this pain.

A few days before its onset, he had packed up his drum kit and loaded it into his car to play a fund-raiser block party with his band. Some years before, he had joined this band—a bunch of writers who practiced in a North Hollywood studio they rented by the hour. They called themselves The Lower Companions. (They took their name, just for fun, from the term used in twelve-step programs signifying people who drag you down.) Once, they played the Writers Guild Christmas party at the House of Blues on the Sunset Strip. We have the video. There's Laurence at his drums under the giant House of Blues logo. But the point of the band was to have fun, so block parties were fine, too, and they had played this one for a couple of years in a row. Unloading, setting up, and reloading the drums were all involved at home and at the other end as well, and within a few days, the pain in his back set in.

I did what I always do. I screamed. "I can't believe you did this! After all we just went through, you had to go and do something so stupid!" Again, not one of my prouder moments.

My tirade became protracted as the weeks passed. And the pain got worse. We wondered if it could be related to the neuropathy. The various doctors suggested Laurence see a pain specialist who ordered an MRI, which revealed nothing. He prescribed muscle relaxers and anti-inflammatories, but they didn't make a dent in the pain.

We segued into massage therapy, physical therapy, and acupuncture. Nothing seemed to provide any lasting relief. Painkillers joined the mix of nerve-desensitization meds which Laurence had been using to combat the neuropathy. There were no signs of the neuropathy fading, but we were willing to wait for that, as long as this pain would go away.

The pain would not go away. We could not get a handle on the pain.

We bought a Zero Gravity chair. The La-Z-Boy was demoted from the bedroom to downstairs, and the new high-tech suede-and-wood recliner took its place. Designed to take all the pressure off your back, it did just that. Laurence pushed the motorized button and sent the chair back to a happy angle. Sometimes he was able to doze off, but it didn't really get rid of the pain.

So there was a visit to a neurologist. And a visit to a urologist. There were visits to a pain management specialist who administered injections directly into Laurence's back and added various drugs to the mix. That helped . . . for a few days.

But then the pain began to migrate. From his back around to his right flank, settling under his rib cage.

I stopped screaming about the drums.

We reassured ourselves. "You're clean. You just had all those tests. You're clean."

But the pain had ideas of its own, enough so that Laurence ended up in the emergency room twice within three weeks. As had been the case immediately following his surgery, the powers-that-be suspected some sort of intestinal blockage (or blockage of what was left of his intestines), but tests and tests and tests revealed none.

There were a few hours during which the doctors considered the possibility that Laurence was having a gall bladder attack, merely coincidental to everything else. Those tests proved his gall bladder, at least, was fine. "You're clean," we said some more. "All clean."

I suggested to Laurence that maybe he'd rather not have the reattachment surgery. He had, after all, been handling the indignity of his current anatomical situation with such finesse. He looked at me like I was crazy. Of course he wanted the surgery. It was what he had been waiting for. I, however, was terrified of the surgical waiting room and more hospital time.

No matter. It was becoming obvious that the surgery was going to have to be postponed regardless of what either one of us wanted. Laurence couldn't go into surgery with pain like this.

After four weeks of the pain—increasing and unrelenting—Laurence ended up back in a hospital room on a Sunday night. We thought it was a better-safe-than-sorry overnight stay. They hit him with some heavy-duty intravenous painkillers to break what was surely some weird inflammatory cycle. Just as a precaution, they ran some new scans. They would show nothing of consequence, of course. They'd been clean just one month earlier.

When I arrived to pick Laurence up early that Monday morning, he was feeling a bit better. The IV had worked some magic. The pain had abated. He was chipper. As he got dressed, he said that Oncology Man wanted to see him in his office.

"How come?"

"I don't know. Just to go over things, I guess."

"Are you sure? Why couldn't he just talk to us here?"

"It's no big deal."

—   —

"You have three tiny nodules."

"Shit," Laurence said. "Fuck. Goddammit."

"And a film around the liver. It's not in the liver. Just around the liver."

Oncology Man must have said something else, I don't remember what. Then—and this I will always remember—he said, "We have three things to deal with. Pain management. Diagnosis. And treatment." In that order.

It wasn't, "We're going after this fucker again. And, by the way, we'll work on your pain." Pain management was the first priority. That meant two things. First, the pain was probably going to get worse. Second, he wasn't saying anything like the first time, just six months before. I was not going to be splitting the semantic hairs between "This is not incurable" and "This is curable." We were going to be managing pain, zooming in on a diagnosis, and then, it seemed, attempting to aim a slingshot at the giant monster in the dark.

Oncology Man muttered the same preamble he had six months earlier about his penchant for telling the truth no matter what. And then he did just that.

"The prognosis is not good."

Looking back on that now, I cannot believe we couldn't manage to process the subtext. I couldn't anyway. Or refused to.

The subtext was, "You're dying."

Foolishly, what I heard was, *Years. We can count the years.*

Oncology Man launched the final salvo. "You will be on some form of chemotherapy for the rest of your life."

That was it. Normal would never be an option again.

We asked about surgery. Can't you cut it out again? *Just get it out of there, all of it. Get it out.* But the answer was no. Surgery was not an option this time.

Hope, like dreams, dies hard. Of all the physical senses, it may be the hearing of the man on his deathbed that is the last to fade. But of his spirit, it is hope that is the last to go, as it is for those who love him.

Oncology Man led us from the examining room into his office where he turned us over to his assistant to schedule a new round of chemo. He was wasting no time. The chemo would begin the next day. I sat on a chair by the door. As the doctor headed out of the room, I grabbed his hand. I said nothing—there was nothing to say. I just looked him in the eye. I would not let him slip from my gaze for several seconds. *Remember, we are people—our lives comprise a whole world.* And then he left the room.

While Laurence dealt with more paperwork and scheduling, I retreated to the small bathroom next door. I pulled out my cell phone and called my sister. I had to say it out loud, tell someone else, to believe it myself.

"It's back."

All the way home, I kept saying, "We can do it again. This is still doable. Promise me you won't give up. Promise me."

Laurence promised.

But when we arrived home, as we walked through the living room, Laurence paused before stepping down into the den.

He stood there a moment and said, "You're going to have to carry on."

"No," I said. "I won't. I'm not going to have to. You promised. I'm not having grandchildren without you."

"Okay," he said. But he was crying now, too.

"Don't give up." Again, I made him promise.

"I won't. I won't give up."

I have regretted my response, daily and deeply. Now, on the after side of before-and-after, I want so desperately to know what my husband would have said if I had answered differently—if I had managed the courage to say, "I will carry on. Tell me how. Tell me now, while you are here. What should I do? What can I possibly do without you?"

But I didn't say that. I couldn't. I wasn't giving up. I wasn't giving in. We may have come up for air for just a very few minutes, it seemed, but I was ready to fight again. Not ready, really; just less ready for the alternative. Another loop on the roller coaster for which we'd never bought a ticket in the first place. *Let us off*, we wanted to scream. *There's been another horrible mistake.*

But, of course, there hadn't been. A biopsy of one of the nodules, each approximately one centimeter in diameter—the size of a blueberry—confirmed what we already knew.

Pain like this could only mean one thing.

Gearing up for a recommitment to the fight, Laurence put all the new paperwork into a three-ring binder. Then he created a cover page to slide behind its clear plastic cover. He spent considerable time fiddling on the computer—distraction in the art of design—creating the page. Classic Laurence.

At the top was printed PROJECT "X." Beneath that, he downloaded a picture of his childhood hero, Commando Cody, Sky

Marshal of the Universe, circa 1952. Cody is poised in attack stance—wide stride, torso angled slightly forward. He wears his flight suit, complete with jetpack strapped to his back and a metallic bullet-shaped helmet. And he brandishes a ray gun. Laurence drew in by hand the ray itself shooting from the gun in an ever-narrowing spray of pinpoints. Beneath COMMANDO was printed ZZZZZAP!!!, the Zs growing in size like the reverse of the focused ray beam. Laurence selected a font remarkable for its dynamism. The very lettering, let alone Commando Cody himself, should have made that cancer cower.

Trying to summon his own brand of Zen, Laurence sat slumped in a sling chair in his home office, staring at another copy of the serial hero he had pinned to the bulletin board. But Commando Cody seemed no match for the pain.

It only got worse.

There had been pain after the surgery, and the chemo-induced neuropathy qualified as pain after a while, but this pain was from another planet.

Oncology Man prescribed a painkiller in a new delivery system, the lollipop. The brand name was Actiq, so perky and effervescent that it sounded more like an energy drink than a painkiller specific to what was termed "breakthrough cancer pain." I thought, *If this drug is meant for that, for breakthrough cancer pain, then surely it will work for Laurence, because that can't be what he has. Not breakthrough cancer pain. That's for when it gets really bad. Yes, he has cancer. And yes, he has pain— horrible pain—but the doctors keep saying his pain appears disproportionate to the "tumor load," so it has to be something else as well—a pinched nerve, or a tiny nodule pressing on just the wrong spot. This is not cancer pain. His cancer is not that bad.*

I preferred to believe he was a hypochondriac rather than dying. Even crazy. Anything but what the subtext implied.

I could hear Laurence unwrap the lollipop in the middle of the night. It didn't work. We paid a visit to the oncology office the next morning and learned he was supposed to swab the inside of his cheeks, not suck. He tried that the next night. It didn't work any better.

He needed heavy-hitting pain relief that no pill or lollipop seemed able to deliver at home, so we began a series of hospital stays for IV pain treatment.

It was during one of these brief inpatient spells that Cami participated in curating an exhibit at her college gallery. For her sophomore year, she had transferred to a school only an hour's drive from home, as opposed to the four-and-a-half-hour flight required by her previous college.

The art show at this new school was the culmination of an anthropology class called Museums and Material Culture. Cami had thoroughly enjoyed the class, and this final project was of the type that particularly spoke to her, combining art and academia in a hands-on experience. The exhibit was called "By the Work of Their Hands: 18th- to 19th-Century Pennsylvania Dutch Folk Arts and Artisans." Cami was so proud of the way it had turned out.

On the afternoon of the grand opening, I left Laurence in his hospital room and took my mother with me, driving what should be the one hour east, but was, in Friday-afternoon traffic, a bumper-to-bumper two and a half hours. I wanted to be in two places at once: Laurence's hospital room and Cami's show. Instead, I was at neither; I was sitting in traffic.

Cami delighted her Gaga with a tour of the campus and details of how the exhibit was assembled. The show was to be up for three weeks, and, as I studied each display, I told her, "You'll have to show Daddy this cool carved squirrel when he comes."

"You'll have to tell Daddy about that butter press."

"He'll love how they spun the flax into linen."

Cami had been on the team responsible for the portion of the exhibit devoted to cookie cutters. Simple but beautiful cookie cutters shaped like birds, horses, fish. Whimsical moons and stars. Special shapes for Christmas and Easter. But year-round, the heart was the most popular. Of course. Love trumps holidays, and even nature.

Daddy would especially enjoy the cookie cutters. We had no doubt he'd make it there before the exhibit closed.

After the opening festivities, Cami, my mother, and I went to a little Greek restaurant in the village neighboring the campus. We chatted about the show and what a good match this school plainly was for Cami, but suddenly, I started to weep. Something was so wrong. Laurence and I worked together and played together. Most of the time, we went to the supermarket together. Life was just more fun that way. But the thing we did the very best together was enjoying our daughter. This gallery opening was not a particularly significant or grand event, but if Cami's daddy wasn't there to see it, all was not right with the world.

SNAPSHOT

When I got pregnant—before I got pregnant, actually—Laurence and I had a secret. We both wanted a girl. We never said it out loud for fear of jinxing our chances, fifty-fifty though they obviously were, but we knew it was true. We adored our nieces, already thirteen and nine by then, and couldn't conceive (pun intended) of not having a girl of our own.

We came home from crib-shopping one afternoon to find a message on our answering machine. It was from the lab. The results of my amniocentesis were in.

First, the nurse told me what was really important. The baby was fine. I don't believe they tested for us many anomalies, syn-dromes, or diseases twenty years ago as they do now, but whatever they did test for, the results were perfect. And then the nurse asked, "Do you want to know the sex?"

"Yes, please." Girl or boy. It would be one of those two words.

Instead, she said, "Female."

"Thank you." I hung up the phone.

"It's a girl!" I said. Laurence beamed. We held each other for a long moment. But then—call it hormones or outright lunacy—I began to doubt what I had heard. I had been so primed for one of those other two words, girl or boy, that this whole "female" thing had really thrown me.

"I think she said female. Maybe I just wanted to hear that. Maybe she said male."

"I'm sure she must have said female," Laurence said.

"You call and ask."

"I'm sure she said female. Why would you think she said female if she didn't say female?"

"You call."

Laurence dialed the number. "My wife is sort of freaking out. It's a girl, right?"

I guess I just couldn't believe we could be that lucky. Neither of us could.

CHAPTER EIGHT

Once again, Oncology Man conferred with the G.I. Cancer Guru at USC, and a new cocktail was agreed upon: Leucovorin, Erbitux, CPT-11, and the good old 5-FU. It was back to the chemo room the very next day. Oncology Man couldn't get Laurence there fast enough, it seemed. This time Laurence was promised an acne-like rash across his face and upper torso courtesy of the Erbitux. The drug came with a pamphlet—again royal blue, like the tote bag handed to us on our first visit to the chemo suite—complete with photographs of the rash and warnings that drying, cracking, and redness of the skin might also come along for the ride.

We waited, not long, and the rash appeared. We decided to be glad for the proof. The drug was doing its job. Even the chemo nurse seconded this philosophy.

"It's doing its thing," she assured us as she lifted Laurence's shirt.

The drying, cracking, and redness were not far behind. These side effects, in addition to the neuropathy in Laurence's fingers and feet, made it painfully difficult for him to do any number of things. Not only could he not button his shirt, but it was sometimes uncomfortable to hold utensils. We began to think that maybe we needed to make sure we were exploring all our options.

We pulled some strings to get an appointment with a head honcho at the City of Hope. Laurence compiled a fifty-page medical history—every test, every report, every regimen—and had it spiral-bound with a clear plastic cover. This time, he selected a no-nonsense font for the title page.

As we neared Duarte, the location of the City of Hope, billboards along the side of the road declared our proximity in the way that pictures of Sleeping Beauty's Castle and the Matterhorn are paced to make a child's blood race as she approaches Disneyland. PROSTATE CANSWER. BREAST CANSWER. And there it was: COLON CANSWER. They were promising us. No matter what body part required it, they had the answer (as well as a first-class advertising team—high-fives all around the day someone came up with that one).

We arrived an hour early. It's an impressive cluster of edifices. An entire city of hope—surely there had to be a scrap there with our name on it.

Dr. City-of-Hope's office was sizable and bright. Evidently, he was a man at the top. He had a beard and wore a bow tie—a man at the top who might just be eccentric and/or pompous enough to be his own man sartorially as well. He would think outside of the box for us if need be.

Laurence pulled his medical history out of its envelope and handed it over, but the doctor wanted the *Reader's Digest* version. I could do that. I clicked into efficiency mode, accessing the mental file in which every fact was etched. Dates, drugs, procedures—whatever was required. (It amazes me now that I was ever able to relay all that information so dispassionately, without derailing into "This is the date when normal disappeared . . . These are the drugs that failed . . . These are the poisons we are trying now . . . These are the drugs for the side effects of the first drugs that have us swirling in this maelstrom . . .")

The doctor listened. And then he said, "What have your doctors said to you?"

This is what I heard: "How long have your doctors said you have to live?"

Later, Laurence told family members that Dr. City-of-Hope had said, "We'd be doing here at this hospital exactly what your doctors are doing."

The doctor had indeed said that . . . after saying all this:

It was difficult to determine if the tumor was refractory to the first line of chemo. In other words, had that chemo protocol been eliminating the tumor or merely keeping it in check? He agreed that the current chemo, the second line, was as aggressive as one could be at that point. He suggested a scan in another two months to give it time to work. If, at that testing, the tumor remained the same or was shrinking, we should continue with the current regime. If it were growing, we should change treatment. Or, he added, we should also change treatment if the side effects became intolerable. And he echoed what Oncology Man had said: Laurence should stay on some form of chemo indefinitely, even if no disease were evident. How had we gotten to a point where lifelong chemotherapy offered the best scenario?

I was silent in the car on the way home, concentrating on the driving to calm my racing heart. Normally—in our old life, our true life—Laurence would have been driving, but I was the constant driver now.

He said, "It's okay, Carla. It's okay."

And I nodded.

"We're doing everything right," Laurence said. "He said we're doing everything." He knew that was all we could do. Everything. But what if everything weren't enough? What do you do then?

A friend whose mother was two months behind us on the journey through colon cancer called shortly after we got home. "How was it?"

"City of Hopelessness," I told her. And then I cried on the phone for an hour, upstairs in the bedroom with the door closed. *I never used to close doors.*

But we kept casting about for places where we could anchor some hope. We sent a copy of Laurence's medical history to a family friend, a doctor himself whose cousin was a renowned oncologist at Sloan-Kettering. When the friend read the report, he called me. "Well, at least you will know this. No matter what happens, you will know you've done everything you can."

This man had lost his own wife to cancer. I wondered if he had spent the intervening years wishing he had done more, or if he had found comfort in the knowledge that he, too, had done all he could. Whichever was the truth of his situation, his words brought no solace. No matter how deep among the trees I found myself—admittedly with no forest in sight—even I could tell that *No matter what happens* was a euphemism.

This I did not repeat to Laurence. What was this world where I censored what I said to my husband? How had we ended up here?

At this point, we probably went a little nuts. I recognize this only in hindsight. At the time, it felt like we were behaving perfectly reasonably. Certainly, the pain knew no reason. Sometimes Laurence lay in bed, legs bent, and shook. He did not tremble; he shook. Because his body could do nothing else against the pain. No holding him, no matter how tightly, would calm the shaking. I tried to think, *Maybe it's the chemo working. This is the last hurrah of all those evil cells dying.* But the shaking came from a place so deep that it could only mean those cells were on the attack.

So, when you are in excruciating pain and you've got three malignant nodes in your peritoneal cavity, and a suspicious coating around your liver, this is what you do.

You keep doing exactly whatever the A-team of white coats tells you to do. But just in case, you contact: a hypnotist, a pranic healer, a cancer mediator, and a practitioner of the healing arts whose card reads PURPLE AURA. On the way home from her New Age office in Beverly Hills, you stop at Whole Foods to pick up bushels of carrots, as prescribed by the lady with the magic healing hands. You embark on a frenzy of juicing. Your refrigerator cannot accommodate all the carrots you have bought, so you set brown-paper bagfuls of carrots, carrots, and more carrots on the Saltillo tile step outside the kitchen where they can stay chilled by the cold autumn night.

You call the cancer clinic which advertises on television when its number appears at the bottom of the screen, and you talk to a consultant there who takes your insurance information and sends you a DVD in the mail.

You meet with a nutritionist at UCLA who tells you not to eat red meat and to concentrate on poultry, whey powder, soybeans, and sweet potatoes.

You meet with a nutritionist at an Eastern medicine institute who tells you to eat red meat and hands you a sheet marked "Guidelines for a Healthy Diet" on which he has circled the names of all manner of seaweed: hijiki, kombu, nori, wakame, and arame.

You have a phone consultation with a third nutritionist who prescribes her standard cure-all: a green soup made by pureeing boiled green beans and zucchini.

You do your own nutritional research and begin spiking everything with turmeric and cinnamon.

And, for good measure, you have a feng shui expert analyze your home. For a few hours, you wonder if there are any laws of nature so capricious that replacing a mirror with a painting or purchasing a fountain could actually beat into submission a metastasis otherwise refusing to behave according to the limited rules of medicine.

You try to remember what that one nurse had recommended immediately after the surgery—some kind of mushroom that sounded like so much voodoo at the time, but now, seven months later, is precisely the sort of thing you're adding to the arsenal.

And you buy a case of Xango juice after listening, rapt, to the cancer survivor hawking the stuff who insists that not she, but someone she knows was cured by doing nothing more than drinking the elixir. With your logical mind, you think, *It can't hurt. Maybe it will give my husband a little more energy.*

You try all this sorcery under the pretense of alleviating the pain. But in your lizard brain, you want to believe that by the time your beloved reaches the bottom of the first bottle, his insides will be positively pristine. What you are looking for is magic.

When Charles Darwin fell ill, he tried a series of quack remedies. If Darwin, that staunch advocate of science, could soak his neck in vinegar, then I could make Laurence drink the maroon juice of the mangosteen fruit imported from Israel, poured from a gracefully shaped bottle with stars imprinted on the glass. If Darwin could starve himself and soak his body in an effort to take the bath cure, then we could get up on a Sunday morning and head to Culver City to peek in on services at the "church" presided over by one of the people responsible for *The Secret*.

Our making that drive was more out of character than any of Darwin's shenanigans, more out of character than any of our own as well, but more than one person, independently of one another, had mentioned to Laurence that he might find something useful there. The origins of all that "Secret" stuff lurked there, we gathered: intention, energy, what we used to call karma. They stop short in claiming a cure for cancer, but they reel you in with the law of attraction theory. If you put it out there that you're looking for a cure, it will come. The flip side, of course, is that you must have put it out there that you were looking for the cancer in the first place, which adds a whopping helping of guilt to the cancer patient's—or any patient's—repertoire. *Shame on them*, I thought. But by then I was fully capable of holding two opposing thoughts in my head at the same time—one rational, one lunatic—especially if one nurtured hope.

In the movie version of *Butterflies Are Free*, Goldie Hawn explains that she was going to go to UCLA, but gave up because she couldn't find parking. We ended up not attending the service that morning for the same reason. It was only fitting; Laurence was an L.A. guy to the core. The parking lot for the church was full, and we, along with a stream of other cars, were directed to a lot several blocks away. As we headed in that direction, I watched the hordes of churchgoers entering the building, and all I saw were millions of germs per person.

Laurence and I looked at each other and laughed as we drove off. So much for our anomalous churchgoing impulse.

Our other craziness did not recede so quickly.

A friend had told Laurence about a Chinese Grand Master who had helped to sustain his girlfriend through breast cancer treatment. She swore by his exercises and herbs. We were not so sure about herbs, but exercises we could go for. And any other magic that couldn't interfere with the big Western magic in which we were putting our lion's share of faith.

The Master's office happened to be located not far from a restaurant Laurence had read about. The place, tucked into the corner of a strip mall, serves Chinese soup dumplings— an exotic culinary treat made by freezing broth, then wrapping dumpling dough around the savory ice cubes. The broth re-liquefies when the dumplings are boiled so that when you pop them in your mouth, steaming hot, they explode into soup from the inside out. Laurence had been eager to try them ever since he had read the restaurant review the year before. Though he was wracked with pain and continually slathering hand cream onto his cracked fingertips, he timed the appointment with the Grand Master for right after lunch so that we could hit the dumpling joint first.

We had to wait thirty minutes for a table, shoved by the door in the lunch-hour crowd. *Too many germs*, I feared. *Let's get out of here.* But I kept my mouth shut. This was supposed to be the fun part of the day. So we waited and were finally seated. Laurence did not—could not—eat anywhere near as much as he would have had we made this pilgrimage a year earlier, but we ordered several different kinds of dumplings and enjoyed the soup explosion in our mouths.

As it turned out, the Grand Master keeps his stateside office in the corner of the second floor of yet another Arcadia strip mall. This one was still under construction, and the escalators were not working. (The Master spends most of his time in Hawaii, proving his masterly ways, because who wouldn't spend most of his time in Hawaii if he was hooked up with the universe?)

The office was sparse, but a fountain gurgled somewhere. The Grand Master didn't smile much. Maybe not at all. He had some grand masterly ways of sizing Laurence up. He studied his face. I believe he gazed at his palms. Then he instructed Laurence to lie facedown on his stomach and he slapped him—hard—across the lower back. He was going to free his chi if it took beating it out of him.

I worried that he was also sending cancer cells flying, but I just sat there, a few feet away, watching, engaged in an inner dialogue about the thousands of years of Chinese practice leading up to this flogging.

He told Laurence to "do everything"—from east, west, anywhere. Laurence's energy, he could sense, was very low. "Low, low, low," he said. "After Chinese New Year, go up, up, up."

A new mantra.

"We just have to make it to Chinese New Year," we told each other from then on. This resonated with Laurence, who had a lifelong love affair with all things Chinese. It was the day before Thanksgiving. February was not so far off. We just had to make it to the day of yard-long noodles and Gung Hay Fat Choy.

The Master proposed his own dietary rules. No poultry, no lamb. A pot liquor of boiled mussel shells and pork bone spiked with black fungus. Goji berries, red date, and green papaya.

Then he led us into another room, this one nearly empty, where he demonstrated a series of exercises Laurence was to do daily, both morning and evening, in two sets of eight pairs. Qi dong, they were called—a set of meditative exercises combining breathing techniques, body movement, and mental imagery to guide the chi throughout the body. The Grand Master faced us and began the sequence of movements. To an uninitiated eye like mine, it looked like tai chi. I did them with Laurence. The slow, deliberate flow was hard for me, requiring an inner calm I could not begin to tap into. Laurence, usually less adept at exercise than I, was immediately good at it. The Master complimented him. Qi dong was as much about intent as movement. Despite the pain squeezing Laurence's back and right flank, he could connect with intent.

Clutching the four sheets detailing the exercises, we said good-bye to the Grand Master, promising to make a return visit in a few months. He told us that in the meantime, we should e-mail him with any questions and he would respond with healing energy from Hawaii. I could think of worse ways of making a living than dispensing healing energy through the ether while enjoying paradisical comfort.

We sat in traffic, barely arriving in Santa Monica in time for Laurence's appointment with the pain specialist. Appropriately, we were traveling from the extreme eastern reaches of the Los Angeles environs to the extreme west. Medicine Man, a short man given to similarly short visits, wielded his hypodermic in a sort of medical drive-by. His nurse prepped Laurence's injection sites (his back and side) with a swipe of alcohol, then instructed him to sit there on the examining-room table holding up his shirt. Medicine Man dashed in, shot, and ran.

We reconvened with him in his office to provide an update on how Laurence had fared with the prescribed drug protocol of the week. I kept pen flying over steno pad as Medicine Man tweaked the schedule, adding new drugs and dropping others. It was all trial and error week to week. He provided the Marcaine injections. At home, we dealt with Lidoderm patches applied directly onto the painful areas; more general narcotic Duragesic patches of various dosages to be changed at various intervals; a nerve desensitizer called Pamelor substituted for Restoril at night for sleep, or used along with the Restoril if desired; Ativan at night for anxiety, but not during the day; Lomotil for diarrhea; Lyrica for the continuing neuropathy; Protonix for the acid reflux from all the other meds; and Toprol if Laurence felt like his blood pressure was up a little (gee, I wonder why . . .).

The next week Laurence would inform Medicine Man that he was still in pain. I would inform him that I thought Laurence was overmedicated. Our agendas began to be at cross purposes, Laurence's and mine. All he wanted was to be out of pain. All I wanted was to have him defogged, to have him back.

I begged him, "Can't you just try to go a little longer before your next dose?"

He couldn't.

I raised my voice. "You're not trying. Do it for me. Do it for Cami."

Sometimes he could make it an extra hour between pills, or go for a couple of days on the lower-dose narcotic patch. I considered those times a victory, momentarily uplifted, for no good reason really. They did not mean the pain was lessening. Its ebb and flow and the brain's own fluctuation in processing the pain allowed him, occasionally, not to give in. And it was Laurence himself trying really hard, in spite of my accusing him of not trying at all. Actually, how hard he was trying was more than I could bear to witness. It was a tug-of-war that was excruciating to behold: the pain versus his will not to be in pain.

All I could do was rail. I am so beyond sorry that I ended up railing *at* him as well as *for* him. It was too scary: the sight of my husband caved into a chair, eyes closed, desperate to be somewhere else—somewhere other than his own body—and having only his mind to take him there.

I badgered him to do the qi dong exercises, striving to convince myself that they held some ancient key to regaining strength. Usually, he insisted the time wasn't right. He was too tired in the morning, too tired in the evening. He was too tired all the time.

When he did manage a few repetitions, I read aloud from the sheets to make sure he was incorporating every nuance of each movement. It was crucial, I thought, that he do them absolutely perfectly, as the instructions cautioned that "the best results can be attained only through doing the exercises accurately."

"Maintain a gentle smile during your practice, a smile that comes from within. It has cumulative positive effects on the energy in your internal organs, and on the appropriate mental state during practice."

Sometimes, when he could only manage two or three repetitions before promising to do more later, Laurence would nonetheless master the Buddha smile. Smiling from within was not his problem.

⌒ ⌒

For the last few months, we had been seeing a therapist to help us through. I am what you might call therapy-resistant. I believe this to be true about myself, and have always believed it, even though I had never before given it a shot. Perhaps it is a purely conceptual aversion. I don't like the idea of someone telling me what I'm feeling, and I certainly don't like the idea of someone putting my feelings into words for me. (Yes, of course, I know there's more to it than that, especially in the hands—or chair—of a skilled practitioner, but an aversion's an aversion.)

However, previous distastes, conceptual or otherwise, applied to normal life. And normal life was a thing of the past. So we went to see a lovely young woman—together, separately, the two of us, the three of us, in all permutations of our little family. Happily, she was not particularly interested in analyzing anything anymore than we were. She was there to help us make it through the day.

I sat on her couch and managed to spew on command, proving that I had left my true self on the home planet.

One Saturday morning she handed me a thick turquoise rubber band imprinted with the words "Positive Popper." She had come to know me well enough to understand I would not respond well to gimmicks, but she also knew that desperate times require desperate measures. I slipped the stretchy band onto my wrist. I had told her I was plagued by obsessive thoughts that looped in my brain. She suggested I think of three of the most disturbing thoughts and compose a counter-thought to each. Whenever one of the bad thoughts scrawled itself across my brain, I was to snap the rubber band and replace the thought with its opposite.

The first one was easy: *Laurence is going to die.* The second one required a few moments' consideration. I came up with: *the best part of my life is over.* I realized that I had lived my entire life certain the best part was just around the bend. Now all that lay ahead was darkness, a pitch so inky that the only surprise it could hold would be one of timing—precisely when the ultimate abyss would yawn in front of me. That brought me to the third thought. *All news is bad news.*

I reported these three thoughts to the young woman sitting across from me and watched her eyes fill with tears.

Then I tried to formulate the counter-thoughts. The first one was quite simple: *Laurence's health is restored.* As the days passed, I refined the mantra. Every morning, before opening my eyes, I tried to repeat it to myself: *today is another day when Laurence's health is being restored.* I went for the present tense. Not tomorrow, not in the future, but right now—today. After a while I realized that I should strive for the active voice as well: *today is another day when we are restoring Laurence's health.* Who knew that when English teachers insisted on the more vital grammatical alternative, they were offering up the gift of real-world power? *Today is another day when we are restoring Laurence's health.* I said it to myself throughout the day. I imagined I might say it to myself forever.

I couldn't come up with anything that could reverse the second thought: the best part of my life is over. Irrefutably. How could it not be over if there were no Laurence to share it with? The best part of my life is over because I cannot imagine experiencing joy without sharing it. Sharing is part of the definition of joy. The kernel. But I said the words anyway, only half believing: *I will create ways to experience joy.* The unspoken end of the sentence reverberated in the room. *No matter what.* Those three words dangled, unarticulated, after so many sentences during those days. I will carry on . . . no matter what. I will continue to be a parent . . . no matter what. I will live . . . no matter what.

Finally, I arrived at the last of the three: all news is bad news. I struggled to flip that one on its head, and finally came up with: *surprises can be good.* I believed that theoretically, in the way that you might believe in the impossible only because you cannot disprove a negative. I could barely remember the time—that was, in fact, so recent—when surprises connoted something marvelous.

A few days later, Laurence spent an hour with this young woman. He, too, came home with a rubber-band bracelet. Later, when I was rifling through the Commando Cody notebook to find a doctor's phone number, I came across a sheet of lined yellow paper. Apparently, Laurence's assignment had differed from mine. He had not sat in her office, identifying plaguing thoughts and creating their corresponding un-thoughts. In a shaky, uncontrolled version of his distinctive printing, he had simply scrawled this prayer:

> *I don't want to be a patient for the rest of my life.*
> *I don't want to be in pain anymore.*
> *This is not who I am.*
> *I don't want to be angry anymore.*
> *I want my life back.*

An acquaintance had suggested that Laurence get together with an old family friend of his who offered an ideal combination of professional qualification and personal experience. He was a psychiatrist and a cancer survivor. More than a survivor, this man had been told, some twenty or thirty years ago, to go home and die. Laurence made an appointment.

I dropped him off. The doctor, now quite elderly, worked out of his home in Brentwood Park, just a few minutes from us. Laurence emerged an hour later appropriately shored up. After all, he was better off than this old fellow. No one had actually come right out and said to him, "Go home and die."

A few weeks later, Laurence and I were wandering our neighborhood supermarket when he nodded toward an older gentleman pushing a cart—a dapper man wearing slacks and a navy blazer, not the standard grocery-shopping wardrobe of the typical Westsider.

"He's that psychiatrist," Laurence told me.

Ah, the survivor. The man who had said "Fuck you" to his doctors and kept on living.

Not only did this man look healthy, with his elegant posture and sure gait, but he looked old. Really old. He had made it to *old*.

An elderly woman, his wife, appeared a moment later and added something to their grocery cart. I wanted to weep with an amalgam of envy and hope. They had both made it. They were old.

Together.

CHAPTER NINE

On the first Friday evening in December, the merchants on Montana Avenue in Santa Monica hold an open house. They launch the Christmas season with free eggnog and hot chocolate, cookies and cubes of cheese on silver platters. Carolers in Victorian dress harmonize in front of festively decorated shops, while a Santa Claus or two widen the eyes of children delighted to be out so late. We have strolled these holiday streets every year for as long as I can remember. It's one of those events without which Christmastime doesn't quite feel like Christmastime.

However, by this Christmastime, Laurence was rarely leaving the house except for doctors' appointments. He was weak. He shuffled. He was an invalid. And he was not eating. Laurence sans appetite—it just didn't compute. I tried to cajole him into eating—just a little bite—the way you would an anorexic teenager.

Whenever I had to leave the house for any amount of time, I mapped out a route that included stopping for favorite temptations: deviled eggs from Clementine, caramelized French toast from the City Bakery, a hickory burger from the Apple Pan. They sat in the refrigerator or in the cupboard, uneaten, until they had to be thrown out.

He began losing weight alarmingly fast. Crazily, we bought a new scale in hopes that seeing its numbers go up, even a few tenths of a pound, would be reinforcing. Every now and then, he gained a pound or two.

"I knew it!" I'd say. "I could tell. You look great."

But the next day, those pounds would have melted off, along with one or two more.

Before long, Marinol joined the arsenal to help stimulate his appetite. But this medical marijuana, a tiny BB of a pill, didn't seem to work.

I dreaded dinnertime, usually so relaxed and chatty and, most especially, yummy when Laurence had done the cooking. Cami had been coming home most weekends, but now she was home for the extended winter break, making dinnertime seem even more aberrant with the three of us around the table. One night, Laurence dragged himself to the table, but he was so doped up and disinterested in food that his head flopped forward like a rag doll's. He was nodding like a junkie.

Even so, he wanted Cami and me to have the Montana Avenue Christmas fun. It was important to him. Reluctantly, we left him in the charge of a young woman who had been doing massage therapy with him and had stopped by for a visit.

"Are you sure you don't mind if we go, Laurence?"

"I'm sure."

"We'll bring you something to eat. Whatever you want. What sounds good?"

Nothing. In a most ironic play on "Be careful what you wish for," Laurence had lost his appetite.

That night in December, Cami and I phoned Laurence from the restaurant where we grabbed some dinner before hitting the shops. Cami read him the menu and he chose short ribs. I ordered them, buoyed by his enthusiasm for the dish. Riding a wave of optimism, I ordered butternut squash ravioli as well, thinking it would make an appealing accompaniment, at least one that would go down easily.

I should have known better. It was easy for him to order from a distance. In his brain, he was still himself. He had a perfectly enthusiastic theoretical appetite; it was the one in his gut that was not cooperating.

It was my first evening out of the house in a long time. You might have to be a Southern California native (or semi-native) to recognize the subtleties of our seasonal shifts, but to us, it was beginning to feel a lot like Christmas. A crisp, cool evening that required the heaviest jacket I owned. Cami and I bought a few presents at a favorite jewelry store, but I was not able to focus on the task. I could not select specific items for specific people on my Christmas list, so we picked up a few generic gifts and called it a night. I was preoccupied. After all, Laurence was home, wait-ing eagerly (I pretended) for his short ribs. It had become so much about food for me—eating heartily so much bespeaking life, not eating at all so screaming something else.

As Cami and I hurried back to the car, carry-out bag in hand, we ran into an old friend whom I had not seen in years. I ques-tioned her for news of her family, hoping to deflect reciprocal questions. But, inevitably, they came.

"How are things with you?"

"Well, Laurence is sick."

"Oh, I'm sorry."

I smiled and we were on our way. I realized after the fact that she probably thought he was home with the flu. Why would anything less benign even cross her mind? I had not been able to say, "Laurence is sick. Really sick. Actually, he might be dying." How could I speak it if I could never let myself think it?

As it turned out, the short ribs did not dazzle in the way that I had hoped. Laurence ate a few bites; I negotiated one or two more—again, so much coaxing—and then we both gave up. We were both too exhausted. Besides, two more bites would not buy normal.

That evening did not herald the start of the Christmas season as the first Friday night in December traditionally did. Instead, it felt like the beginning of the end.

Oncology Man had continued to confer with the USC G.I. Cancer Guru who had been consulting on Laurence's case from the start. Ten days later, we made an expedition to USC to meet with the guru in person. Off to see the wizard.

The scans performed a few days before had shown that the second line of chemo was doing less than nothing. While the nodules appeared the same, there was some disease progression of the coating around the liver. We had phoned a specialist at Sloan-Kettering in New York who had performed surgery on a friend of a friend. We faxed her all fifty pages of Laurence's history and waited. The word came back from her assistant that she would only see Laurence if and when the disease actually invaded his liver. This shadowy coating didn't count. We supposed that fell into the be-grateful-for-small-favors category.

By mid-December, Laurence was in agony most of the time. The pain was both more intense and more widespread. I remembered that when I was pregnant, I believed that labor pains would be isolated, like menstrual cramps. The actual pain, of course, was staggering; I experienced it across and through every centimeter of my body. That was happening to Laurence, only there would be no prize at the end. But he did not complain. Mostly, he just wanted to be left alone with his drugs.

On several occasions, I drove him to the chemo room at Oncology Man's office for an intravenous hit of Dilaudid, a major narcotic that seemed to provide some relief. His special chemo nurse would usher him into one of the few private rooms so that he could lie on a bed while the medication was administered. The recliners were no longer comfortable. Nothing was comfortable. Secretly I wondered if he looked too frightening for the other patients in the communal rooms.

The day we went to see the Guru at USC, I gave Laurence a pep talk. "Try to perk up a little, sweetie. Please." I wanted to entice him back to this planet, but I would yank him if I had to.

I cannot remember if I just thought or actually said, "You have to seem like someone worth saving." I wanted to beg him, *Show the fight on the outside that I know you still have on the inside*. But all he could really focus on was getting through the appointment so that he could be hooked up to some Dilaudid right there in the USC chemo room. The Dilaudid had become his best friend; his pain was that great.

The moment the Guru's nurse walked into the examining room, Laurence felt understood.

She looked at him and said, "This is unacceptable."

Laurence relaxed a bit. The Guru would have ways to address the pain.

And indeed he did. From the moment he appeared, the Guru inspired confidence. His accent was as thickly German as his name, and I thought, *Hallelujah! Let him stormtroop through the cancer!* He suggested many alternatives to the pain regimen we'd been trying, unsuccessfully, to hone over the previous several weeks. What about methadone? What about other oral meds whose names swarmed us? What about a saddle block that could alleviate the pain but keep the mind unclouded? We were ready to try them all—one at a time, or all at once. Bring them on. Please.

He ordered a slide of the original tumor removed in the surgery nine months earlier so that testing could be performed on it. Chemo-sensitivity testing would discover which therapies were effective against this particular cell structure. Finally.

Then he took out a blue folder containing various drug pamphlets and he scribbled a list on the front. Four different chemo protocols, some already in clinical trial, others experimental. He ticked them off one by one.

"If this one doesn't work, we go to this one, then this one, then . . ."

I looked the Guru in the eye and nodded. *Yes, that's what we want to hear. Tell us more. Tell us a story of possibility.*

He was going to be our magic man.

It took enormous effort to remain focused, to ask questions. "Are these double-blind studies? Is there a possibility Laurence will get a placebo?"

"No," he promised. Laurence would get the real thing until it did the job.

Suddenly, there was hope again. That was all we needed. A taste of hope. Laurence would begin the first clinical trial on the list the very next day.

Finally, the Guru confirmed what we had hoped might be the truth, an unspoken truth we had been clutching so tightly. Despite three tiny nodules in the peritoneal cavity. Despite a coating around the liver. Vital organs uninvaded. His accent crisp, he said matter-of-factly, "What's to kill you here?"

Laurence smiled. It was a question that penetrated the fog. It was a question that penetrated the pain.

And there was more out there to try. We would keep trying. All Laurence had to do was stay alive until we found the magic treatment.

We called Cami the minute we got in the car.

"He said, 'What's to kill you here?' That means there's nothing. There's nothing to kill him here. And he's got four or five trials that Daddy can do! 'What's to kill you here?' That's what he said! Isn't that great? 'What's to kill you here?'"

Laurence and I repeated that question to each other countless times every day.

We just assumed the wrong answer.

— ～

Laurence began the new chemo protocol—the third—the day after our visit to USC. A different IV drug—shipped to Oncology Man's office in Santa Monica—plus an oral medication. While we waited for them to work, pain management remained the issue of the day—every day, every hour, every minute.

So the next few weeks were punctuated with overnight hospital stays. Some mornings when I arrived, instantaneously feeling like I had never left, I momentarily forgot which room Laurence was in, like when you emerge from the grocery store or the dry cleaner, places you frequent regularly, and cannot remember where you parked your car on that particular day.

Between hospital overnights was a blur of doctors' visits. The names of MDs etched into stainless-steel plaques on door after door. Stale magazines, blond wood, flecked linoleum. Artificial wood-grained cabinets with drawers full of latex gloves. Cylindrical waste receptacles, shiny chrome and three feet high. Chalky pastel walls meant to soothe. Doctor after doctor rolling closer to Laurence on a wheeled stool to poke or prod or palpate and have a closer look. When we sat in these examining rooms waiting for the doctor to appear, I froze at every ring of the phone outside, every hushed tone, every intercom announcement, assuming they all concerned us, concerned Laurence—secrets too heinous to be spoken in our presence.

Our world had shrunk. I studied the faces of the people in the oncologist's waiting room—the non-patients—and wondered if they felt the same way. The waiting room was always full. There's a lot of cancer going around. Patients and their loved ones ringed the room, usually in pairs. Some of the non-patients were obviously helping their elderly parents. I envied them. Middle-aged sons and daughters in disbelief at how the father who had tossed them in the air had grown so frail, or how the mother who had kissed their boo-boos better had withered so.

There were a few pairs—patient plus one—who were less easily defined. I wondered if one woman was the wife or daughter of the man sitting next to her. And then I looked at Laurence and wondered if people were wondering that about us. Were there people who assumed I was the dutiful daughter? Did he look that bad? I didn't think so. I couldn't see it, but still, it was possible. Or did I look too drained, too afraid, too desperate, to be the daughter? So many of the spouses in this room were the more haggard of the couple. Our husbands, our wives, were struggling to get from moment to moment while we fought to maintain myopia, strenuously avoiding the big picture.

One morning as I was studying the players in the waiting room, inventing their backstories, a young man bounded through the door. He was strapping. There was no other word for him. I tried to match him up with one of the older patients. Whose son was he? He was actually young enough to be a grandson. But then I noticed the purple elastic tied around his arm, indicating that he had just given blood at the lab across the hall, as had Laurence. That's the drill before they can administer your chemo. Cancer, the equal opportunity attacker, had turned this fit-looking young man into one of the patients in this room.

When an older man, maneuvering his cane, approached the door, the young man leapt across the room to open it for him. Effortlessly and with such energy. It was impossible to reconcile the elastic around his arm with his vigor. Like Laurence during the first go-round.

The young man returned to his seat. I listened as the woman seated next to him struck up a conversation.

"I think you're one of my customers," she said.

He asked where he worked, and she explained that she owned a health food restaurant.

"My daughter's a vegetarian," he told her. "She'd probably know the place."

A sound caught in the back of my throat. This young man had a daughter, probably a middle schooler—the age when many young California girls flirt with vegetarianism on their way to personhood. This young man had a family. Making up the stories of these people's lives was one thing, but unearthing the real stories was quite another.

When the nurse called the restaurateur out of the waiting room back into the doctor's office, I was astounded. I recognized her name because her restaurant, a well-known institution in health food circles, bears the same name. If this woman, who had devoted her life to making sure everything that goes into her mouth is organic and sprouted and nutrient-rich, could not escape a spot in this office, then how could anyone else?

When the nurse called Laurence in—"Mr. Starkman"—he didn't want me to go in with him. For the first time, he said, "It's okay. I'll go in by myself."

"Are you sure?"

"I'm sure."

Clichés become clichés for a reason. At that moment my blood ran cold. What had he not been telling me? Where did it hurt now? What question did he want to ask that he would not be able to utter if I were sitting beside him? And how chilling, how surreal, would the answer be?

I stayed in the waiting room, seated across from an older couple. The woman's hair was in pigtails, gray straw shooting out like a geriatric Pippi Longstocking. She chattered at her silent husband about upcoming holiday plans, complaining that she could not come to terms with the idea that they were no longer the caretakers of the family. She was chagrined that she could no longer drive, that they had to be chauffeured to family celebrations like children.

Finally, her husband spoke matter-of-factly. "That's the way it is."

And, alone in that waiting room, I thought, *Isn't that just the truth for everyone in this godforsaken room.*

— ∽

Early on, I expended a lot of mental energy on continuous calculations of time—how far along we would be by this point or that. I thought a great deal about Christmas. *We will be two scans clean. The second surgery will be over. There will be so much to celebrate.*

I had often said to Laurence, "Just think. Once we've accomplished this, we won't have to worry about doing anything else for the rest of our lives."

Yes, Christmas would be magnificent. That's what I had thought in August and September. I would buy gifts for the entire team of doctors and all the chemo nurses, gifts of thanks for a job well done . . . a job completed. But instead, as I taped the cards onto their packages, I silently imbued them with supplications to keep going—to not give up.

Cami and I delivered the presents. I circled the block while she dashed into the various offices. We tried to pretend it felt like other Christmas ho-ho-ho delivery days from years past. We listened to the same Christmas tape in the car that we have played since she was four years old. But we knew that nothing was the same this Christmas, even if her childhood favorites,

Sharon, Lois, and Bram, were singing, "When it's Christmastime in Hawaii, all the little elves do the hula . . ." This year, we weren't singing along.

By now, the Dilaudid had moved in. Laurence's drug of choice, closest to being up to the job. It dulled the pain, occasionally bordered on erasing it. But relief came at a price, for me as much as for him. It took him away. The only place without pain was so far away, too far away. He couldn't go there and still be here.

Our dining room table was overrun with medical equipment so that Laurence could administer the drug at home on his own. He was so motivated to have control over the medication's availability that he learned how to hook himself up, a task normally left to medical professionals, or at least, paraprofessionals . . . or junkies. There were pumps. There were tubes. And tiny multicolored pieces of plastic. I didn't know what they were all for. The dining room table became Laurence's purview. Ashamedly, it was too much for me. I let him sit with the visiting nurse and learn to prep the site—his port—and then flush the lines and hook himself up to the drug.

In our refrigerator were bags of saline and of the drug itself—a controlled substance for which we had to sign when it arrived at our doorstep by courier in a cooler. Nurses from the infusion center came daily, I think. (Like an infant's feeding schedule, you think these facts are etching themselves into your brain forever—all you think about—but they are soon deleted by the next round of crucial information.)

The constant reminder that was the pain regimen made me cranky. Though we were still battling the common enemy, in some warped version of transference, I shifted my rage from the disease to Laurence himself. I cannot bear to think of it now, these many months later, but he was driving me crazy. Out of sheer exhaustion and its ubiquitous companion, despair, I lost the ability to separate Laurence from the disease. The disease was robbing him of who he was, bit by bit. He sat for hours, his back against a heating pad, with headphones on. Now, after the fact, I am so grateful that those moments seemed to bring him some peace. But during those days, I was enraged. Sometimes he was so inaccessible that I panicked. He was strung out.

Despite the various books people offered on caregiving, all of which discussed the caregiver's inevitable resentment toward the patient, the fury only split me further. I was angry and I was guilty and I was ashamed. I was out of control. What broke my heart most was realizing that if I felt that way, how must Laurence's guilt and anger—intense beyond words, beyond measure—have made him feel? Because at the bottom of all this gnawed a horrific presumption: this didn't have to happen.

I called my sister nightly and she listened. (That is all anyone can ever do for someone who was in my position. All one can do, and the best one can do: listen. When there is nothing that can be done, there is nothing that can be said; listening becomes its own kind of advice, its own gift.) We pretended we were having a normal conversation. We talked about how men are such horrible patients, as we might have if either of our husbands had been nursing a cold. We invoked, "What's to kill you here?" and said repeatedly that Laurence just had to try a little harder. But I would be so tired of coaxing and cajoling him to eat, to try, to just be present, that I ended up saying, "This is what's going to happen: I'm going to save his life, and then I'm going to divorce him."

We both knew I didn't mean it. It was just another framework, another excuse for saying the first part out loud, the saving-his-life part. I had thought the bargaining phase had long since passed, but it was appearing again in this new form. *Just let him live and I'll let him go.* Of course that wasn't true, but if the universe was playing fast and loose with the whole bargaining concept, so could I.

Still, there were days when hope did not seem misplaced. Early in December, Laurence and I went Christmas shopping for Cami. He hooked himself up, took a nice hit of Dilaudid, and off we went. Given the planet we now inhabited, it seemed a perfectly sensible way to begin the day. We headed east to Melrose where we stopped at Johnny Rockets. Laurence ate his whole burger. Maybe we were turning a corner.

When we were out and about, stopping in and out of shops on Larchmont Boulevard, it was easy to forget that Laurence had, just an hour or two earlier, been receiving heavy narcotics through a plastic disc embedded under his skin. We had made this expedition eastward because there is only one store in town that carries Wee Forest Folk, the tiny handcrafted mice Cami has collected since she was in preschool. It could not be Christmas without a new mouse in Cami's stocking. (Yes, Cami was nineteen years old, but holiday traditions have always loomed large in her life. She still hangs a stocking; she still leaves cookies for Santa; and Santa still leaves her a note, thanking her for being such a good girl.) This was our normal, and clinging to it became even more critical as the holidays neared.

Laurence studied the tiny ceramic mice in the case. He chose a snow scene featuring a baby mouse poking out of an igloo as the mama, bundled in a pink, fur-trimmed creation, adds another snowball to their home. Now, when I dust the shelves of mice, each holding a memory of a birthday or holiday, I can't help but be struck by the fact that this last miniature includes only the mama and the baby in their iridescent home.

It would be the last present Laurence would ever pick out for Cami. When she opened it on Christmas morning, I made sure she knew. This year it wasn't from the North Pole. Not out of Santa's sack. No elves involved.

"Daddy picked it out," I said. "Look how beautiful. See how the snow sparkles. Daddy picked it out."

By that Christmas morning, nothing much felt like Christmas. We had turned down every party.

"Next year. We'll be there next year."

And, of course, we didn't throw our own annual party, an extravaganza that traditionally took months in the planning and a solid week devoted to preparation. No talk of menus or flowers or twinkle lights in the tent enclosing the backyard. This year, the dining room table held no carving boards bearing spiral-sliced ham; no platters of cookies; no candles that looked like ornaments. Just containers of sterile needles. And tubing. And painkillers.

No matter; on the twenty-third of December, Laurence surprised us. He announced we were going to Mr. Chow's to celebrate his birthday, which was the next day. And that we did.

We arrived in Beverly Hills a few minutes early. As I handed the car over to the valet, Laurence spotted a sale across the street at a swank shoe store. He insisted we go. He bought himself a pair of black Beatle boots—like nothing he had ever owned or, as far as I know, wanted to own. But he was drawn to them and when he tried them on, they looked great.

"Buy them," I said.

"Buy them, Daddy," Cami said.

I wondered if my shopping impulse was contagious. Was he also trusting my mantra? *If I buy them, life will come.*

"They'll be great when we go to San Francisco," I offered. A visit up north was long overdue. It would make a splendid first stab at traveling again when the next scan came back clean, or maybe after the next two clean scans. Whenever that would be. Maybe after Chinese New Year? As we crossed the street to Mr. Chow's, it felt like a time for celebration might still be lurking in our future. It felt like the future might still be lurking in our future.

Laurence enjoyed his birthday dinner. All the Mr. Chow's specialties, notably a Peking duck, Laurence's favorite. He ate heartily and happily, no coaxing required. The three of us were dressed up. We felt celebratory. On my way to the ladies' room, I whispered to the waiter to put a candle in a dessert. Laurence was relaxed and smiled his old smile. I thought, *Okay, this curing-cancer thing is doable after all. We're doing this. Next year on his birthday, we'll have the biggest party ever.*

I could have begun planning that party right then—Laurence looked that good as we sat there at Mr. Chow's on December 23rd. Cami told me later that he had confessed to secretly planning this celebration for days. I didn't allow myself to realize how much psyching up it must have required. He rose to the occasion with such élan. He managed to let his old self inhabit his body for that one evening. Though we were celebrating his birthday, he gave the real present to Cami and me.

Before returning home, we cruised Beverly Hills to take in the Christmas lights just as we had every year since Cami was a baby. It seems that each year fewer and fewer houses are decked out, but we knew where to find the reliable standbys. It warmed our hearts to spot them in their full holiday regalia, as though we had never before oohed and aahed over the Rockette line of Santas or the giant reindeer springing toward a chimney. Laurence was tired when we got home, but it had been a good night. Cami and I would remember it as a great night.

Cami would tell me later that one night during that holiday week, Laurence and she were watching television together. *Scrubs,* a shared favorite. In this particular episode, young doctor Turk had forgotten to bring his wife's suitcase to the hospital when she went into labor.

Turk grabs his pal JD's hand.

"What are we going to do?" asks JD.

"Sometimes if you shut your eyes and pray really hard, a miracle will happen. Help me out."

They shut their eyes and clutch each other's hands, and, sure enough, Turk's dog runs into the hospital and sets the suitcase at their feet.

Cami grabbed her daddy's hand. "Let's close our eyes and pray really hard."

They faced each other and closed their eyes so tightly that their heads vibrated.

SNAPSHOT

The ride was called the Wacky Soap Box Racers, but it was one of the tamer attractions at Knott's Berry Farm. Cami must have been about six on this particular trip, and her cousin, Emily, nine years older, came along, which made any outing extra fun for Cami.

We stood in line waiting for this nonthreatening roller coaster. Sort of a roller coaster in training. There would be no whipping around hairpin turns or precipitous drops. This roller coaster was, in fact, so easygoing that it may have been located in Camp Snoopy, the area of the park designated for its youngest guests.

As we approached the front of the line, Laurence announced to the girls that he might sit this one out. "It's a little too zippy for me." They thought this was hysterical.

He did not sit out the ride, and forever after insisted he had just been making a joke, upping the danger quotient to make the feeble ride more thrilling. Regardless, for the rest of the day, we all badgered him about whether this ride or that might be too zippy for him.

By the time we arrived home that night, he was Uncle Zippy. And Uncle Zippy he stayed, to his nieces and then, years later, to their children.

Some fifteen years later, at Emily's baby shower, we ladies cooed as tiny onesies and whisper-soft blankets were pulled from pastel boxes. Upstairs, Uncle Zippy—one month before diagnosis— entertained the two-year-old daughter of our other niece, Alison. I went upstairs to bring them a plate of cookies. There they were: Uncle Zippy and little Mila, jumping on the bed and singing along with the Beatles as "A Hard Day's Night" played on the TV.

CHAPTER TEN

When I look back on those December weeks, I realize that we were doing our own version of hospice, though no one ever used the word. Our days revolved around drug protocol. Nurses came and went to make sure all was well with tubing and needles. Delivery men rang our bell with drugs that needed to be rushed to the refrigerator. Laurence moved from the couch to the recliner to the canvas chair in his office.

When you have been with someone as long as Laurence and I, you don't really see what's happening. In the way that a mother always sees the baby, the toddler, the schoolgirl, in the young woman standing in front of her, I still saw Laurence as a young man and a new father. Even as he sat, medicated into limbo, slumped into the Zero Gravity chair, headphones playing Bob Dylan or the Yardbirds or Bo Diddley, or drumming the beat of a Boston song on his thighs.

Finally, however, I could not help but see the dying man. As Laurence's pain became more and more unmanageable and sleep less and less attainable, I tried sleeping in Cami's room. But when she came home from college for the monthlong Christmas break, I moved back to our room. We bought a new easy chair—one that opened into a single bed. It was meant for the occasional night when I had to move out of our bed. But once we opened it, we never closed it again. It became my bed.

I lay in it night after night listening to Laurence a few feet away in our bed. He was in constant motion, searching for a position that might, even just for a few moments, be remotely comfortable. The sheets rustled all night long. And he was plagued by those hiccups, so ferocious and long-lasting; they exhausted him. Every hour or so he would get up to go to the bathroom or just to relocate to the Zero Gravity chair or to a different venue downstairs—the office sling chair, the La-Z-Boy, the good old couch. From where I lay on the cot-sized bed, I watched him shuffle to the bathroom before heading downstairs, each foot's contact with the carpet, then the bathroom tile, tentative and unsure.

"Do you need some help?" I'd ask him in the middle of the night.

"No, I'm okay."

Sometimes I said, "Maybe if you tried to move a little more normally, you'd feel better."

Again, how embarrassing. I don't even know what that meant. Maybe, *You move like a dying man and that's too scary for me. Please try to stop that. Maybe if you moved differently, like your old self, you'd feel better and then you wouldn't be a dying man anymore.* I was insane. I said insane things.

And I was terrified every time he got up. The neuropathy had made the soles of his feet dangerously numb. He had already fallen once in the shower, crashing with a thud, letting out a shriek, "Goddammit!"—more fury even than pain. I ran to the bathroom to find my husband in a heap on the shower floor. *Could this be it? Could this be how it happens? After all this—with a bump on the head?*

Family Doc was out of the office, so that emergency visit was to his associate. He examined Laurence and said he looked okay, but ordered an MRI of his head to be sure, given . . . he paused . . . given all that he was going through. His head was indeed fine. But mine was not. I could not erase the sound—the weight of Laurence's body hitting the shower floor full force, the crack of skull hitting tile, the echo of his scream. After the fact, I realized I had thought I might find him dead.

So I went a little more insane.

You can't avoid going insane when what you see in front of you no longer matches the reality in your heart. I watched my husband from my narrow chair-bed and tried to comprehend that the moment had come when I could no longer see my boyfriend, my young husband, my daughter's young father. No matter how much he rallied during the day—which varied from day to day, from hour to hour—in the middle of those nights, he looked like none of those things. He was a man fighting a terminal disease. And losing.

Even then, clock ticking as though we were counting down to high noon before a ghost-town gunfight, I couldn't understand how it could be possible that we might lose. Americans in particular are bred to believe that right prevails. Doing everything right, including working hard, earns you the American dream. The drug companies know we believe this. They perpetuate the myth in order to pad their pockets.

"I'm ready to fight," says a woman with short-cropped hair,

steeled for her fight against cancer as she looks right into the lens and into your eyes through the television screen.

"I'm ready to fight," says a man, similarly steadfast.

"I'm ready to fight," says another, this one of some non-white ethnicity.

They're all ready to fight.

By December, we had been fighting for nine months. We had recently added one of those ready-to-fight drugs to the arsenal in order to keep Laurence's blood counts up, resistant to infection, and able to withstand the chemo. Now we were not only doing what the doctors said and a fair amount of what the non-doctors suggested, but following Madison Avenue's two cents as well.

Add to this combo my personal history, and I just couldn't figure out how we could be losing. There was the example set by my father, after all. In him, stubborn Eastern European stock blended with a particular predisposition toward interpreting neutral facts as a personal challenge. My father was a man who took a high-cholesterol reading as a dare.

I grew up assuming that mind-over-body worked regardless of whatever havoc was being wrought in the body. Laurence's being sick—this sick—made no sense. So there I was. When what you believe comes face-to-face with what you see in front of you, and they cannot coexist reasonably, all you can do is lose your mind.

I know of one oncologist (not Oncology Man) who uses the term "the narcissism of the cured." This is the "after" half of the before-and-after pictures that serve up all those ready-to-fight spokespeople. "Survivors" parade their survival (and more power to them—I am envious, after all). Their friends and family point to their fighting spirit as the critical element in their victory. The thing that made the difference. Fine. But where does that leave those of us who had fighting spirit enough for a hundred victories and still lost? Where does that leave those of us who had confidence in our ability to prevail? Does that make us more the loser or less? Or does it just make us the ones who caught a bad roll of the dice?

———　～

Since there would be no Christmas party and no guests, putting up the tree lacked its usual cheer. Only a few days before Christmas, and for the first time ever, we hired someone to haul the thing in and string the lights. Aptly, he called himself Dr. Christmas. Of course. There were nothing but doctors in our life. Even Christmas had its own specialist.

Laurence joined my father on the couch in the den, directing the placement of ornaments rather than participating in their actual hanging. Frank Sinatra sang from the stereo ("I love those J-I-N-G-L-E bells . . .") as he always has for my family, and we all tried our level best to make merry. When my mother opened the refrigerator to retrieve the eggnog, she pretended not to notice the two shelves piled with plastic bags of saline and narcotics. For a moment, when Laurence got up from the couch and reached high to place the star on the top of the tree, I thought there would surely be many Christmases to come when he would do the same.

Early on, we had argued about Christmas trees. We were living together, as yet unmarried, in the Westwood condo, and throwing what would be the first round of our holiday parties. We had the same conversation every December. We both wanted what we were used to, what we had grown up with. I wanted a tree and Laurence did not. We settled on decorating the living room ficus in an uber-eighties color scheme of silver and rose. Year after year, I managed to elicit a promise that we could have a Christmas tree when we had a child, but I think our first tree appeared the year before Cami was born.

Laurence was hooked. If he was going to do something, he was going to do it right. We began to collect ornaments, Laurence as enthusiastic about each magnificent one as I. Whatever he did, he did with style. Even if he had been a bar mitzvah boy (yielding a hilarious photo album, if not the desire to ever again set foot in a temple), he was going to have a knockout Christmas tree.

For two people with an equal disaffinity for religion, we turned out to be very much committed to imbuing our tiny family with our own sense of tradition. Raised on old-school Disney fare, I often thought of the line in the original *Parent Trap*, when Hayley Mills inhales her grandfather's smell—a mix of tobacco and peppermint—and declares that she is "making a memory." *That's what we're doing*, I sometimes thought. *Making memories*. I just never knew how soon Cami and I would need them. I always assumed there would be so much time to grow more.

The trouble with doing something the same way year after year is that when you no longer can, it shines a spotlight on how out-of-order everything is.

On Christmas Eve, Cami retreated upstairs so that Santa's elves could do their thing. She was never a child who rummaged in closets or shook mysterious pre-Christmas boxes. That would spoil the fun. And big fun it was. Christmas morning has always been something of an obscene display in our house, I admit, and its surprise value—the evidence of Santa's visit sprawling beneath the tree—requires a fair amount of dashing about the night before.

This year, there were none of Laurence's teasing reprimands: "You've overdone it again." He didn't even supervise from the couch.

He padded upstairs to watch TV while I moved, nearly possessed with my solitary mission, from closet to tree, cupboard to stockings, stowed shopping bags to den. I didn't realize I was crying until I myself had to play Santa—traditionally Laurence's job—and nibble at the cookies left in front of the fireplace (yes, by our nineteen-year-old daughter). Laurence had a gift for this task, leaving the perfect pile of crumbs, the exact slosh of cocoa at the bottom of the mug, aptly jagged tooth marks in the reindeers' carrots. I tried to duplicate the remnants of a snack well enjoyed, but had to give up when it came to getting the hot chocolate down my throat. I poured it down the kitchen sink and replaced the empty mug on the hearth. The scene—presents beneath the tree, stockings stuffed, Santa's leftover crumbs—looked like every Christmas past. I sat alone in the den for a long moment before heading upstairs, terrified that what it felt like was Christmas future.

Despite the phantom in the corner, Christmas morning was Christmas morning. Laurence snapped photos. Cami opened her stocking stuffers first. We moved to the presents under the tree. I had wrestled with what to buy for Laurence, trying to come up with gifts that he would enjoy and use, but which did not scream "patient," mainly books (including cookbooks blatantly designed to whet his appetite) and DVDs. Other boxes held soft cashmere gloves and socks. I hoped they were luxurious enough to counter the obvious implication. They were intended to alleviate the worsening miseries of the neuropathy.

Laurence and Cami gave me a necklace, a fine gold chain

from which dangle two small charms. One is the Eye of Horus, the ancient Egyptian symbol of protection and indestructibility, believed to assist in rebirth. The other is a Hamsa, that stylized hand with thumb and pinkie of equal lengths, both flaring out to the sides. It, too, is believed to ward off evil and offer protection. These particular two charms have tiny sapphires in their centers, sapphire being the gem for the month of September, the month of our anniversary. This would be the last present Laurence would ever give me. Amulets to watch over me and hold my hand when he no longer could.

After opening gifts at home, we trundled off to my sister's house nearby for more family Christmas. I cannot remember if I allowed myself to wonder if this would be our last Christmas. I don't think I believed that. The worst still meant that there were no longer an infinite number of Christmases stretching out ahead. That seemed undeniable.

But not our last.

I phoned Dr. Christmas on December 26th. "Get the tree down."

CHAPTER ELEVEN

People pray for you in whatever way they can. From the moment friends and family learned of Laurence's diagnosis, we received word of prayers rushing out on his behalf. Laurence's cousin tucked a slip of paper bearing his name into the Western Wall. An acquaintance—barely more than a business associate—incorporated his name into her daily Buddhist meditation. Our Christian friends prayed to the God in whom they believe with all their hearts. And then there were all the other prayers that may not have been called prayers but were equally pure. The friends who pictured Laurence bathed in white light, haloed in golden energy, already well and whole.

We were grateful for it all.

Jim, Laurence's dear friend and one-time partner in the film title business, took him on excursions to art museums. Other friends took him to lunch. One of Laurence's oldest and closest friends, Uncle Larry to Cami, dropped everything and came from his home in Reno when we needed him before Laurence's surgery in March. He came to celebrate with us for that ten minutes in October when we thought we had something to celebrate. And he came at the end.

I don't pray. I hold good thoughts—or try to. And I can give the white light thing a go when desperation takes hold. But I have such a pestering interior monologue, even dialogue when I'm feeling particularly schitzy, that the impulse to quell the brain mania is far stronger than any to engage another party. I suppose that proves how little I know about praying. I know; it should come from the heart, not the brain, and it should bring peace, not more frenzy. I figure the universe knows the state and intention of my heart, if it cares, and by the end of December, I felt fairly certain that it did not much care.

So, by this time, my prayer took the form of a concoction. Cottage cheese and flaxseed oil, plus a handful of frozen strawberries and a squirt of honey to make the goo more palatable. I had read about this miracle mixture in a book cataloging unconventional cancer cures. Something to do with creating a sulfuric environment sufficiently unfriendly to cancer cells to halt their proliferation. The only way I knew to pray was to *do*, to keep in motion, to keep the demon from the door, and, as it turned out, to dump stuff in the Cuisinart.

Laurence was game, but despite his promises, he couldn't manage even a few spoonfuls. I implored him to take a bite every now and then; it seems so beyond-silly now. But the Tupperware container remained full day after day until, unable to determine the shelf life of such glop, I mashed it down the garbage disposal.

I was out of tricks. And out of prayers.

This new chemo clinical trial had to work its magic. That's all there was to it.

On January 5th, I dropped Laurence off at the chemo clinic and went to meet Cami, her friend, and her friend's mother for lunch. When I got back in the car, I phoned Laurence to find out what time he needed to be picked up.

"They couldn't do it," he said. For the first time, his blood work was not perfect. His white count was elevated just enough to prohibit receiving his chemo and to require an antibiotic. He started taking the oral antibiotic immediately.

We had had a tearful scene that night, the three of us. It was all about his effort. Cami and I pleaded with him to try harder. We screamed—not unusual for me, but most unlike her. It makes no sense now, but still, Laurence promised to try harder.

Cami would tell me later that that night, after I had gone to bed, the two of them were bundled on the couch in the den, watching television. Her daddy assured her, "It's still me inside." Then he smiled, almost sheepishly, and nodded slightly—convincing her, convincing himself.

The next morning, he appeared recommitted, energized, almost chipper. "I feel pretty good today," he said. Wouldn't it be funny, we wondered, if all he'd needed was an ordinary antibiotic to make him start feeling better?

But the twenty-four-hour blood work had shown an infection that, according to the powers-that-be, warranted IV antibiotics in the hospital. We figured it would just be a couple of days and that he'd feel that much stronger, strong enough to resume the chemo. That's what I was singly focused on. Not skipping a chemo beat.

He checked in to the hospital on January 6th, whereupon a new parade of doctors joined the squadron. At first, it was the infectious disease guy with his questions about foreign travel. *If only Laurence had contracted an exotic disease in the tropics*, I thought. It appeared obvious to me that a different sort of port was the culprit—the one implanted just under the skin below his collarbone, which he had been accessing himself in our dining room for the past several weeks.

When we had moved the infusion center into our home, I had been deeply concerned that all those needles would be an open invitation to infection no matter how many precautions we took. I had remained uncharacteristically silent on the matter, since Laurence felt there was no choice, and he was the one in pain. But now, I was certain that I had once again worried a physiological phenomenon into being.

Or maybe not. Maybe the infection had just happened, needles or no needles. Who knew anything anymore? All I knew for sure was that Laurence had not contracted a romantic ailment on a hip vacation to Costa Rica. I also knew that these were the things that get cancer patients. The secondary ailments, the disease tributaries.

Pushing those thoughts aside, I remained fixated on continuing the experimental chemo, counting each day he was overdue. I asked every doctor when he thought Laurence would be able to resume the regimen.

The pain specialist, Medicine Man, dropped by with greater frequency than he had during previous hospital stints. I asked him about the other pain-relieving options suggested by the USC Guru—methadone, a saddle block. He said, "That's for down the road."

I tried to take that as a good sign. If there was more down the road, then we weren't at the end of the road yet. But I wondered how many bends in the road Laurence would have to round before he could try some methadone. At the same time, I wondered how much more of his self the methadone would take while it was busy taking away his pain.

— —

And then, after a few days, another specialist appeared. The lung doctor. Apparently, Laurence had not contracted malaria while on safari, but he had managed to contract pneumonia while in the hospital. It was determined that it was not bacterial pneumonia, but rather aspirational. He had inhaled some particulate matter into his lungs. I remembered a few days before, Laurence had been given a chalky white tablet (Mylanta or some such) to chew for general digestive discomfort.

He floated at the edge of a highly medicated semi-stupor much of the time, and his mouth was miserably dry from many of the medications that kept him there. In that state, he had choked on the tablet, sputtering and spitting and gasping for air as the white powder sprayed from his mouth. That had to be the moment. He must have gasped in a speck of the powder, just enough to settle into a lung and percolate into pneumonia.

This will be the thing that does it. If it's not the blood infection, it will be this. Pneumonia. Isn't that the complication that always sounds so manageable but ends up being *it*, the thing that tips the scale?

More antibiotics. Less appetite, if that were possible. *Of course, it was possible,* I thought. *Nobody wants to eat hospital food.* There was no point in offering treats from the outside, but I couldn't help myself. I brought smoothies and other calorie-dense drinks that might go down easily despite his lack of appetite. No go. This was now more than lack of appetite. My husband—lover of all things culinary, from barbecue to ethnic to five-star—had become food-averse.

Though I understood that the pneumonia was not viral— Laurence had contracted it, not caught it—I became even more determined to keep germs at bay. I scrubbed my hands thirty times a day. Every time I touched something, I spent several minutes with soap and hot water until my hands were raw.

I lost the ability to concentrate altogether. I turned the pages of magazines and stared at blank Sudoku grids. I made trips to the hospital cafeteria, returning with cardboard containers of soup which I inevitably emptied into the sink in the nurses' kitchen across the hall from Laurence's room. It was marked STAFF ONLY, but no more than one or two nurses ever gave me a hard time. Most of them knew me so well from our stays over the past months that they didn't seem to mind. Pretending a sudden craving might awaken in Laurence's gut, I stashed all flavors of smoothies in the refrigerator there—peach, vanilla, strawberry. And I made myself endless cups of tea, temporarily British, apparently, in my conviction that a cup of tea could fix anything.

I sipped my tea while watching Laurence sleep, or try to sleep. I spun the dial on the remote for the hospital TV. So much nothing-to-watch. In spite of his lack of appetite, Laurence man-aged to complain about the annoying absence of our usual fall-back channel, Food Network, from the hospital lineup. It was his gut that was betraying him; his brain was still his.

It's a frightening thing, how insidiously the rhythm—or rather, the non-rhythm—of a hospital day sucks you in. It's a lot like being in a casino. You find yourself whooshed into the same sort of time-space vortex, except, unlike in a casino, you spend a great deal of time watching the clock. And if you spend enough time in a hospital, you forget that you're not sick.

It came to me in a flash one day. I don't know why, but for some reason I suddenly took stock of my body. Maybe I moved a certain way in the bedside chair or stood quickly and realized that nothing hurt. The previous year I had endured several months of back pain after lugging an enormous purse over one shoulder for five days in New York. (Oh, this will make a great travel bag. It's so big . . . and so heavy.) After a few months of physical therapy, at-home exercises, and tincture of time, the pain had lifted. But on a muscle-memory level, I was still on guard. Then, I realized the pain was gone, long gone. And I thought, *I'm not in pain . . . anywhere*. Undeniably, I was suffering from cancer, but I did not have cancer. I had cancer at one remove.

Even so, I realized in a startling epiphany, that I was not actually sick.

Laurence's diagnosis was my diagnosis. It was the diagnosis for his body and, unexpectedly, in the previous few weeks, it had become a diagnosis for his spirit, too, no matter how he fought against it. And, most certainly, it was a diagnosis for our life. But not until then, all those months in, did it hit me that it was not a diagnosis for my body as well. A guilty euphoria washed over me for a split second. It was too sweet to bear any longer than that. Just long enough to formulate the thought, *I am healthy. I have energy. If I wanted to, I could walk out of this hospital and move through the world.* It was a revelation. *I am not sick.*

And then I got sick.

Laurence had been in the hospital for a little over a week when a stomach virus felled me. Our nieces, Alison and Emily, had come into town with their husbands and babies to visit their

Uncle Zippy. Laurence had nixed visitors during every other hospital stay. Over the course of our life together, he had chastised me whenever I'd mentioned to anyone, friend or family, that he may have had a cold. He did not want to be the cancer patient. He especially did not want friends—even those friends who knew—to see him lying in a hospital bed.

But now, this time, he didn't bristle when I said, "The girls are in town. They might drop by." They came en masse on a Sunday morning. Little Mila (named after my sister, her grandmother) was only three and a half. She was palpably apprehensive, though also happy to see her uncle. She offered up a drawing to her Uncle Zippy and then retreated to her grandfather's side before deciding that it might be fun to go outside and wave to Uncle Zippy through the window. It was a scary room for a three-and-a-half-year-old.

The babies, Stella and Charlie, were not yet a year old, and too young to know the difference. Charlie did his tricks.

"How big is Charlie?"

"So big!"

His arms stretched to the sky in response. We marveled at his brilliance, but somehow none of us made eye contact. If we didn't make eye contact, we wouldn't cry, and, equally, we wouldn't have to acknowledge what was happening. That everyone had come to say good-bye. There was a lot of high-pitched joviality and a lot of kisses bestowed on Uncle Zippy's cheeks and forehead. What I do not remember at all is what Laurence himself said or how he behaved. I don't think I could look at him. I couldn't bear to know what he was thinking.

When our niece Emily had visited alone, the night before the rest of the gang arrived, he had held her hand the whole time she sat with him. He smiled at her and kept saying the same thing over and over to the nurse.

"Isn't she beautiful?" he said. "Isn't she beautiful?"

What could he be thinking now, surrounded by the nieces and babies he adored? Did he know he would not be seeing those babies grow up?

That night, Cami and I left the hospital briefly to meet the family crew for dinner at a nearby Mexican restaurant.

I awoke at midnight violently nauseated, so violently that my first instinct was to nudge Laurence so that he might help me to the bathroom. During all his hospital stays, I had never before awakened, mistakenly believing, for even a second, that he was lying there next to me. I usually awoke with my heart pounding as though from a nightmare, even if I could not remember having had one. But on this night, the nausea was so great that it bypassed my brain. My first thought was, "I need Laurence. I need help."

At first I assumed I had food poisoning. Tacos—even largely uneaten—plus vomiting must equal food poisoning. But after vomiting every half-hour for six hours and then spiking a fever, I began to think otherwise. I was just plain sick.

I lay on the cold tile floor of the bathroom for a few hours, unable to drag myself back to bed, thinking, *This is what my life is going to be. No one to hold my head. No one to cradle me back to bed. No one to take care of me in the middle of the night.* It wasn't entirely that I felt sorry for myself, though I surely did, but it was more a stunning awareness of reality, of simple fact.

I phoned Laurence's hospital room at seven a.m. "I'm sick."

I waited for him to say something comforting, something he would have said before. I wanted him to say he was so sorry, to hold me through the phone.

He said, "You better not come."

I had been clinging desperately to the illusion that he and I were still living in the same universe. But at that moment, I knew that this was no longer the case. The agonies inflicted on him by his body—avoiding them, buffering them, escaping them, confronting them, succumbing to them—dictated his world now. He could only interpret events in terms of how they would impact his own private hell.

I spent much of the day at home, on the phone, trying to track down the tumor sample requested by the USC Guru those weeks before. A few days earlier, I had checked on the progress in analyzing the tissue. Only then, because of my call, did we discover that, apparently, the sample had gone missing. I navigated the maze that is the bowels of St. John's Hospital, seeking out the appropriate people to talk to—the shipping folks. The sample had been requested four weeks earlier, and I pressed to find out if and precisely when it had actually been sent. Over the phone, I pestered the Guru's assistant and various other USC personnel to find out if there was any record of it having arrived. My detective work was largely unproductive. The best I could figure was that it had gone out, but had never reached its destination.

I was stunned to learn that the tissue had been sent via regular U.S. mail. Lost forever, no doubt. I ranted over the phone from my sickbed. "If you had told me you were going to send it by mail, I would have hand-delivered it myself!"

My stomach virus only lasted for twenty-four hours. The next morning I was back in the hospital basement, badgering everyone there in person, this time attempting to discover if there was, a) enough tumor remaining to send another sample, and b) if so, could they find it? After I parked myself in a chair in the corner, they finally unearthed more tumor tissue and packaged it. I was set to deliver it to USC the following morning when, miraculously, the original sample was discovered in a pile somewhere in a corner of a lab at USC. We were furious; we were exhilarated; we were relieved.

But our relief was short-lived.

The Guru's assistant clarified the purpose of the sample. Though Laurence and I had both been led to understand otherwise, it was not intended for chemo-sensitivity testing. It was not going to help us pinpoint the most effective treatment. They wanted it only to acquire data for their records about the specific nature of its heinous cells. The sample which had taken several days and countless phone calls to track down had everything to do with research, but, as it turned out, nothing really to do with Laurence.

SNAPSHOT

It was just a piece of pink flannel edged in the same shade of satin. Maybe fifteen inches square. But for the mother of a child who had no gift for self-soothing, it was more than a piece of material. It was a talisman.

It was my baby's blankie.

She would have nothing to do with a pacifier. On those few occasions when, out of sheer desperation, I guided her tiny thumb to her rosebud mouth, she could not have been less interested in that either. I had read that some babies find soothing the feel of the silky trim on blankets. It was worth a shot. I enlisted my mother's talent with needle and thread, and twenty-four hours later, Cami had a blankie and a spare, also pink, but with lavender trim. That also-ran remained on a shelf in her closet for at least a dozen years. I missed the point in time at which alternating it with the original all-pink item would have produced two equally seasoned speci-mens. So it was the pink blankie and the pink blankie alone that did the trick, nap after nap, night after night.

Inevitably, over the years, the blankie went missing from time to time, but we always found it. Crammed behind a sofa cushion. Stuffed into a bucket of LEGOs. Clinging to a towel still warm from the dryer. Once Cami had outgrown her crib, it was commonly wedged between the mattress and the wall. It might have taken some searching, but we always found it.

But one night, we could not. After several hours of hunting, all three of us were forced to realize that the blankie was not in the house. There was only one explanation. It must have fallen out of the stroller when we'd taken a walk earlier in the day. Oh well—the backup with the lavender trim was still waiting in the closet.

Daddy decided the blanket-in-reserve could stay there in the closet for another hour or so; he was going to cruise the neighbor-hood. He grabbed his bike off its rack in the garage and took off. He pedaled up and down the blocks, eyes glued more to the sidewalk and neighboring lawns than to the road ahead. I considered it an exercise in futility. It had been hours since our walk. Dusk was rapidly turning into night. Why bother?

About forty-five minutes after he had set out, Daddy walked through the door. Return the conquering hero, he was waving the pink flannel square. We would sleep well that night after all.

As the years passed, Cami continued to sleep with what was gradually degenerating into a threadbare rag. That pink square traveled the country. It made trips to Hawaii and Sedona, Boston and San Francisco. In New York, we had to phone Housekeeping at the Plaza to hunt for it, fearing they had bundled it up with the dirty linens, but we ultimately found it stuffed in a drawer full of T-shirts and underwear.

I often asked Cami, "Is that blankie going to college with you?"

"Yes," she answered matter-of-factly.

And so it did.

By the end of Cami's freshman year, life had changed. Daddy had cancer. I forgot to remind her to make sure she had packed her blankie, and in her preoccupation with getting home to her father, she did indeed forget. We ran our hands through every empty tote bag and duffel, feeling for the softness of nineteen-year-old flannel, but it was not lurking in any zippered pocket or hidden crevice. Cami called her roommate who was still occupying their dorm room for a few more days.

"You know my little pink blanket . . . ?"

But there was no blankie. Anywhere.

No blankie anymore.

CHAPTER TWELVE

"I'm concerned about Laurence's attitude," his brother said to me over the phone. He had just spoken to Laurence in the hospital, as he did daily. "He's usually so upbeat. But the other day he said, 'When I get out of here . . . if I get out of here . . .' That's not like him."

"No," I said, "but it's completely appropriate."

He's got nothing to be upbeat about. He feels like he's losing. That's what I was saying. When challenged, I could say it to someone else. *You fool, can't you see what's happening here?* I just couldn't say it to myself.

I attempted different versions of this acknowledgment with different people. "I think maybe I should be preparing myself," I would manage over tea sipped from a Styrofoam cup in the hospital cafeteria. Friends were constantly offering to pick me up and take me to lunch. I could only go as far as the hospital cafeteria. Even then, by the time I had steeped my tea, I wanted to get back to the room, in the way that you can think of nothing but returning home to your baby when you leave her with a sitter for the first time, regardless of how much you presumed with great anticipation that a dinner out would cure your muddledness.

Usually, however, I deflected these offers. The very concept of small talk demanded too much energy, and I couldn't face the big talk. But occasionally I accepted an invitation for a fifteen-minute break from the hospital room. The few steps in the fresh air between the new north wing and the cafeteria were always shocking. How strange that the sunshine was so bright one day, or that the air was so chilly another. Friends brought me pieces of the world, offering them up in the form of newsy tidbits. I tried to remember what life used to be like, though the act of remembering itself ached too excruciatingly. There was no part of my psyche that wasn't too tender to the touch to be in the company of anyone outside of that hospital room.

Dear friends, crazed with the urge to help, asked what they could do.

"If you don't mind," it occurred to me, "could you buy a baby hairbrush?" Like his hands and feet, Laurence's scalp had blistered and cracked from the chemo, and he could no longer tolerate his usual brush. I met my friends outside the hospital on the corner of Santa Monica Boulevard and collected the small brush with its baby-blue plastic handle. I ran my fingers over its bristles, so soft and from a distant time.

"Thank you. This is perfect."

They were happy to have done something—anything—no matter how small. I knew they wished they could have done more. Everyone did.

In fact, I learned a great deal about friendship during those days—about the fine line between when to ask and when to just do, about stepping in and stepping back. Finessing that balancing act is a gift, and I was—and am—beyond grateful to those people who even attempted it, let alone managed it so gracefully. E-mail goes a long way toward facilitating that art. Indeed, staying in touch with someone who was in my position—whatever position that was—may be the highest purpose e-mail could ever be called to.

Overflowing with goodwill and the best intentions, friends told me to take care of myself, using the dreaded word, "caregiver." *I am not a caregiver,* I wanted to shout. *I am his wife.*

What I said was, "I will take care of myself. I am."

I shuddered whenever I heard the word. *Caregiver.* So reductive, so redolent of bedpans and sponge baths. So not the grist of what I was doing, of what our relationship was . . . is. *Don't call me that. Call me cheerleader if you must, or comrade in arms, but not caregiver. Not when I am taking my very life from every tiny sign of improvement, even if I must fabricate it. Don't make me a glorified nurse. Do not call me caregiver.*

Gradually, I began allowing friends to poke their heads into Laurence's room. The pretense under which we all operated—the various friends, Laurence and I—was that they had just walked me back from the cafeteria. Laurence always rallied for those few minutes. He complimented one of my girlfriends on her jacket. He asked another how her son was enjoying his first year at college. He chatted for several minutes with our dear friend, Deborah. (When I bitched to her about the rigmarole of medical paraphernalia having taken over our house—how it was inescapable and terrifying—she soothed me with her vestigial North Carolina lilt: "Just think of it like he has a broken arm and all that stuff is the cast; it's just what he needs to get better right now.")

When a friend and business colleague, Blair, stopped by, Laurence even managed to pitch her an idea we'd been entertaining to turn an old screenplay of ours into a play. She commanded him to get out of that bed and get to work on it. Her enthusiasm energized him so, I believed he might.

These brief impromptu drop-bys segued into planned visits.

"My parents feel horrible that they haven't seen you in a while. I have to let them come," I told Laurence, going against his edict of no visitors.

"Fine." We had been a family always together—abnormally, ridiculously perhaps. Weeks felt like a prolonged period to have not seen one another, an aberration that even Laurence could no longer ignore.

My sister brought them, helping my father up the stairs from the parking lot and down the corridor to Laurence's room. I had cajoled Laurence into shaving and letting me wash his hair. It had taken a great deal of persuasion. Suddenly the stuff of everyday hygiene seemed altogether too daunting a task to him. He wanted to sit up in a chair for their visit. My mother chirped well wishes. My father sat, silent, until it was time to leave. Then he kissed Laurence on the forehead and said, "I love you very much."

Mila would tell me later—a few weeks later, a lifetime later— that Laurence had told her on several occasions how sorry he was for what he was doing to the family, the entire family. He was so grief-stricken. Not for himself, but most especially for Cami and me. I didn't know about these talks at the time. The talks in which he apologized, and she assured him everyone would take care of Cami and me. How could I not lift my head out of the foxhole long enough to sense that these conversations were taking place?

A few days later, our friend Larry was passing through town. As teenagers, Larry and Laurence had dressed alike one night to take a pair of identical twins on a double date, ever after delighting in telling the tale of how many heads snapped as the foursome passed. Larry became a comedian-magician. Laurence, the go-to for all things remotely architectural, had helped Larry design and build countless props, not to mention originating the role of one of the Flying Cavettis in Larry's gonzo magic troupe during college days. (A performance on *The Gong Show* netted us several years' supply of elbow macaroni and antifreeze.)

I had warned him that Laurence was not good. Larry was steeled for the worst. It was dinnertime when Larry arrived, and Laurence asked his old friend for a cloth from the bathroom to wash his hands.

True to form, Larry gave him a hard time. "Warm or cool?"

Laurence gave him a hard time right back. "Tepid."

Larry delivered the washcloth. "Is that satisfactory?"

Laurence raised his hand and motioned swatting him—forehand, backhand—across the face. "But that's all right," Laurence said. "I won't make you sleep with the goats."

Later, Larry told me he didn't know what I was talking about. Laurence had seemed a little weak, but completely himself. For a moment, I allowed myself to wonder if I had been overreacting.

A morning or two later, the lung doctor arrived bright and early. He had just read Laurence's most recent set of chest X-rays. Laurence was still a little groggy. Preoccupied with the discomfort in his belly, he began to describe the sensation to the doctor.

"No, Laurence," I told him, "this is the lung doctor. You want to ask him about any lung issues." To which the lung doctor said, "There are no lung issues."

Amazingly, the pneumonia had completely cleared. Just like the blood infection the week before. Neither one of those supporting players was going to kill him. He'd fought them both and won. We were ecstatic. For at least ten minutes, I forgot that the lead villain was still gathering its troops in the shadows.

We ventured a walk or two in the halls. But this time, it required an effort Laurence had never had to exert before. We crept. We paused. We didn't joke about the signs on other patients' doors. Now, we were the people the other patients eyed sympathetically. As we turned around, aborting our circle around the floor, I realized that nothing was pure or true in the decor of the place. Walls were painted buff, but not quite; alcoves mauve, but not quite; another statue of Jesus—a lamb draped around his shoulders like a stole—meant to be serene, but not quite. Now, we were not-quite people. Of the world, but not quite. Hanging on, but not quite. Alive, but not quite.

The lung doctor may have been able to excuse himself from the case, mission accomplished, but he knew what was happening. All the doctors did. Scary Surgeon Lady pulled up a chair at the nurses' station and sat with me for half an hour. Push had come to shove, and she was suddenly not so scary. She told me about when her father was ill (I don't believe she said *dying,* but I can't remember for sure) and required hospice care. I startled at the word. She told me what it entailed, how it all worked. Now she was looking at me the way I looked at her the day we'd first met in her office. Now *she* was thinking, *We are both women . . . We are both mothers . . . Let me help you.*

Meanwhile, Oncology Man had performed a disappearing act. During previous hospital stays, he had popped in nearly every evening, lingering past the point of medical necessity to exchange jokes and banter with Laurence. Not this time. The official word was that there had been a redivision of labor in his practice. A young woman—Russian—stern but brilliant, had been assigned sole custody of the practice's hospitalized patients. We had interacted with her often in the past months, particularly during hospital stays, and the transition had been smooth. She was there every day, often twice a day, answering questions and offering support.

Though this was no longer his official domain, I often spotted Oncology Man in the hospital corridors after office hours, usually between five and eight in the evening. I would see him duck into one patient's room or emerge from another's, and I would think, *He'll be stopping by our room next.* But after a certain point in time, he never came.

He had been true to his word. He didn't sugarcoat anything. He just disappeared—down the hall, into other patients' rooms.

Then he phoned me at home one morning, early enough that I hadn't yet left for the hospital. "I need to ask you," he said, "if you want me to have an end-of-life conversation with Laurence."

I managed a sharp intake of breath, just enough wind to respond.

"No. Please don't." *Please don't say that's what's happening.*

I should have asked questions. *How long? How can you be sure? How long? How much more pain? How long?*

"Your brother-in-law thought that maybe it was time . . ."

I already knew that Tom had cornered Oncology Man in the hall one evening, and while I was not sure of the specifics of their conversation, I figured it had gone something like that.

The assailant in Laurence's body had begun to flaunt its power in a new and horrifying way, impossible to ignore. His abdomen had become taut and swollen. He had first noticed the bloat one night when he'd caught a glimpse of himself in the bathroom mirror.

"We better call the doctor!" he'd said, his voice urgent and panicked, not like him.

I was terrified, too, but tried to calm him. "We'll show the doctor first thing in the morning," I said. *What was happening here? Couldn't someone make it stop?*

Within a day or two, his abdomen had grown hugely distended, a pregnant belly in time lapse. They took him away—out of the room—to drain the fluid pooling there. I waited, desperate to do something. Anything. They had rolled him out on his own bed, not transferring him to a gurney. The vacancy revealed a floor full of dust bunnies. I spent the next hour bunching paper towels into wads, dashing back and forth to wet them in the bathroom sink, then using them to scrub the floor on my hands and knees.

When they returned Laurence to his room, he was more comfortable, less four liters of fluid. But there was another procedure ahead: the insertion of a PICC line into his arm (Peripherally Inserted Central Catheter). How odd that now I can't remember why the line was needed; he already had the port.

I stood in the hospital corridor, talking to my sister on my cell phone. Finally, I managed to say it. "He's dying, isn't he?"

"Yes," Mila said, "he is. He's dying."

Then I knew it was the truth. I knew that if there were any way my sister could tell me otherwise, she would. She would continue to cheerlead as she had for the past ten months if there were any way possible. She would point to other treatment options, to waiting miracles, to a flicker of hope, if any existed. They did not.

So, now, this early morning, sitting on the edge of my bed talking on the phone with Oncology Man, it should have been no surprise that he was using the phrase "end-of-life." Except for the fact that it continued to be a surprise every time I articulated the thought in my own mind. An absolute shock, every single time.

He took me at my word. And I let him off the hook. *Don't have the talk; don't tell him what he must already know.* And that was the end of our conversation. And, though I don't know for sure, I don't believe he ever spoke to Laurence again.

Laurence never mentioned Oncology Man's retreat. Hospital days blend one into the next, and time does that funny Vegas thing. He may never have noticed. And if he did, Oncology Man had that "some kind of genius" thing going for him. Laurence would have understood how busy he was. In other patients' rooms.

Instead, Laurence lay in his hospital bed watching *South Park*. One afternoon, he seemed particularly deep in thought.

"What are you thinking?" I asked him, an atavistic question. When we were young—so young—and eager to probe every corner of each other's minds, we must have asked each other that question several times a day. The question did a slow fade over the years, of course. A glance—not even—explained everything. But that night, I needed to know.

"I'm thinking," Laurence said casually, "that I'll change the channel."

Then, at some point later, the conversation turned to one of Laurence's favorite topics: Los Angeles institutions long gone. With equal parts enthusiasm and nostalgia, Laurence provided the nurse with the recipe for replicating a perfect Orange Julius.

As it turns out, those are the things you talk about when you're dying. And why not.

Laurence was that little boy who was always drawing or constructing a model or painting that model. When Hawaii became a state, the whole country went wild with island mania. So did Laurence. He was seven years old, and tropical scenes began overtaking his drawings. Volcanoes. Waves splashing on the shore. And palm trees, which would become an automatic doodle that stuck with him for the rest of his life. He, like so many other boys and girls around the U.S., wore a tiki around his neck on a leather cord. Its eyes glowed in the dark. Hawaii must be a magical place. He had to get there.

Thus began an ongoing plea. One of Laurence's salient memories of his childhood was of begging his father to take the family to Hawaii.

They never went.

But we did. Once, before our daughter was born, and then several times as a family. Remarkably, the air and the beaches and the sunset more than lived up to Laurence's lifelong imagining. Often, when we hadn't been to Hawaii in a year or two, one of us would turn to the other and say, "I feel the call of the islands," eventually abbreviated in that shorthand that families develop to "Call of the islands."

The young therapist who had been holding our hands through the previous months arrived at the hospital one afternoon. We were beyond therapy, but she hoped to take Laurence's mind out of his body for a brief while, to leave the pain behind, along with the drug-induced fog.

He was sitting up in a chair when she walked into the room. She pulled up another chair and sat a few feet away, facing him. "Where would you like to be right now?"

"Hawaii."

"How does it feel?"

He closed his eyes.

"Warm."

"What's the water like?"

"Warm and soft."

"What color is it?"

"Blue-green."

"Okay," she said. "You're in the blue-green water where it's soft and warm."

He nodded.

Deep greens and blues soothed Sweet Baby James. Maybe they could weave a lullabye for Laurence.

When we left the room and I walked the young woman to the parking lot, she said, "We need a miracle."

I believed that I understood my husband was dying. But I also thought, *Fine, then, let's get ourselves a miracle. Where do I go for one of those?*

—　—

A power failure had hit our neighborhood while Laurence was in the hospital. He had to talk me through resetting all the clocks and electronics in the house, but he couldn't remember how to reset the telephone answering machine without laying eyes on it. One night when I got home, the urge to tackle the damn thing overtook me despite my antipathy for anything electronic, digital, or, worst of all, a combination of the two. I tried communing with the machine, attempting to follow its instructions when it spoke to me. But we were not understanding one another.

In my head, I kept hearing Laurence tease me: "You're the only person who thinks the computer is being sarcastic when it talks." And his ongoing diatribe: "If you'd just give me five minutes, I could teach you how to do these things once and for all." The truth was, even if I had given him the five minutes and concentrated with all my might, I knew I would never have retained the information. Because I didn't need to. Laurence would always be there to do these things for me.

It was late, and it had been another long day at the hospital, but after nearly thirty minutes, I managed to make the answering machine respond with the correct time. I debated whether to call Laurence and tell him, wondering if he would interpret this achievement as code. Would he think I was telling him I would be okay without him? I would not, of course, but did this mean I would survive? Or simply that I would disintegrate in a house where every clock displayed the correct time?

"You're going to be so proud of me," I told him when I called. "I set the answering machine."

"Good for you." No sarcasm. He meant it.

By then, Laurence and I were communicating in subtext.

I choreographed a few more visits with a chosen few friends, never explaining why. He acquiesced, never explaining why. I spent long moments in the hospital hallway, ostensibly chatting casually with these dear friends, but actually weeping with them. There was a different reality out in the hallway, but I didn't know which was the more true.

Our friend Donna put her arms around me and we held on to each other for what seemed like minutes on end. She said, "He's still so in there." And that was precisely right. He was trapped. And so were we all, trapped, between the hallway where we acknowledged what was happening, inexorably happening, and Laurence's room, just the other side of the door, where we joked and reminisced, and Laurence was the one to remember an old colleague's name. Trapped.

That Saturday night, shortly before I left for home, Laurence said, "I guess we've just been unlucky."

I knew what he meant. We'd faced countless professional disappointments during our career. More than our share of carrot chasing, as many deals dangled as signed. And now this. Other people have cancer treatment work. Other people are lucky. Why not us?

An hour later I was back home for the few hours of night, practice hours in missing him in the way that a mother begins missing her child before she starts kindergarten or has left for college. I was attempting to read the mail when I suddenly had to tell Laurence something. I didn't want to wake him, but this was urgent.

His voice was thin and raw when he answered the phone.

"I've had an epiphany," I told him. "You're so wrong. We've been the luckiest people. How many people find someone to spend their life with when they're so young, and then get to do it? Actually get to spend their whole lives together?" I listed all the people we know who are still looking for someone, or getting divorced, or sharing stale air with a spouse.

"Don't ever think that again." I made him promise.

"You're right."

"Promise. Promise me you won't ever think that again."

"I promise," he said. "We're the luckiest people in the whole world."

I didn't know that I would cling to that moment for the rest of my life. And I certainly didn't know that the rest of my life would begin so soon.

‒ ⁓

Cami had driven home most weekends during that fall semester. There were a lot of reasons why. Her apartment was too noisy, so she couldn't sleep. Art history field trips required that she visit the Los Angeles County Museum of Art. And the ever-popular college classic: it was easier to do her laundry at home. But there was an underlying reason. Her daddy was sick.

So, like clockwork, she returned home on the first Friday afternoon of the new semester, having just gone back to school after the long winter break. Daddy was still in the hospital bed where she had left him a few days earlier. He was eager to hear about her new classes. They talked a bit about her Media Studies class on Sound, and she picked his brain about what sort of a project she should do. He suggested shooting a video and adding different soundtracks to demonstrate how drastically sound can alter the emotional content of the visual. It was the perfect idea. "I'm so excited," Cami said.

Daddy was, too. *Too excited to be on his deathbed. That wasn't possible. This couldn't be happening.*

When Sunday afternoon rolled around and it was time for Cami to drive the hour back to school, I followed her home from the hospital to help her pack up her car. But suddenly, she was overcome with exhaustion and decided to take a nap before driving. As I headed back, she told me to call her in an hour to wake her up at five o'clock.

Cami did not go back to school.

A few moments after I'd arrived back at the hospital—I'd been gone no more than forty-five minutes—Family Doc arrived. He palpated Laurence's abdomen. The fluid had reaccumulated almost immediately after being drained just three days before. And there was more. He could feel, right beneath the skin—everywhere—the hard and evil masses. Our doctor grimaced ever so slightly, straining not to. He listened to Laurence's heart. His heart rate had been speeding all day. By now it was over 160.

And the pain. There was no need to ask about the pain. It was obvious that it was overtaking him.

When I pressed later, I would hear words which I could bring myself to research only many, many months after. Tachycardia—increased heart rate. Ascites—abdominal fluid retention. Sepsis—whole body inflammation—often used interchangeably with "blood poisoning," which can lead to malfunction of the circulatory system, then to multiple organ dysfunction syndrome . . . and to death.

None of these words, however, were used at the moment. Instead, Family Doc looked back and forth between Laurence and me. After a long pause, he suggested that since Laurence was no longer getting relief from pushing the on demand button for the morphine, which administered a metered amount of the drug, maybe he would be more comfortable with a morphine drip. Laurence was not as medically savvy as I. He always hated all that medical stuff. Right then, in that moment, he was just looking for relief, and a steady stream of morphine sounded good. I don't think he knew what the drip meant. I wished I didn't. I hope he didn't. I'll never know for sure.

I followed the doctor into the hall.

"I thought I was ready," I said. "But I'm not. I'm not ready."

He nodded.

"Can we wait till Cami gets here?"

"Sure."

As if on cue, Mila and Tom burst around the corner, arriving home from a few days spent visiting their daughter and her family in Berkeley.

Mila looked at my face. "What's wrong?"

We decided that Tom should drive to our house to pick up Cami. When he finally rousted her, he said, "You're not going back to school."

Tom had her back at the hospital in a few minutes.

"What's happening?" she asked me.

"They're going to start a morphine drip for Daddy. Whatever we want to say to him, we should say now, because that's going to make him out of it."

"Forever?"

"Yes, forever."

She said, "Won't he think it's weird that I'm back?"

"No, sweetheart. I don't think he'll think about it. He's a little out of it already."

Cami hadn't been feeling well that weekend, and we had done our best to keep her out of breathing distance from her daddy. "Won't he wonder why I can get close to him now?"

"I don't think so."

We held each other so tightly I'm sure it was impossible for a passerby to discern where one of us ended and the other began. I whispered, "Mommy's here," which was all I knew to say, though utterly useless. We needed Daddy to be here.

Family Doc backed up against a wall in the corridor, clutching Laurence's chart, not knowing where to look. A screenwriting trick for heightening the emotion of a scene is to place private moments in public places. It can be a difficult trick to make believable. Who really acts out scorchingly intimate moments anywhere but behind the most tightly closed doors? I discovered the answer to that question at five-thirty that Sunday afternoon. When everything else fades away, you don't care who's watching.

By the time Cami and I had reentered Laurence's room, he was no longer fully conscious. I suspect he'd been pushing the morphine delivery button continually, although it was programmed to only administer a dose at prescribed intervals.

Cami and I talked to him for an hour.

She started, leaning over him. "You're the best daddy in the whole world."

SNAPSHOT

Removing those training wheels was not easy. Cami must have been five or six when the time came to take them off. You think you're going to remember all those benchmark ages forever and ever, but some of them fade. You're left with "Cami must have been five or six," like an old grandmother trying to remember her first kiss while rocking on a porch.

Laurence had been running behind her, one hand steadying her ride, for what seemed like months. We live on a cul-de-sac, convenient for impromptu practice runs, and Cami wanted to hit the road every chance she got. She was determined, if a bit tottery. Before dinner, after dinner, anytime they found a spare ten minutes, Laurence strapped Cami's helmet under her chin, settled her onto the seat of her royal-blue bike, and steered her onto the road.

Gradually, his grip on the back of her bike loosened, as all fathers' do. But she wasn't quite ready for him to let go. So he jogged behind her, steadying her wobbly path, as she pedaled to the end of the block and back.

It was a dad thing. Just as driving lessons would be ten years later.

But one late afternoon, I ended up on bicycle practice duty. Laurence was working out of the house at that particular time. I don't remember what the job was—designing a title sequence, editing a montage, shooting a documentary. Whatever, Cami couldn't wait for him to get a few practice minutes in, so we wheeled that bike out of the garage and hit the road.

After several trial runs, I let go.

Ultimately, that's what you have to do, isn't it? Just let go of the bike, hold your breath, and see what happens.

She pedaled. The pedals kept going around. She pedaled some more. And she stayed upright. She was bicycling down the street.

At the exact moment when Cami realized she was doing it, actually doing it, Laurence's car rounded the corner of our block. Cami was bicycling toward him. He was driving toward her. He slowed, then stopped. From behind his windshield, I could see his eyebrows go up, his eyes widen, and his jaw drop. He got out and Cami kept pedaling. Right to her daddy. She made it all the way to his open arms.

It was impossible to tell who was more excited. Or proud.

CHAPTER THIRTEEN

I went to get the nurse to start the drip.

"We're ready," I told her. "You can do it now." Or course, we weren't ready. We would never be ready.

The nurse on call had been Laurence's nurse several times over the previous months, and had tended to him a great deal in the preceding weeks. She couldn't start the drip, she said. She just couldn't do it. Not on him. She was crying. She apologized, but she would have to defer to another nurse.

So a different nurse entered the room. At six o'clock on a Sunday evening, a different nurse—one we didn't know—hooked Laurence up to a continuous drip of morphine.

Mila and Tom ultimately went home for the night. They had phoned our friend Larry and he arrived a few hours in.

And we kept talking, running on empty, Cami and I. We talked to Laurence—my husband, her daddy—for the next thirty hours. Sometimes Laurence responded. Other times he did not. Sometimes he made perfect sense. Other times he did not.

I invoked the blue-green water, soft and warm.

"You're swimming," I told him.

And then, later, when he grimaced against the pain, I put my lips close to his ear, as close as I could, and whispered, "You're swimming. Go ahead. Keep swimming. It's okay."

What I wanted to say—what I was screaming in my brain—was, *Turn around! Swim back! Don't leave me!*

What else we said, the three of us, belongs to us.

Around midnight, Laurence, having been on the drip for six hours, defied expectations, if not medical science, and got up out of the bed. "Get me out of here," he said.

That clinched it for Cami. She had been lobbying to take him home for several hours. Clearly, she had given some thought, in the most shadowy recesses of her mind, as to how her father's death was going to play out, and she refused to let it be in the hospital. It had to be at home, in the home he had created and which he enjoyed so enthusiastically. (How many times over the years did the two of us comment on how much we loved our house, the warmth of the den or the serenity of the bedroom?)

At five a.m., I walked down the hall, hoping that the social worker who could begin the discharge process might be in that early. Of course, she was not. So I ran back and forth between Laurence's room and her office every ten minutes until she arrived an hour later. It took until five p.m. for everything to be in place.

During those twelve hours, I continued to run back and forth, countless times, entangled in the red tape of hospital bureaucracy. The process at once distracted and infuriated me. Paperwork. Ordering an ambulance. A lengthy interview with a hospice coordinator.

She sat in Laurence's room with us and filled out forms. She didn't belong there, I thought, but I was not going to adjourn to the "Family Room" down the hall where Laurence and I had spent so many hours in the past ten months, stopping for a change of scene along our walks, waving to his doctors as they passed and smiled or paused to chat. Laurence had been doing so well.

The hospice coordinator, an overweight bleached blonde in a red suit, made check marks and filled in line after line on form after form. Her air was brusque. This was her job. She arranges for people to go home and die. I discovered later that she had thought I was Laurence's daughter. I wondered if she would have dialed up her sympathy meter had she known I was his wife.

A friend whose husband had survived cancer the year before had told me that the side effects of treatment made her feel like she was watching her husband age in fast forward. Apparently, that had happened to my husband; it had happened when I wasn't looking, and so quickly. It had happened in the last few days. Now strangers thought I was my own husband's daughter. My friend had continued, marveling at how you get to watch him come back, to have the hands of the clock spin in reverse. I had been looking forward to that springtime. More than that, I had been living for it. Now I sat at Laurence's bedside, knowing, *There will be no springtime for us.*

The blonde in the red suit finally left us with our instructions. Because Laurence was on morphine, we had to have a hospice nurse waiting for us at home, so Mila went to our house to meet him when he arrived. There were discussions about the pros and cons of renting a hospital bed and various other logistical issues. There was no way of knowing if he would be home for hours or days or weeks.

We had an appointment scheduled with the USC Guru for that very day, that Monday. On Friday, just three days earlier, the young Russian oncologist who had inherited our case had assured me we would get Laurence to that appointment no matter what. We would go by ambulance if need be.

Though part of me wanted to strap Laurence into that ambulance and drive him across town, I called USC to cancel the appointment.

"Is he not doing well?" the Guru's assistant asked.

"No. No, he's not," I said. He's not doing well at all. *He's dying. Can't you feel it those few miles away? How can you not feel it?*

When the Russian doctor entered the hospital room, Cami was curled up in bed at her father's side. She instinctively sat up.

"No, honey, that's all right." The stern young Russian woman had dissolved.

"I need you to tell my daughter that we did everything we could," I implored her.

"We did, honey. We did everything. We did more than everything because he's so young, and because he wanted us to."

Cami cuddled back in, her head on her daddy's chest.

— ~

A friend stopped by unexpectedly. I don't know how the smoke signals had gone up alerting friends. He sat at Laurence's bedside and talked to him briefly, and when it was time to leave, he said, "I just wanted to come and say . . ." He paused, unable to say what he had really come to say. "I just wanted to come and say hello."

At one point Tom took Cami to the cafeteria. She would tell me later that he did a good ten minutes on why he likes Jell-O. Frank Sinatra may submit that "You're riding high in April, shot down in May." But I say, *That's life, right there. You talk about Jell-O when your beloved brother-in-law is dying.*

And then, Cami told me later, after the discourse on Jell-O, Tom said to her, "You're doing everything right."

In fact, she was. She continued to insist that her daddy be brought home even when every doctor who entered our room flinched at the idea. They suggested Laurence might become too agitated and that the pain might flare up. The ambulance ride could be "too much for him." I thought, *I don't want him dying on Wilshire Boulevard in rush-hour traffic.* But Cami held firm.

Finally, I said, "It doesn't matter to me. And it won't make any difference to Daddy. But I can see how much this means to you, so we'll try it. But if it looks like it's too much for him, we're not going to go through with it."

She agreed. Somehow she knew it would be fine. And she knew that I was wrong. It would make a difference to Daddy. It would make a difference to all three of us that was, at that moment, incalculable.

Even as Cami pushed to bring her father home, she talked about someone who knew someone who knew a healer. Maybe we should try contacting that person.

So I did. Realizing I'd been looking for magic all along, I made the calls. But the "healer" was hours away in San Diego. We could attempt a telephonic miracle for half his regular gargantuan fee. It was the perfect capper to the Purple Aura lady and the Xango juice and the pink goo that ended up down the drain.

Enough.

Telephonic healing was not going to be an option. I was simply waiting. *Right now, that is what I'm doing. Waiting. Waiting for my husband to die.*

— —

When the ambulance men arrived, time shifted gears. The twenty-three hours before, since six o'clock the previous evening, had been long and slow, though simultaneously dissolving with lightning speed, one into the next. I was desperate for them to end, but out-of-my-mind terrified of the moment when they would.

Laurence had stretches of calm, interrupted by spells of agitation and pain. We summoned the nurse who had been instructed to up the morphine as needed, and she obliged. There is no word for the state he was in. He was not awake. He was not in a coma. Or even a semi-coma. He was in an altered state—somewhere between those three—somewhere else, but somehow so with us, too.

The minute the ambulance guys appeared, everything sped up. An action sequence stuck in a Fellini film. A blur of activity. Hugging the nurses good-bye. Seeing them cry. Thanking them. This time, we would not be back again.

Tom and I blasted through the room, packing up like people suddenly called away on a trip, as though Laurence would need his Chapstick, his quilted vest, the books on the nightstand, once he got home. He was reading Richard Dawkins's *The God Delusion,* and using as a bookmark a flyer hawking premium Wagyu beef, "for a healthy and stylish life."

As the paramedics lifted Laurence onto the gurney, I thought, *Be gentle; don't hurt him.* But beyond that, I thought, *He would be so ashamed. He would be so humiliated.*

Cami and I followed behind as these two hale young men maneuvered Laurence down the hall. We held his hands in the elevator and told him we were going home. Then we followed at a near run through the maze of the hospital basement out to the waiting ambulance. We two climbed in as they lifted Laurence into the back.

I had never been in an ambulance before. Inside, it was tight, cramped. Cami and I sat on either side of Laurence, cradling his head. "We're going home, Daddy. We're going home."

It was five o'clock in the afternoon. Traffic in Los Angeles is generally thick at that hour, but also unpredictable. There had been a fair amount of discussion between Tom, the ambulance driver, and me as to the best route to take. Once in the ambulance, I prevailed. We headed east from Santa Monica on Wilshire Boulevard.

Cami provided location updates. "We're at Bundy, Daddy. . . . We're crossing Barrington, Daddy. . . . The light's green. We're going to make it through this green light."

(I had begged the driver to turn on the siren when we first climbed into the ambulance, but our situation, we were informed, was not siren-worthy. We were just another vehicle subject to the rush-hour rules of the road.)

"Daddy, we're almost there. We're in our neighborhood. We're almost home . . . We're home, Daddy. You're home."

— —

I wanted them to get Laurence into the house as fast as possible. Again, all I could think of was how humiliated he would be if the neighbors saw him. The paramedics maneuvered the gurney out of the ambulance and I ushered them inside. But the gurney was too wide for the staircase up to the bedroom. He was going to have to be carried up the stairs without the gurney. We needed another body to help.

I had spotted one neighbor in front of his house down the street. As I ran outside, he was approaching our house to see what was going on. "I need to ask you a favor," I told him. "We've brought Laurence home to die."

He rushed into our house with me. Already the paramedics were gathering the sheets encasing the gurney into a sling around Laurence. Mila and Tom were holding onto ends of the sheet as well. Our neighbor grabbed another end.

Cami and I watched as they carried him up the stairs—she moving in front, I behind.

"He wouldn't be able to stand this. He would hate this so much," I said.

How could the boy I knew at Oakwood have become this tortured shell being hauled up a flight of stairs like so much cargo?

— ~

There is no way of knowing definitively if Laurence knew he was home. But we believe he did. He became more communicative, more relaxed. We placed him on the single foldout bed in our bedroom that I had been using. And we talked to him.

We were exhausted, yet coursing with adrenaline. We talked and we talked and we talked to him. I marveled at how my baby girl knew exactly what to say. "We'll be together forever, Daddy. Forever . . ."

How can it be that forever *is starting so soon? How can it be starting now?*

Laurence looked up at Mila and Tom and said their names. "Mila . . . Uncle Tom . . ."

His brothers arrived. They said their sister would be catching a plane in a few hours. When his brothers left, Laurence said my name. "I'm here," I answered.

Now it was just the three of us. Except for the hospice nurse, a specter in the corner of the room.

We curled around Laurence, Cami and I, as close as we could be. *More than anything, I do not want you to feel alone. Because I don't want to feel alone through this. Not alone. Not yet.*

Time passed, though we felt out of time. We were out of time.

Laurence's breathing was changing, but he seemed strangely hyperaware, his eyes wide.

"Goddammit!" he said, with so much fury that we will always know how fiercely he did not want to leave. He did not go gentle. He blew kisses to Cami, whose face remained inches from his. "Good night," he said.

After a few hours, Cami slid a DVD into the player—a compilation of old home movies and samples of her father's work. She and I lay on the big bed, watching a movie—originally shot in Super-8—of the year Laurence and I met.

Our senior year of high school. About ten years ago, Laurence had dug up the footage he had filmed throughout that year and set it to the Traffic song, "Dear Mr. Fantasy." Though he lay dying, I absolutely knew that when he heard that music, he could see the images playing in his mind's eye. The shot of me walking in front of the school in what must have been a fourteen-inch skirt with hair down to my waist. A shot of him talking into a microphone, narrating some wonderful teenage moment.

After a while, I went into Cami's room to use the bathroom away from the male hospice nurse. I sat down at Cami's desk for a minute, I'm not sure why. I was staring at the screen of her computer, blankly, when I heard the nurse say my name. There was no urgency in his voice. He said it with such nonchalance that he might have been asking for a glass of water.

I stepped onto the landing between Cami's room and our bedroom. There was the nurse on his way to get me. "Carla, you better come."

It had been a year of continually lowering the bar. First, wanting real, true, normal life in all its sweet ordinariness. Then, hankering for a semblance of normal life as we accommodated the treatment into our existence. Then, no pain. Then, just life. And so suddenly—*not now, not this day, not this moment.*

Once again, just like in the hours first following my husband's diagnosis, I was confused. How did we get here? I had been waiting for a neon sign—no, a digital tote board counting down. I thought I would know when the process had officially begun, but somehow I never did. And now, here we were, and it was already ending. I wanted our life to flash before my eyes. I wanted those images to replace the real one:

Cami standing over her father like a wild animal, shrieking. "I'm so sorry, Daddy! I'm so sorry this happened! Oh my God! Oh my God . . . I'm so sorry . . ."

A minute later, what had been set in motion those forty-nine weeks earlier came to an end.

I searched for my husband in his green eyes. How could he not be there? I placed my fingers on his eyelids to close them and felt a strange and unexpected resistance. When Cami was born and the obstetrician had handed Laurence the scissors to cut the umbilical cord, Laurence had said how much tougher it was—literally—than he'd anticipated. No simple snip. And now, this. The fibers that bind us to the people we love hold tight. In birth, and, as I was on the threshold of discovering, in death.

Though Laurence's death was proof positive of a random universe, the fact that the exact moment I left the room is when he "let go" could not have been coincidence. Cami would tell me later that she had just begun to drift off to sleep, after two full days awake—more than awake, in hyper-drive—when the noise coming from her father had changed. His breathing, previously rhythmic, though shallow and labored, shifted. Both she and I had disengaged ever so slightly. The tiniest step back. A momentary easing of connection. That was when he could leave.

I suppose I believe those people who claim they see a magnificent peace wash over their loved one at the moment of death. It must happen if so many people report the phenomenon. I cannot say the same. Laurence was, unequivocally, pissed off. Until the end. Beyond the end. Yes, the pain was gone. But so was he. It was not a fair trade. Not even for him.

I don't know what happened to the next few hours.

Mila and Tom returned, and Tom, in his official capacity, pronounced my husband dead. The hospice nurse took care of business, whatever that was. The strange men in black suits from the mortuary slithered in, ghoulish and silent. I did not watch them take him away. They were removing his body; he was already gone.

Cami and I lay in our bed, the room suddenly so empty, to weep in the dark. Choking through sobs, she asked, "How will we ever eat food again? How will we ever listen to music?" That, of course, would be the crux of the challenge of surviving: how to carve our way through anguish to find joy in all the myriad places he had found joy. How to even hope to? How to even want to, when I knew that the experience of any joy that may lie ahead had been transformed, instantaneously and forever, into a half-life of joy.

At dawn, Cami left our bed and lay on the narrow foldout where her daddy had died. Dying is such hard work, made all the more strenuous by the battle against it, that the sheets were still clammy, even gamey with his sweat. But it was only there, on that bed, that Cami was able to finally, if just for a bit, drift off to sleep.

A little less than three months earlier, when the recurrence was diagnosed and the prognosis officially declared grim, I spent a sleepless night engaged in a hot-and-heavy round of bargaining. For years before Laurence got sick, he and I had discussed the pesky business of adulthood: wills, estate planning, cemetery arrangements. We were not good at that stuff, but we had managed to address the first two orders of business with equal parts brio, black humor, and knocking on wood. We were reluctant grown-ups by virtue of being members of our particular generation, but more so, by temperament and interest. Laurence was, after all, the only one of his siblings who did not succumb to their father's urging to get that all-important MBA.

After cancer required us to join in its ménage à trois, we never again discussed that third element: cemetery arrangements. But that night, the night of the recurrence, I lay awake. *If we had bought our cemetery plots, we wouldn't have to use them.* We had missed the chance to buy cosmic insurance. Could I secure it now?

The next day, I informed my sister I needed her to come with me for moral support. I had to buy some real estate. Fortunately, *where* was not the issue. Laurence and I had gotten that far in our talks years before, choosing, without contest, a tiny cemetery that resembles one of those lovely little private English gardens. Tucked unobtrusively and unexpectedly behind a movie theater, it is only five minutes from our home.

Mila and I sat across the desk from the mortuary lady.

"I'm so sorry," she said to me, that day in November.

"Oh, it's okay. My husband's just sick."

She explained to me that the small area in which I was purchasing this piece of ground, this pair of plots, was being renovated and would not be ready until April.

"That won't be a problem," I promised. "In three years, I'm going to bring my husband here and show him which plots I picked, and he'll scream at me for picking the wrong ones."

Laurence was not a screamer, but I pictured him so alive, alive with a vengeance, that in my mind's eye, he had been transformed into one.

I handed over the check, having never before made a decision of that magnitude without consulting Laurence. It felt like a betrayal. But now I had my insurance policy. Surely this meant there was no way I would have to use it.

Suddenly, this short time later, I was sitting across from the same mortuary lady. "I'm so sorry," she said again. And this time, not quite three months later, all I could do was nod.

Those months ago, I had assured her with such certainty that it would not matter if the small area of the cemetery was not going to be ready until the spring. Wearing her black suit and speaking in her modulated tones, she explained that my husband would be temporarily housed at another cemetery, one in Westminster, wherever that is.

"If anyone would want his accommodations freshly remodeled, it would be Laurence," I said. I didn't mean it to be a joke. It was just the truth.

There was paperwork, of course. The first stack I would encounter of the many stacks that would arrive from lawyers and accountants and banks over the next year. And then the lady dressed in black introduced me to her colleague, who appeared with a glossy coffin brochure in hand.

I flipped through the pages, desperately hoping to find just one that did not include some hideous feature that disqualified it instantly. I turned the pages, one after the other, unable to silence the voice in my head: *I'm picking out a coffin for my husband . . . I'm picking out a coffin for my husband . . .*

Just then, the mortuary man leaned across the table.

"You know," he whispered, almost conspiratorially, "I used to be a hairdresser, and your color is fabulous." It was so *The Loved One*. Laurence would have loved it.

This was the first time I formulated that thought, a new staple of my internal monologue. *Laurence would love this.*

Riffling through the coffin catalog only added to the black comedy. It was just too bizarre to feel like anything else, surely not my life. Selecting a coffin was not difficult. There was only one acceptable candidate in the entire pamphlet. I pointed to the picture of the one whose materials were remarkably like those Laurence had used in designing our office: cherry wood and pewter. Then I said to the mortuary man, "You're lucky this wasn't the other way around. If my husband were sitting here, he'd be saying, 'I want the wood from this one and the hinges from that one and the handles from the one on page twenty.'"

Mila laughed; it was absolutely true.

What I did not say was, *The truth is, I wish it had been the other way around. If only I could have made it be the other way around.*

Because although there was some relief, albeit fleeting, in Laurence's unspeakable pain coming to an end, what now was I supposed to do with mine?

SNAPSHOT

Everybody needs to play hooky now and then. When Cami was in preschool, Laurence originated the "playing hooky" tradition. If we were working on a screenplay at home, a hooky day probably didn't look a whole lot different from any other day. But if Laurence was in the middle of an editing job or a graphics assignment, it meant taking an actual day off from the studio or the camera house where his animation was being shot. And Cami would take a day off from the preschool grind. It was our little family secret. When I called the school attendance office to explain Cami's absence, I would never report her sick, being a bit squeamish about bad karma. I simply pled "family business." The truth was, Daddy and Cami were playing hooky. And what do you do when you play hooky?

Go fishin'.

I would pack a picnic and they'd load up their gear. Red tackle box. Cami's Mickey Mouse fishing pole. The net for scooping a fish or two right out of the water if you got lucky. Everything you'd need. It was downright Mayberry.

The two of them headed off to parts northwest—slightly northwest—Agoura to be exact, to a place called Troutdale, a stocked lake (more like a pond) where Laurence had gone as a little boy. There was a small shack on the premises where they sold bait, shocking pink and fairly stinky. Laurence helped Cami bait the hook of her Mickey Mouse pole and then they'd settle in for a day of good ol' fishin', punctuated by trips to the vending machine, which was stocked with more candy than the lake was stocked with trout. Laurence would buy Mike & Ike and Good & Plenty, the candy of his childhood, which Cami found utterly fascinating.

Then the waiting began. The first time they went fishing, Laurence wondered if Cami would be bored. But, like her father, Cami was good at waiting, even at age four. They both enjoyed the company of their own imaginations. Mostly, they both enjoyed the company of one another.

It was with enormous glee that Laurence related the story of the first fish Cami ever caught. With a bit of help and much cheering, she yanked the struggling creature out of the water. Laurence had maneuvered the hook from its mouth, leaving a gaping, bloody gash as the trout flopped in the bucket. Laurence checked for Cami's reaction, fearing that she would be upset by the gore.

"Have you had enough?"

"No!"

What on earth was he talking about? She was overjoyed. She was proud. She was hooked. "Daddy, let's stay all day."

And they did.

All day, at least once a year, usually two or three times, until, sadly, missing a day of school meant missing actual work, and Cami decided the tradition would have to be replaced by others. A Saturday excursion to the lake just didn't pack the same punch, lacking in forbiddenness as it would be.

But those days at Troutdale were worth a lot. More than a spelling test, or a play rehearsal, or conquering long division.

Everybody needs to play hooky now and then.

CHAPTER FOURTEEN

You are the one who can make us all glad,
But doing that, you break down in tears.
Please don't be sad, if it was a straight mind you had;
We wouldn't have known you all these years.
                                    —"DEAR MR. FANTASY"

Cami and I bounce around the house for the next few days like
pinballs. A sort of manic exhilaration. Strangely, there's a sense of
accomplishment. We walked through fire, our whole selves consumed by flames. Anything else we encounter in life can be no
more than a little smoke wisping at our ankles. The scenario that
had sprung to mind the instant Laurence had been diagnosed,
which we had fought against for those long months, had come
true. Yet I was still alive. Being alive suddenly meant something
entirely different, alien, but I was alive whether I wanted to be
or not.

I just didn't know how to be.

If only Laurence were here to tell me how. I thought back to that day when we returned home from the doctor's after the recurrence had been discovered. Laurence had said, "You're going to have to carry on."

"No, I won't," I'd insisted. "I'm not going to have to. We can do this."

He had been opening the door and I had refused to step through. The blackness on the other side was too frightening. And now he could no longer tell me how to face it. At that moment, denial felt like courage. Now I knew it was the exact opposite.

Courage would have been saying, *Yes, I promise. I will carry on. Tell me how, now while you can.* I promised him while he was dying, actively dying during that twenty-eight hours, that I would carry on. But it was too late to receive his advice. I had missed the moment when he could have held my hand and walked me through his own absence.

One morning I pause to listen to Randy Pausch on the radio. A professor of computer science at Carnegie Mellon, he is famously battling the pancreatic cancer that will soon take his life. He tells the interviewer, "My family's going to be pushed off a cliff, and I won't be there to catch them." With enviable maturity and the clear-sightedness accompanying his scientific bent, he adds, "This gives me time to make a net."

Where is my net? I wonder.

Three months ago, I should have turned around and looked over my shoulder to see how close the precipice was, but I did not. Even if I had, I wouldn't have believed a net possible. I could not say to my husband, "Weave me a net." The only safety net I ever knew was Laurence being here, being in the thick of it with me, reminding me of who we were together.

So now I free-fall.

I had thought that the pain of the initial diagnosis was unbearable, then the pathology report, then the recurrence. A chain of the unbearable. But Laurence had always been there to make it seem all right. He was the one suffering, but he was making it better for me. Now it is clear. Those were all just dress rehearsals.

Sometimes the scream chokes its way out of my throat: "I can't do this without you." Life's cruel, ultimate catch-22.

At other moments—so many of them—I feel like I am losing my mind. I actually attempt to hold on to those flashes, because losing my mind feels like the only way out of the pain. But they are only flashes; I cannot sustain any real delusion. Maybe I used up my ability to perpetuate delusional thinking during the course of Laurence's illness. Instead of finding the solace of insanity, now I ride the wave of adrenaline. Like a mother lifting an automobile off her child, there are moments when I feel I could lift the death right off of him, so that he could just slide right out from under it and slip back into life. But then the weight of the reality, the horrible foreverness, falls.

A friend from the distant past hears the news and calls.

"Stay open," he says.

I try to grasp the idea. I can indeed feel the hatches closing one by one. Everything closing in. My body shrinking. My chest tightening. A vise squeezing at my temples. Panic, almost claustrophobia, laying siege. Get me out of here.

At first, I allow myself to feel grateful that I left nothing unsaid in my husband's last hours. But that small gratitude cannot cancel out the guilt that, in the preceding months, I surely kept him stuck in a ghastly spot, an awful space between his intuition about what was happening to his body and not wanting to frighten me. It must have been a lonely and fearful place. I am so sorry I trapped him there. Even after he is dead, I say it out loud repeatedly. "I'm sorry. I'm so sorry."

Just as I had said while he lay dying. "I'm so sorry. I didn't understand."

I didn't allow myself to understand. How horrific the pain was. How impossible, what it meant. The truth is, of course, I did understand. But the chasm between what I understood and what I acknowledged was so deep and jagged that there was no climbing to the surface where rational, admirable behavior might be possible.

So, at the end, all I could say was, "I'm sorry I didn't understand. I'm sorry."

From deep behind the morphine drip, Laurence had answered me.

"It's okay," he breathed. "It's okay."

I instruct someone, I don't remember who, to phone various agencies in search of one that will pick up the paraphernalia—syringes, tubing, latex gloves—strewn across the dining room table along with the bags of narcotics lining two full shelves of my refrigerator. I move through the house, dragging a lawn-sized garbage bag from room to room, tossing in all the other medications: those lollipops (such a deceptively cheerful moniker), patches, pills, pills, and more pills. They fill the medicine chest, of course, but also the refrigerator, and the drawers of the bedside tables—both sides of the bed. They are scattered about so many random surfaces. I need a second bag.

How could so much medicine have done so little?

I will be coming across bottles tucked into strange places for months to come. And scraps of paper, sometimes whole steno pads, on which I'd scribbled various days' medication schedules and reminders as though I were in nursing school or chemistry class. They are strangely cryptic now, hieroglyphics from another time.

One page is headed "Re: Dilaudid Pack."

"Put 50 mg patches back on @ 7:30 p.m."

"E = error = disconnect"

"High Pressure = Kink."

"1 mg Dilaudid every 30 minutes."

"2:45 p.m. 5 ml–1 mg / every 30 min."

"Ask for Angela at the pharmacy where the Dilaudid comes from."

"PCA = patient-controlled analgesia."

I keep the page on my desk for one entire day, then let it slide from my hand into the trash can, noting that I always capitalized the word "Dilaudid," the name of the drug, willing its power.

I am spurred on to a rampage of cleaning out cupboards and closets. Everything but Laurence's stuff. I get rid of my own old clothes, but can't touch his. I get rid of Cami's old clothes, but can't touch his. I try to, standing in our closet, staring at the rods of pants and shirts. I study each of his eighteen Hawaiian shirts, a splendid collection: the vintage Reyn Spooners, the soft muted ones, the wacky black one with the highball glass print. Laurence's band had a good run for a while there—a string of Saturday nights at a seedy Culver City joint called Johnny Foxx's, which amounted to their glory days. For these gigs, he often wore that black Hawaiian shirt with the LeRoy Neimanesque buxom beauty spilling out of a martini glass.

And then I spot the shoebox tucked in a corner. Inside are the Beatle boots. Unworn. Forever shiny and uncreased.

I purge the pantry and the refrigerator, but cannot throw away the exotic risotto mixes or the jar of strawberry jam that always resides at the back of the second shelf of the fridge. I don't like strawberry jam. Neither does Cami. But when I spot the jar, I cannot toss it. It's not the usual French import with the checkered lid, but Swiss, its lid ringed with strawberries. The brand name is Hero. I hold the jar for a moment. It is three-quarters full. A few toast crumbs cling to the outer edges of the lid where Laurence had last swiped his knife. I replace it at the back of the second shelf.

When we had first bought our house twenty years ago and were in the throes of remodeling, we gave some friends a tour of the semi-demolished site. Laurence explained precisely where everything would be and how it would look as plainly as if he saw it before him. Because he did.

At one point during the tour of the kitchen, he said, "The breakfast bar will be here. And the toaster will be right there, so I can sit here and eat slice after slice of hot, delicious toast." For years afterward, the couple asked Laurence how he was enjoying his slice after slice of hot, delicious toast. He was enjoying them quite a bit, thank you very much. Usually with strawberry jam.

I wonder if jam grows mold. I decide that if it does, I will dump out the jam, wash out the jar, and return it to the refrigerator. But maybe jam doesn't grow mold, in which case the jar will remain exactly as it is, waiting for the next slice of hot, delicious toast.

That couple got divorced. As it turns out, he was sleeping with the housekeeper who worked for friends of theirs. Surely a punishable offense. I keep wondering, what was ours?

— —

One week after Laurence's death, Tom and I drive an hour south to Westminster to watch as they bring Laurence to his temporary accommodations. *He never did anything like anyone else*, I think. *No final resting place for him until the place is perfectly spiffed up.* He is, after all, the man who drove a hundred miles in search of a black soap dish to be built into the master bathroom the first time we remodeled our home.

This temporary cemetery is nothing like the lovely little one in Westwood. It is vast and sprawling and, to be blunt, tacky.

I wear a powder-blue sweater dusted with tiny crystals because it looks celestial. I have no idea why that matters, except for the fact that I have, in this past week, begun scouring the material world for signs, and am generally desperate to participate in symbology. Little indications of enduring connection.

I clutch a scrap of paper with the building number, the section number, the vault number.

Tom and I arrive early and explore. A feeble fountain trickles over papier-mâché rocks at the front of the building. A few of the bronze vases bolted to the markers contain dusty plastic flowers. A poor man's Disneyland of mausoleums. We find one empty slot draped with a burgundy velvet curtain.

It's okay, I remind myself. *This place is just temporary. He's going to be dead a long time.* I say again what I will end up saying countless times in the next several months: "If anyone would have wanted his spot newly remodeled, it would be Laurence."

When the hearse finally drives up and the ex-hairdresser/mortuary man arrives, he accompanies Tom and me to the cloth-draped slot. We watch as the workmen raise the coffin on its metal gurney. This is not a picture in a catalog; this is the real thing. Transformed by grief into primitives, Cami and I have sent along to the mortuary a few items to be tucked away with Laurence. I watch the coffin slide into the wall. Inside are these totems. Inside is my husband.

I rest my head on the end of the coffin for a moment before they draw the drape.

"That's not him, Carla," Tom says.

"I know."

But I don't really know. It was him all his life. It's been him virtually all my life. How could it be that suddenly that's no longer him? And if it's not, then where is he? And why can't I be there?

⁓ ⁓

As the frenzied days pass, the cleaning rampage continues, excepting Laurence's clothes, which I still cannot bring myself to remove from the closet, though I will later have dreams of gathering piles of empty hangers. Instead, I turn my attention to his work life. Countless samples in all formats: professional three-quarter-inch, old Betas, standard VHS, as well as actual celluloid and the newer DVDs. Shelves upon shelves of these line the closets of our two home offices, his and ours, not to mention a dozen or so moving boxes packed with more of the same. The sheer bulk of the task is daunting.

I enlist Larry's help and we set out to discard the enormous number of duplicates, making certain to keep at least one copy of every single piece of work: student films, title sequences, montages, documentaries, short films. Everything. I need a second set of eyes to make sure that nothing gets thrown out accidentally.

I can hear Laurence in my head, "You're always so quick to throw things away."

Larry and I spend several hours emptying boxes, filling others selectively, double-checking ourselves and each other. We finally finish around ten o'clock at night. At least a dozen, maybe closer to twenty boxes, are filled with duplicates.

Larry leaves, but I remain possessed. Need compels me. The need to be in motion, to feel like I am accomplishing something, to be numb with activity. I need to get those boxes out of the house. With Cami's help, I load the boxes into the backseat and trunk of my car, and we set out to cruise the dark neighborhood in search of a construction site. It is the Westside, after all. A Dumpster must be standing, half-full, in front of some nearby remodel in progress.

We drive a few blocks and find one—a good-sized bin. But neither of us can manage the leverage to chuck these heavy boxes up and over the side of a Dumpster. We each try and try again, but finally give up. We encounter the same difficulty at the next Dumpster a few blocks away.

We need another plan.

It is a Monday night—trash night. Garbage cans line the streets. Surely enough must be half-empty to make this mission possible. It's a scene from a caper movie as I pull up alongside a row of garbage cans and kill the headlights. Cami jumps out and finds a can with enough room to toss in one box. We drive from block to block, in the dark, tossing cardboard storage boxes full of Laurence Starkman commercials, films, sample reels into strangers' garbage cans. A half-hour later they are all gone.

We return home, spent. One or two copies of each piece of Laurence's work remain. That will be all we will need.

SNAPSHOT

In the late 1990s Laurence created two cable television series for the Disney Channel, Magic Shop *and* Joke Time. *He reveled in every aspect of their production. He handpicked each tchotchke for the background of the magician's set, placing colorful silks and a stuffed Sorcerer's Apprentice, the Mickey version, just so. He designed the* Joke Time *backdrop against which kids stood to tell their jokes (building the prototype himself), tweaking the colors to Disney's specifications. The Channel's demand for "Mickey red" and "Donald yellow" made him shake his head and laugh, but he provided them happily. Laurence understood perfectionism well enough. While industry insiders often balk at the challenges of working for Disney, Laurence enjoyed it thoroughly.*

When we'd pass an adorable toddler on a neighborhood walk, Laurence would say, "I love the little people." The Disney shows were more than a job.

Producing Joke Time *took him around the country to various Disney parks and local Disney-sponsored events where, over the course of a few years, he filmed thousands of children telling their favorite jokes. The summer Cami was ten years old, Laurence shot at Disney World. At that time, Cami dreamt of becoming a Disney Imagineer when she grew up. The timing was exquisite.*

We found out about the Florida trip while Cami was at summer camp in Northern California for a month. It was her first summer away from home. Laurence and I had flown her to San Francisco and handed her over to waiting counselors at the airport. During the taxi ride from the airport into the city, we were clobbered by a nasty case of child-withdrawal, but spent the next three days acclimating to our new status, albeit temporary, before returning home. We must have mailed her ten postcards in those three days. We had never been apart from her for more than a weekend, and that, only once or twice.

By the time we drove up north to fetch Cami at the end of July, we were beside-ourselves excited to lay eyes on our baby girl. The camp provided strict instructions. No parent should arrive on the premises before nine a.m. on the appointed pickup day. We spent the night before at a bed-and-breakfast a few minutes away, the only dot of civilization within an hour of the camp. Predicting what desperate characters we would be by then, we had booked our night at the inn at the same time we had enrolled Cami at camp.

Laurence told me later that he had pictured his little girl running toward us, as flushed with the anticipation of the moment as were we.

Not quite.

We arrived ten minutes earlier than the appointed hour, and spotted Cami across a field. Bedraggled and dirt-encrusted, she wore the bottoms of her red-and-white-striped flannel pajamas, the pair that matched her American Girl doll, a green fleece pullover, and hiking boots. It looked like a brush had not made it through her hair during her entire stay. She was flanked by two other girls, in equal states of disarray. They were all weeping.

It took a split second, but we gave up our fantasy of having been missed and joyfully replaced it with the obvious thrill this camp experience had been for our daughter. Cami's tears flowed, as all happy campers do on that last day. Then we headed off in the car, dusty footlocker shoved in the trunk. Laurence and I had agreed ahead of time that we were not going to mention the upcoming trip to Disney World—a dream come true for Cami—until we got all the way home. We wanted to hear everything about her adventures and her new friends, how she had milked goats and batiked t-shirts and chopped wood to heat the water for the showers. We didn't want to shift the focus from her month at camp until every detail had poured out.

That plan didn't last very long. We stopped for lunch at Spenger's, a landmark seafood restaurant just off the freeway in Berkeley. I sat next to Cami in the booth and, over her fried shrimp, she put her head on my shoulder and began to cry again. Along with new best friends and a heady sense of self-sufficiency, she had picked up a raging case of impetigo. The scabs on her face rubbed off as she wept, and blood streaked my T-shirt where she buried her face.

"Is there anything we could do to make you feel a little better?" I asked.

"I guess we could go to Disneyland when we get home," she sobbed. Laurence and I looked at each other. It was too perfect a straight line to pass up.

"Well," I said, "I don't know about Disneyland. But we are going to Disney World."

Over the years, Laurence spoke many times of the look— or series of looks—that flashed across his little girl's face at that moment. Disbelief. Confusion. Ecstasy.

A month later, Cami and I covered every inch of Disney World while Laurence filmed child after child telling their favorite jokes.

By late afternoon, Cami and I often dropped by the set to watch the proceedings while we caught a second wind.

An endless line of kids snaked around Downtown Disney. Each child stepped up to the microphone and received Laurence's undivided attention.

"Do you have a joke for me?"

"What's your favorite joke?"

"I bet you know a really funny joke."

If the joke was funny but the child was nervous, Laurence encouraged him. "That's so funny. Can you tell it to me again?" And again, and again, till the kid nailed it.

If the joke was feeble but the kid was great, Laurence fed her a joke. "You know what? Have you heard the one about the interrupting cow?" And then he'd ask her to tell it back to him. He'd nod and smile.

"That was so great! You did such a good job!" He was never phony, and he put the kids at ease. He made them feel they were really doing a great job. The kids beamed as they stepped away from the mic and the Disneyfied backdrop.

At a certain point each day when he had just begun to lose the light, Laurence would size up the queue and send an assistant back two-thirds of the way down the line to tell the kids and their parents that he would not be able to shoot anyone beyond that point. A handful of kids peeled off, but invariably the bulk of the line stayed put. After all, this was going to be their moment in the sun, even if the sun was setting.

And so, Laurence stayed into the night, night after night, encouraging each child as he or she stepped up to the microphone.

"Have you got a funny joke for me?"

"What's your favorite joke?"

"*That is so funny!*"

He waited to wrap until the very last child had given it a shot. The children never knew that with the sun long set, their director was no longer running film in the camera. He was just giving them a moment to remember, then thanking them for a really great job as he sent them on their way, before ushering the next child up to the microphone in the darkness.

CHAPTER FIFTEEN

Till death do us part.

That's nonsense. Literally. It makes no sense. Or else demands a superhuman feat. There is no switch to flip. *What happens to the love I keep sending out? All that energy that has no target anymore. Where does it go?* It leaves me feeling like I'm bleeding uncontrollably, hemorrhaging energy that is desperately trying to take root somewhere.

The prevailing wisdom about grief (with actual statistical data . . . how do they measure such things?) points to the fact that it is the yearning that persists. Not the anger or the bargaining, not the denial, certainly not the acceptance. The yearning is the bitch. A longing that does not subside, so crushing that it demands a voice; it makes me scream out loud in the middle of the night, "Come back! Please come back!"

In the first few months after Laurence died, my life becomes about quieting that scream just enough to be able to function. The yearning will always be there, like the engine noise on a jet—always there. When we travelers are occupied, absorbed in chatting or reading or eating our airplane meal, it fades into the background and becomes part of our journey. But when we hit the smallest patch of turbulence or our mind wanders from the page in front of us, the noise shoves to the forefront again and becomes all we can hear until the turbulence passes or we return to our conversation, our book, our anemic chicken. Perhaps the best you can hope for is that eventually the grief, like the engine noise, will propel you forward even as it roars.

The mania continues for days, into weeks. I am slightly buoyed to be back in the world as though having returned, if not from the dead, then from a protracted quarantine. Another one of those clichés that are clichés for a reasons. It is remarkable to find that the world still turns. How is it that it didn't grind to a halt or shift with a jerk that sent it permanently off kilter? How is it that everyone else is going about their business as though nothing has happened? Only I seem to be walking around in a parallel universe. I try to reenter normal life, but it feels like such a long time has passed since I have navigated the outside world. I cannot catch the rhythm, like trying to jump into a complicated pattern of Double Dutch.

The more I rejoin the living, the less it makes sense that Laurence is not here.

Frenzied, Cami and I turn to each other repeatedly.

"I don't want to remember him that way," Cami says.

"I can't get it out of my head," I say.

Laurence's spirit shone as pure and true as though a glow had been digitized around him, but he was no longer him. He was evaporating. So we say to each other, *Not that. Not that image.*

Remarkably quickly, that dying vision begins to recede. Within the month perhaps, the real Daddy—comfortable, easy, profoundly whole—replaces the dying Daddy in our minds' eyes. Partially because we launch into bingeing on videos and photographs, but partially, too, because we have to erase that image out of self-preservation, nature's gift.

But recalling the healthy Laurence presents a double-edged sword. If that was my husband, if that was Cami's daddy, then where is he? Why isn't he walking through the door? Why isn't he sitting with us at dinner? Why isn't he lying in bed with us, watching TV? The more we remember him the way we want to, the less we can make sense of his goneness. Dying Daddy didn't belong here. We could almost come to terms with that. But Real Daddy does. It becomes more and more difficult to process the forever part. For the rest of your life is a long time, and I begin to worry that all I will ever want from the rest of mine will be to get to its end.

There is so much business (as in busy-ness). The canceling of credit cards, the removal of his name from checking accounts and car insurance, the transference of household accounts to my name only. I am on the phone for hours with the gas company, the cable TV provider, Verizon. Someone advises me to make sure that his airline miles get transferred. I do as I'm told, and spend days attending to this—phoning, faxing, explaining. The stuff of life that has always made us curse adulthood. I sign legal paper after legal paper on lines designated for the "surviving spouse." True only in a manner of speaking.

I must also cancel Laurence's cell phone. I spend nearly two hours with customer service, explaining exactly which phone numbers I am keeping and which single one I am canceling, and how the name on the account should now read. Finally, the actual human person I have managed to make contact with seems to understand.

AFTERIMAGE

But then, suddenly, as I hang up, I realize this means they are about to turn off Laurence's cell phone. I run from room to room, calling for Cami's help to find a tape recorder. We must record his outgoing message, capturing it from wherever it exists in the cell-phone ether. Cami and I dash through the house, throwing open cabinets and drawers, until we find a clunky old Panasonic. We don't bother to check if the tape in it contains anything important. We call Laurence's cell phone and play his voice into the tape recorder—once, twice, three times.

"This is Laurence. Leave me a message."

At that moment, I cannot imagine living without being able to play his message at will. Oddly, I will not play it once in all the months since, but in that instant, I am so afraid a time will come when I cannot conjure his voice.

For now, he is so everywhere. We feel his presence in the house so strongly that I almost become a believer in ghosts. He is so with us.

It is as though he just stepped out. Scraps of paper next to the telephone make me weep. His handwriting scrawling a number or a name, random scribbles made while talking, a pencil never at rest in his hand. His trademark doodles of palm trees along with arrows and spirals and whimsical, quasi-mechanical figures. I scramble around the house on a treasure hunt for more.

I undress for bed and open the bottom drawer in the bathroom to toss in my socks and underwear. One side of the drawer received my socks and underwear, the other his. Now there are no jockey shorts. No white sweat socks. No charcoal men's socks.

These tiny things split open my heart with laser precision.

While, in other arenas, calluses have begun to form. Months earlier, I had stopped watching medical shows on television. No

217

more that guilty pleasure, *Grey's Anatomy*. Once George's cancer-riddled father showed up in the hospital, predictably a goner, I checked out. But now I tune back in. The suffering of a bunch of TV characters? What of it?

The first show I happen to catch appears to be a ratings grabber. It is February sweeps after all. Having missed part one the previous week, I am thrust into the middle of the melodramatic mayhem—bloody bodies, lost children, grief-stricken family members identifying loved ones from Polaroids snapped in the morgue. So what. I can handle this. *Bring it on*, I think. I, who normally cry over Hallmark commercials.

Bring it on.

Anything with a commercial break cannot touch me. Kid stuff.

In fact, there is part of me that turns the saga of the last few weeks into something more closely resembling fiction than life. The story takes over. Embarrassingly (and truly uncharacteristically), I suffer Ancient Mariner syndrome, driven to tell and retell the tale of the last day of Laurence's life to people with whom I would not ordinarily share anything remotely intimate. My mouth shifts into gear and my brain disconnects, and I tell the tale. How Cami insisted we bring Laurence home, how we believed he knew he was home, how I will be grateful to my daughter forever. I blather on, automatic pilot fully engaged, frenetic and wild. I cannot decide if I am desperate to transform my new reality into a story or trying to force myself to actually, finally believe the whole of the tale I am compelled to recite.

I am relieved to discover this is an acknowledged phenomenon. It happens to men who have been to war. Elyn Saks remarks in *The Center Cannot Hold:* "If and when they can, people who have been traumatized will tell what happened to them, over and over." Much of the time, most of the time, I feel like I'm doing an impression of myself. Out of body, watching myself transform into this new creature: a widow.

A week after Laurence dies, the dryer breaks. Life's mundane preoccupations continue, oblivious. When the repairman arrives, I stand nearby, pretending to supervise. In this strange new world, I will have to learn what's going on with household appliances, both major and minor, or at least look like I care. The repairman informs me that I should purchase a ventilation spacer. I write it down: ventilation spacer. I consider telling this man standing in my kitchen with his name on his shirt that ventilation spacers are beyond me, that I am a widow, but I cannot speak the word.

I try on the word occasionally, at first with a certain ironic detachment, as if to say, *How could such a word possibly apply to me? It doesn't fit.* I search for a permutation that might suit me better. *Widowette,* perhaps—more diminutive and casual—like a kitchenette in a studio apartment where a twentysomething is trying out life on her own. But no. Like pregnancy, there are no degrees of widowhood. So I just use the word, incongruous as it may be; obviously there must be so much distance between that word and me. But the real irony is that there is no longer any distance at all. That is who I am.

I understand widows from the old country, head-to-toe black proclaiming their occupation. *I am mourning,* they tell us. *I am missing my husband. All else that I can manage is to breathe. Leave me alone. Expect nothing from me. This is all, all that I can do, maybe for the rest of my life.* For those women, their mantillas or the shreds of torn black cloth pinned to their black dresses say, *I am waiting to die.*

And what am I waiting for? How do I reconcile the oxymoron that is young widowhood? I have gone from baby boom to kaboom, finally a grown-up. Do I wait for a glimmer of life to return, or presume it never will? Or do I, as a friend or two suggest, reinvent myself, as though I were Madonna, as though I could just lift the film on the Magic Slate that is my self? I cannot decide which is the more realistic approach—the Sardinian widow's or this modern, anything-is-possible one—nor which, if either, offers any comfort.

Whichever, this is not your grandmother's grief.

The ever-so-brief relief vanishes. I was so exhausted during those final weeks that I thought I could not take any more. I formulated that thought so many times: *I can't do this anymore; it's too much.* But within a few weeks after Laurence's death, I am desperate to keep going at it, to keep him going. I don't care how many more doctors would need to join the team or how many more hospital stays it would take. I could do another year. I could do another thirty years of keeping him alive. I could do that single day, that last day, over and over again, if need be, like the movie, *Groundhog Day*.

Who do I see about getting a do-over?

There is that split second when you stub your toe or step into scalding hot bathwater, when you know that a signal is shooting to your brain—pain is on its way—but it just hasn't arrived yet. You brace yourself—here it comes, here it comes. Right before the whammo comes the awareness, the dread. That was how I lived—those split seconds strung together like a strand of beads choking me.

As Laurence struggled to achieve some measure of comfort in our bed and I lay in the foldout at two in the morning, listening to him breathe, listening to him move, did I half-wish it would be over, no matter what that meant? Did I invite death in for tea, like the old woman in *The Twilight Zone*, terrified that her time was nearing, but nonetheless opening her door to Robert Redford, death in disguise, so solicitous and handsome? And if I did, can I take it back?

— ~

I have no doubt that bereavement groups help many people. I could not drag myself to one. I am loath to join even a book club. How could I join a death club?

Well-meaning friends mention how friends of friends found these groups helpful, especially for the children of. So, after a few weeks, in a glaring example of caring more for my daughter's well-being than my own (and in the great tradition of Do-as-I-say-not-as-I-do), I press Cami to make an appointment to visit a group for people her age who have lost their parents. When the day arrives, she insists she cannot bring herself to go. I urge her. She does not go, but schedules another appointment. When that day arrives, she becomes hysterical.

"No one will understand. Daddy was special. He wasn't like other daddies. Our relationship was special."

I tell her that I am sure everyone there will be thinking the same thing. But she refuses to go.

And then I drop it. Because that's precisely what I've been thinking. He wasn't like other husbands. Our relationship was special. I don't want to have to try to explain it. And I don't want to hear about anyone else's relationship. All those other relationships are irrelevant.

Cami adds, "I don't want to talk to anyone who didn't know him."

Enough said.

There is no describing her father. She knows it and I know it. Laurence was one of those leaders of the tribe. He would never have acknowledged that, but it was true. He was rarely the most talkative person in the room, never the most attention-hungry.

My niece's husband, with the vantage point of an outsider entering our admittedly wacky family said it well. "There are a lot of strong women in this family," he remarked, "but when Laurence spoke, I always wanted to hear what he had to say."

Friends called him with more questions than any single person should know the answers to. Aesthetic judgment calls during remodels. His trick for that barbecued chicken they'd had off our grill. His video expertise in compiling sample reels for friends of varying talents, as well as for friends' children, hoping to demonstrate dance or musical ability to prospective colleges.

Some of this help took a few hours; often it took days. It was creative—and fun—but it was work. Frequently, he offered as favors what he did for a living. The bigger truth is that Laurence was a nicer person than I am. When I'd find him at his computer, editing into the night on a project that was not even his, I would often say, "What has that person ever done for you?"

He would shrug. And keep on working. It didn't matter to him.

Laurence was the go-to guy—in his own way, a leader of the tribe. He knew his stuff. So much stuff.

The answer to so many different questions will catch in my throat for the rest of my life: "Ask Laurence." Or to Cami: "Ask

Daddy." Instead, I will remain silent as my throat constricts and my chest tightens around my heart to make sure it holds together where the fault gapes.

I now check our joint e-mail account every morning. Laurence used to do that. I accidentally open one of those Internet scam requests from an "international businessman" in search of a U.S. citizen eager to stash his money for sizable compensation. For some reason, I read the bullshit. It begins with an account of how the gentleman in question is going to die soon because his cancer has "defiled" all medical treatment. More truth is told in typos.

I scan the rest of the slug lines. They offer the tiniest pieces of the puzzle of who Laurence was. Tikievents, Avid film editing updates, Los Angeles Conservancy, Musician's Friend, Recipe of the Day, doctor@dictionary.com, and ironically, Daily Health News, to name such a very few. And the magazines that arrive in the mail: *Conde Nast Traveler, Saveur, American Cinematographer.*

The subscriptions will run out one by one over the course of the next year. The piles of magazines in Laurence's home office, on his bedside table, on the kitchen counter—so recently just so much clutter—will disappear; the nothing there—on his desk, on the table, on the counter—reflecting the nothing here.

It makes me feel ashamed. What are my myriad interests? What passions excite me enough to subscribe to magazines and daily e-mail updates? My husband had no passing interests. If he was interested in something, he wanted to know everything about it.

Laurence was not the go-to guy for any reason other than his joy in doing a task right, in doing it—whatever it may have been—with his particular style. What he never knew, and what really never mattered to him, was how much people appreciated him for that. In short, how much they loved him.

The days following Laurence's death bring not only flower arrangements and coffee cakes and pots of soup, but mail, too. So many letters that I buy a special box to keep them in. And then another, when the new pile becomes more than a pile, becomes a sprawling mass of envelopes. It is remarkable to me how, for minutes at a stretch, I am actually able to find comfort somewhere, no matter how modest. But there it is. Unexpected comfort in these envelopes, where I discover how much other people loved my husband.

I e-mail friends who moved east some twenty years ago. We have not seen them in all these intervening years, though we have remained in touch. The husband writes back immediately. He thanks me for letting them know, commenting that it would have been particularly awful to learn of Laurence's death from the Hollywood trade papers. Despite the twenty years that have passed, he assures me that the East Coast is awash in their tears.

"He was the best," he adds, "and you had him."

He's right; I never had to settle for apple.

Others—several, in fact—remark that they believed we led a charmed life, Laurence and I, so that his death is all the more shocking. This Capraesque revelation stuns me. You never know what your life looks like from the outside as you go about living it. And where is Frank Capra when I need him to serve up the revelation and then reverse the tragedy before the fade-out?

SNAPSHOT

My father had a mustache when Laurence first met him. My father was an actor, and mustaches, like twenty extra pounds or a brown felt fedora, came and went with my father often in the service of a part. That particular mustache may have been a remnant of a duly forgotten Western called Wild Rovers. *Whatever the reason, he had a mustache when Laurence, still a teenager, first walked through the door. As Laurence would confess years later, it made his girlfriend's father all the scarier.*

It would not take long for Laurence to discover there was not much to be scared of there.

Some thirty years later, my father accepted what was destined to be the last job of his career: a guest shot on the television series, The West Wing. *No mustache. No riding horseback. But, like several somewhat iconic roles that had been part of his career, another priest. The president's priest—called upon to consult with the president as he wrestles with a decision regarding the death penalty. One of those hours the networks dub "a very special episode."*

My father had not worked in a number of years. Well into his eighties, he felt a bit rusty, and, ever the perfectionist, more than a little nervous. He wanted Laurence to go with him the day he shot.

"What do you say, Larry? Want to come?" he asked. Only my father called him by that nickname, but Laurence never minded.

Laurence drove him to the studio and spent the day with him, quietly running lines, making sure he took time to eat, hanging back when the camera rolled.

The end of the scene called for the president's priest to pull out his Bible and offer to pray with the president. My father had brought along the Bible he had used when he played the priest in On The Waterfront. *Laurence listened as, during the course of blocking the scene, my father mentioned the history of the little black book which he produced from his pocket. Laurence watched as various actors from far-flung corners of the set flocked to lay eyes on the thing. It radiated beyond the waterfront priest to a golden age of movies; it radiated Marlon Brando and Elia Kazan. Could they touch it, please?*

The next day, my father insisted on doing something special for Laurence in thanks for his help. "He was great," he told me, "so great. I couldn't have done it without him." They settled on buying a new jacket, and the following week, they spent a morning at the Century City shopping center. Together they chose a sport coat: coffee and black tweed. Laurence's West Wing jacket.

Laurence often wore the jacket when we were going out to dinner to celebrate a family birthday or anniversary. "Look, Pop, this is the jacket you gave me. Looks pretty good, huh?" He might run his hand down the front, tracing a lapel, as if to emphasize its sharpness. He'd cock his head and raise an eyebrow as if to say, "Pretty snappy, eh?"

But it was the Bible anecdote that was his favorite souvenir of the day. He told the story a number of times, consistently bemused. Those funny actors—whom he himself took such pains to cast whenever he was directing—those funny actors, so desperate for magic. Don't they know, he often wondered, that the mustache may make you look scary, and the Bible may glow like a totem, but the magic has to come from somewhere else?

CHAPTER SIXTEEN

There are drawbacks to being together forever. High school sweethearts—such an archaic phrase. To be candid, there are moments when you wonder what you missed, *if* you missed, but the media creates those more than your own heart. When you grow up together, you grow together like a grafted tree.

Laurence-and-Carla. Carla-and-Laurence.

I know that is how everyone thought of us. Among the couples we know, there will be husbands who absently use the phrase—our names fused together—for months to come, maybe years, and wives who shake their heads in disbelief when they do. I sit across the dinner table from these people at restaurants all over town. Their faces tell me I am an amputee, minus more than a limb, minus my other half. The truth is, there were not two halves in our kind of math. Laurence-and-Carla. Carla-and-Laurence. The hyphens were just for show.

In the coming months (it may well be for the rest of my life), friends remark on how often they think of Laurence. They tell me they quote him. ("I have no problem with change. I just like things the way they are.") They wonder what he would do in a given situation. (Freeway or surface streets, Laurence knew best.) For some, the senselessness of Laurence's death shines a spotlight on the teetering they are currently experiencing in their own lives. Marriages sinking, midlife angst mangling self-definitions, preoccupation with health concerns overwhelming reason—whatever their individual scenarios, they speak of my husband and they smile.

I am surprised to discover how these moments make me smile. I take solace in knowing that other people—not just me—feel an emptiness where he should be in their lives. Remarkably, these are often not just our closest friends, but people we had seen infrequently or not in a very long time. In so many different ways, people tell me the world shifted on its axis when Laurence died. They hesitate to confide this, fearing their pain will magnify my own, but the opposite is true. I cannot get enough of hearing what they all say: "We lost one of the good ones." I cannot get enough of hearing what he meant to other people.

It means that he was here.

And if he has left such a big hole, he was here in such a big way.

Most of the time, I am living in that hole. In the negative space of his life. Laurence believed he didn't have the goods to make a career in fine art, but he was a talented artist. As we strolled through galleries, I often said, "You could do that," because he could. He told me once (probably more than once in all our years) about how sometimes you had to paint the negative space, the space between. I'm sure that is no revelation to artists. It was to me. It implied a new way of looking at the world that resonated beyond painting.

And now I spend my life dog-paddling through negative space, the space between what used to be and what is, occasionally bobbing up for air, but mostly just trying to keep in motion against the weight of the water. The weight of now.

— —

I find myself playing a twisted game with my own memory. I force myself to picture Laurence sick and dying. Those images were the last I had wanted to recall. I had been desperate to have them evaporate. But gradually, I find that I need them. I find myself calling them to mind repeatedly. They provide the only way I can make even the slightest sense of his not being here. It remains too impossible to picture him healthy and not have him here.

It takes me a while to realize that not only is he dead, but that he was dying for all those months. The images remind me. We had fought that reality fiercely. While I had failed at so much, I had succeeded in repressing that simple fact. Not just during those last thirty hours, but over the previous several months, my husband was dying. Even on a good day, he was dying.

Even when he ate a whole burger at Johnny Rockets, he was dying.

Even when he masterminded the bouillabaisse we served to our family on Christmas Eve, he was dying.

Even when Cami leaned in to kiss him good-night one evening as she left the hospital and he said to her, "Don't worry. I'll see you at your wedding."

Even then, maybe especially then, he was dying.

She had begun to weep the moment we'd stepped from Laurence's room into the hallway, repeating what he had whispered to her.

She was certain that meant he was going to be okay.

"He's never lied to me," she insisted.

Like my father, who had promised me, "He's going to be okay."

"He's not lying," I assured her.

But I didn't know what he meant. After all, he did not say, "I will be there at your wedding." He promised only that he would see her. And Cami was right. He never lied to her.

— —

Grief is exhausting. It's a lot like patting your head and rubbing your stomach at the same time. I am reading a book, but what I am really doing is grieving. I am talking to a friend over lunch, but what I am really doing is grieving. I am watching a movie, but what I am really doing is grieving. I look like I'm in motion— I *am* in motion—but what I really am, deep at my core, is still. Frozen. *Kine*—for motion. *Stasis*—for still.

Grieving brings a constant state of doing two things at once, which requires an enormous amount of energy. Plus, you are expending even more energy trying to force the main occupation—the grieving—into the background as you go about the other, surface activity. It's no wonder the grief-stricken retreat to their beds. That is all we have energy to accomplish, because we are still going about the business of grieving, even then, buried beneath the covers. Especially then.

It takes enormous effort to live *as if.* To get out of bed in the morning as if the day held promise. To take a bite of a sandwich as if it did not turn to dust in my throat. To have a conversation as if I can follow a train of thought.

Some acting coaches proffer the "Fake it till you make it" trick. Go through the motions until you feel the emotion. Now I am faking the stuff of daily life in hopes that going through the motions might salve the emotion. Go through the motions to numb the emotion.

Grief is exhausting.

That is why the actual grief-related business offers a strange kind of relief. At least while going about that business, I am all in one place. Mind, body, and soul.

Like the business of planning the memorial.

Actually, we end up with two memorials. There is a hue and cry among Laurence's relatives to do something quickly. I am happy to acquiesce. Since a number of them may be distressed to discover the event will be areligious, I want to accommodate them as best I can.

So, six days after Laurence's death, some seventy-five people—mostly his relatives, but also friends of his siblings—arrive at our home. The obligatory deli fare covers the dining room table, so recently dedicated to medical paraphernalia. Starkmans mill about, reconnect with relatives they haven't seen in years, and reminisce.

Various uncles and cousins tell me stories about Laurence at different ages. One cousin, a woman a few years older than Laurence of whom he was particularly fond, takes me aside and says, "Laurence was always different, you know. He wasn't like the rest of the Starkman men."

"I know."

"Whenever we were all together," she continues, "I always used to think of that *Sesame Street* song. 'One of these things is not like the others; one of these things does not belong.'"

I smile. I knew that. He knew that, too.

In old family photographs, Laurence is often the little boy standing apart, with a look in his eye that suggests he had a secret. A look that said, "I'm thinking something no one knows."

He used to say that he looked like a concentration camp victim when he was a kid—skinny, with dark circles ringing his deep-set eyes. Even at his sickest, as he grew thinner and cut his hair short, he didn't look quite like that little boy in the striped T-shirt. But what he did have in the last month or so was that ironic look in his eye, a look that suggested he had a secret, just like when he was a little boy.

A different secret, to be sure. Perhaps it was, "It may not look like it, but I'm fighting." Then, "Leave me to my own mind. I've found a spot in here that's not so bad." And finally, "This isn't me. I'm not this disease."

After a few hours, I cannot move among this crowd anymore. At parties we had thrown over the years, Laurence and I generally circulated separately, as hosts do, mingling and guiding people to the buffet. But during the course of the evening, we tended to check in, help each other refill a platter or change the music. Now I am emboldened by widowhood. I no longer care about etiquette. I retreat to Laurence's office and close the door.

— ~

With that first "rehearsal" memorial over, Cami and I become obsessed with planning the perfect gathering for all our friends. Years before Laurence got sick, maybe ten or fifteen, we were driving home from a funeral and Laurence said to me, "When I die, just throw a party. A really great party."

We never discussed it again, certainly not once he was diagnosed. But I had not forgotten his offhand comment. Of course that's what he would want. There is no doubt.

That becomes our mission. A fabulous party.

We entertain a few options for the venue. For about twenty-four hours we settle on the Community Room at Cami's old school, which has rallied around us with remarkable warmth and generosity. But soon we decide the event has to be at home. "He is so *here*," Cami and I say repeatedly. There really is no other choice that makes sense.

Cami makes a list of her daddy's favorite foods, starring those on which, she informs me, there will be no negotiating. Before I fax the list to the caterers, I warn them of its eclecticism. The menu runs the gamut from Chinese dim sum to mini barbecued pork sandwiches to chocolate-dipped strawberries. I explain the situation: "We've even got Rice Krispies treats on the list. It's a long story." In fact, it's not very long. Cami and Laurence used to make them together from the time she was tiny.

The caterer understands. The menu evolves, but Laurence's favorites remain.

Meanwhile, Cami begins work on a video to screen at the memorial. This is what her daddy would have done. She plunges headlong into the project, sitting in Laurence's office, at his desk, in his chair, hour after hour. The second chair—the one where she used to sit and watch him work, or work together with him on a school project—remains empty. She has moved into her father's chair. She hears his voice. She feels, she tells me, as though she has a phantom limb, fully present though missing.

I hear her there at two and three o'clock in the morning. She is utterly lost in the project—selecting photographs and clips from home movies, scanning the photos, entering data into the computer, executing computerized moves on the pictures, creating a rough cut, then tweaking it until it is exactly the video she sees in her mind. That is the way her daddy worked. "You see it all whole, and then you just make it turn out that way."

Cami falls into what Laurence used to call the black hole of editing. Hours turn into days turn into weeks.

I say, "Go to bed, sweetheart."

"I will. I'm coming."

Another two or three hours go by. She sits at the computer still, absorbed.

I know that story well.

— —

A casino complete with slot machines. A campsite surrounding a pitched tent. Firework displays. Exotic dancers. Inevitably, we baby boomers have grabbed hold of funerals and lit them up like so many flickering lighters at a rock concert. We refuse to concede gentleness to that good night before, during, or after meeting it. Jim Morrison is going to sing us out. Break on through to the other side.

I do not go so far. No bar-mitzvahesque theme for Laurence. What our day has is bunches of celadon orchids and periwinkle hydrangea and white roses. Our day has abundant food—mini pulled pork sandwiches, dim sum, and yes, Rice Krispies treats. We have great music courtesy of Laurence's iPod, and truly good friends filling our home to overflowing. Filled with laughter and tears—if not in equal parts, then at least of equal spirit. Our home filled—remarkably—with Laurence.

I wander through our house. So many people have never been crowded into this space in the twenty years we have lived here. I pick up snatches of "Laurence stories," and the continuing thread of utter disbelief.

Laurence's older brother remembers the little boy with the crew cut and the cowboy outfit.

Laurence's childhood friend, Mark, talks about the grade schooler on the Sting-Ray bicycle and the teenager who introduced his friends to Bob Dylan and modern art.

His friend and colleague, Jim, speaks of how Laurence was one of those rare people who spent his life doing work he felt so passionate about that it was not work. "We all felt he had a charmed life and he knew it. He was grateful for it. We went to a job," Jim says, "and he went to the country club. He thought we all were at the country club. Because he thought working in film was a country club. "

Our nieces speak of their devoted uncle. Alison remarks that he was always there. "For birthdays, holidays, graduations, weddings, dinners out, dinners at home. And more than that, he was always really, really happy to be there. He made me feel like a gathering with our family was the best possible place to be." Emily says, "People know him for all of his amazing talents, but I know him for what I think was his best talent—loving his family."

Everyone speaks not only of the man they loved, but even more enthusiastically, if possible, of the man who loved—simply, without show, and well.

And Laurence speaks for himself. A day or two after he died, I come across a file on the desktop of his computer. It contains a smattering of miscellaneous notes, what would normally be of little consequence. But now, no scribble, no matter how random, is inconsequential. Every word is precious. And in this file is a list.

It is another one of Laurence's homework assignments from the therapist. Laurence had written:

I am so grateful for:
1) My wonderful friends—they have shown so much kindness and support.
2) My beautiful wife. I know she is going through hell, but she won't give up on me.
3) My beautiful, sweet daughter who makes the world turn.
4) My music, it takes me beyond time. I have heard the voices of angels.
5) This beautiful green earth. I know where heaven is.

My sister reads Laurence's words at the memorial. But even before that, everyone knows he is here.

Cami, looking so much like her father—the shape of his eyes, the angle of his jaw—is the last to speak. She introduces her video, cut to the Byrds' version of "My Back Pages": "Ah, but I was so much older then . . . I'm younger than that now." Everyone gathers around the monitors positioned throughout the house and in the yard and watches images of a life well led, a life never squandered, just cut short.

One of Laurence's band mates finds me in the hall sometime after. "Cami will never be on a shrink's couch wondering if her father loved her," he says. I think, *That is the highest compliment anyone could pay Laurence. That is what he most would have wanted to hear.*

Another friend—an acquaintance really, the wife of an old colleague of Laurence's—corners me in the kitchen. She is weeping.

"I was debating whether or not to say anything to you," she says. "I know we don't know each other that well. But I just have to say that Cami's speech and her video made me realize . . ." This woman has a daughter exactly Cami's age. I am sure she is going to tell me how precious her husband holds his relationship with their girl. Instead she says, ". . . They made me realize how Mitchell doesn't have a relationship like that with our daughter. Not at all."

Heartbroken beyond the events of the day, she continues to weep nearly uncontrollably. "Maybe Mitchell will get it," she says. "Maybe it's not too late."

I move into the living room and visit with another friend, but I cannot focus on what he is saying. I am wondering if that other father and daughter just might have a new start because of this afternoon in our home. Or is it too late? Various shots from the video flash across my mind. For that other father and daughter, their moment on the swings—gone; their moment in the hammock—gone; their moment flipping early-morning pancakes—gone.

We still have those moments, our moments. Those moments will always belong to my daughter.

One friend wonders aloud to another, "Does this mean we have to be grown-ups now?"

"Laurence," I answer, "would say 'absolutely not.'"

Astoundingly, it is a great day. The exact day Cami and I had hoped for.

One old friend from high school shows up with a boxed apple pie. He has crossed out the words on the label and written instead, SHLEMMA PIE.

And then it is over.

And so is the planning. No more production. No more losing myself in the details—the placement of the caterer's equipment, the size of the video monitors, the removal of furniture to optimize the standing-room-only space. Just a looking-glass version of everyday life.

The infinite regress that is grief gradually begins to take on a new layer. I grow terrified that I am beginning to remember my own memory of my husband rather than the real human being, in the way that you are unsure if you remember an actual incident from childhood or just the image you spun in your mind's eye after years of hearing the story told.

Laurence is losing dimensions, one at a time. He exists on paper, in notes he has left scribbled on scraps tucked into drawers. He exists in photographs. He exists in home movies. Because he was usually behind the camera, even in those, he most often exists as a disembodied voice, Cami's offscreen playmate or the family documentarian.

But still, he exists, his afterimage hovering before me. Afterimage—a scientific phenomenon, that particular optical illusion which allows us to see something that's no longer there. We turn off the television in a dark room, and still we see its incandescence. Afterimage—the glow that floats in front of us when we have looked into a bright light, a light so bright that neither the setting of its sun nor the closing of our eyes can extinguish it. We do not merely think we see this image; we *do* see it. Our eyes and our brain conspire to trick us, to make us second-guess reality. So now, my mind and my heart conspire to preserve this afterimage for as long as possible, even if it means hurtling into madness during those moments when I can no longer distinguish between the afterimage and all that came before.

Little by little, I find my thoughts occasionally morphing from present to past, as though I am experiencing my own self dissolving into the past, leaving just this illusory version in its place, like the fading photograph of a vacation. I catch myself thinking of the only life I have known as the life I once had. Sometimes it is like remembering a dream, a dream so vivid you are certain you will always remember it when you first open your eyes in the morning, but which only tickles at the outer corners of your brain by the time you are brushing your teeth.

In *A Grief Observed*, C. S. Lewis tells me I am not losing my mind, or, if I am, I am in his good company. ". . . Then comes the tragic figure of the dance in which we must learn to be still taken out of ourselves though the bodily presence is withdrawn, to love the very [him], and not fall back to loving our past, or our memory, or our sorrow, or our relief from sorrow, or our own love." The relationship dance—this phase—simply presents a new series of steps to be learned. Most days, however, I am executing a pirouette on a balance beam between the pathology and the comfort of being lost in memory.

CHAPTER SEVENTEEN

Cami has taken a leave of absence from school for the semester. With the memorial behind us—along with all its preoccupying details—we need something new to focus on. Something to plan.

A trip to Europe seems ideal. Ironically, we had just begun planning such a trip when Laurence was diagnosed. The three of us were going to visit France as soon as Cami was on summer break following her freshman year. Now, it will be the two of us.

I could enumerate many reasons for this trip. Who knows when we will have such an opportunity to travel together again, a window of time in such desperate need of filling? It is the off-season; there will be fewer tourists and, possibly, pleasant spring weather. We pretend that museums and excursions, five-star hotels and three-star dining will help us mend. Of course, we know they cannot. We are not going in order to mend. We are going to escape, though we know full well that flying thousands of miles will not distance us from the pain. No escape from this pain, an inevitable stowaway. It doesn't matter. The truth is, I have to get out of Dodge.

I begin to think of it as the Heartbreak Tour, as though the phrase should be emblazoned across the side of the plane, announcing our fragility before we ever step off. Beware. We may weep as we stroll the Champs-Élysées. Tears may splash into our bone-china teacups in London. We may choke as we say for the thousandth time, "I know someone who would love this." We are on the Heartbreak Tour, after all. It might as well be scrawled across our backs.

It falls to me to choreograph our trip—a task normally under Laurence's purview. His voice directs me, but from within me. I am amazed to discover that I have absorbed his way of doing all kinds of things, from small household chores to researching this trip. Apparently, I was paying attention when I didn't know it, all those years. I want to tell him, *I got it! Isn't that funny? I gave you a hard time. I kidded and teased about overdoing, overresearching, overpreparing, but as it turns out, I got it.*

I wonder if I will spend the rest of my life inventing projects that require enormous amounts of advance preparation. The business of day-to-day living no longer absorbs me sufficiently. I carve daily existence into little chunks of time to make it manageable: afternoons, evenings, hours, the next ten minutes. And at the end of each day, there is a small feeling of accomplishment to still be here, to have gotten through it. But there is also the creeping realization that each day does not get me closer to a time when the hollowness will disappear. I feel like I am biding time. But I am not biding time, because there is no endpoint. This is it. This is what time is now.

I play mind games with myself, endeavoring to work up some enthusiasm for the whole proposition that is life. I play, *What if I were diagnosed with . . . ?* I fill in the blank with any number of miseries—even the big one, the victor—to see if imagining a hideous label smacked across my forehead causes some deep-down, primitive life force to lurch in protest. Sometimes yes, sometimes no. Sometimes it just feels like relief.

Two months after Laurence died, I drive to my sister's house for dinner. Pulling into her driveway, I think, *Oh, Laurence will be here to surprise me.* At that moment, a surprise return feels like the only explanation for what has happened. This is not denial. Just the subconscious trying to make sense of something that makes no sense—a sort of reflex of the imagination.

The segue from normal life to cancer life made its own peculiar sense. It involved a mission. But this new segue catches me up. I am stuck in the cancer life. I am standing at the checkout stand at the grocery store when I spot a *Newsweek* cover story: "How I Live With Cancer," by Jonathan Alter. *I didn't know he was in the club.* I pause. I hesitate. Then I throw the magazine into my cart. I can barely take the few minutes to unpack the groceries when I get home. I am that eager to read the article. My husband is dead, but I cannot break the habit. Maybe this article will hold a secret, *the* secret. A doctor's name, a clinic, a magic potion. I read the words, more focused than I have been at any other task in weeks. I know—Laurence is dead. But I am compelled to read, to see how to cure his cancer and make him live.

I speed-read through the article, nodding in recognition at so many shared experiences. At the end, Alter quotes a line from *The Shawshank Redemption:* "You can get busy living, or get busy dying." Alter writes, "For me, it's no contest." It has been eleven weeks, but still, I do not feel like the contest is over. My reflexes are still in battle mode. I am still fighting to save my husband's life.

I begin to experience occasional palpitations. No big deal. The sensation of my heart flipping inside my chest like a pancake. I've had mini versions of these in the past, but not as persistent or intense. They used to frighten me. No longer. Now I wonder, *Is my heart actually broken? Is this sensation the coming attraction for a heart attack? Wouldn't that be interesting? Would it be enough to do me in?*

I figure this cardiac mambo probably stems from so many months in fight-or-flight mode. I discover there is, in fact, something called Broken Heart Syndrome; the heart tissue is not dead, just stunned. The patient presents as though having a heart attack, but blood tests reveal levels of stress hormone severalfold higher than those of a heart attack patient. I presume I have some version of that. I also self-diagnose with post-traumatic stress disorder.

Treating both drives me to do things wildly out of character. Desperate to take the edge off, I acquiesce and try antidepressants, slicing the tiny pills—already the lowest dose available—into halves with a steak knife. I determine to ride out the side effects and wait one week, two weeks, three, until, sure enough, I am aware of the tiniest blunting of the sawed edges. It doesn't exactly feel like me anymore, but I suppose that's the point. I discover I am, at least, no longer waking up crying. The tears don't come until actual thought sets in, several seconds later. I figure that's progress of a sort. On the other hand, one morning, I find myself squeezing the toothpaste tube without removing the cap.

I am promised that popping this tiny chip of a pill every morning should earn me some sleep at night, but not so. I doze if I'm lucky. Even then, the nightmares are continuous. I come from a family of women whose sleep is plagued by nightmares, each of us possessing our own unique banshee cry. Just as you are often aware that you are dreaming, you know, too, when you are screaming in your sleep. There is a part of you somewhere in the back of your brain that knows the screaming signals the end of the nightmare. It means you are about to be awakened by the person sleeping next to you.

But now, my preliminary moans go unheard. I break into short, stabbing shrieks that still no one hears. And finally, I am screaming, full out, until I wake only myself, heart pounding, in a cold sweat. I glance at the clock. I have been asleep for less than an hour. I lie awake for the rest of the night, hoping I might doze again, maybe when the sun comes up. It's a topsy-turvy world— my husband is dead; I might as well fall asleep at dawn.

I wander the late-night airwaves. So many channels, so little to watch. I must truly be old. I wonder whatever happened to the good old days when insomnia meant spending the night in elegant black-and-white with Humphrey Bogart or Cary Grant. Now, I am pitched the benefits of an age-defying skin-care line, or must consider whether I am interested in making a killing in real estate. (Skin care—yes. Real estate—no.) If I am ready to "begin a relationship with Christ," there is an 800 number I can dial. Even Nick at Night offers only reruns of '80s shows I never watched in the first place. Where's Dick Van Dyke when you need him?

So much for Zoloft-promised sleep. I flush the pills. They are not going to help me. I am not depressed. I am heartbroken.

Further out of character still, I meet with a "grief coach." The proactive ring of her title suggests she is different from a therapist. As before, I am not interested in an archaeological dig for the right words. Words rattle against my skull incessantly.

Permanent. Forever. Impossible. Never again. Gone.

"He's gone," I said to my mother when I phoned her that night, the first time I had to say it, having no clue, as yet, what it really meant.

The rest of my life.

Loss—such a strange word, as though I'd just been escorted off the stage of a game show. Maybe, I venture, a coach will do me some good, cheering me on from the sidelines, whipping pom-poms high above her head and shouting, "Get up! Get dressed! Eat dinner!"

She turns out to be a woman with her own tragic story that more than qualifies her for the job. In keeping with the take-charge bent of coaching, she assigns me homework, including something she calls a "relationship review." This involves charting my relationship with my husband onto a sort of a graph marked by highs and lows.

For all those months I had repeated the refrain—to Laurence, to myself, to both of us together: "We can do this. We can do this. This is doable." I was wrong.

I know from the start that this relationship review is something that is not doable. First of all, I cannot distinguish between our relationship and our entire life. My life, our life—it's all the same thing—the highs and lows so woven into its fabric that were I to pull the thread of one, the entire tapestry would unravel. For the first time in what had been a compulsive academic life, I do not do my homework.

The truth is, there is no relationship review to be done because the relationship is not over. I find myself in an ongoing relationship with a dead man. Rationally, I suppose I don't want to go through the rest of my life married to a dead man, but the alternative happens to be worse, because, as it turns out, I more fiercely do not want to go through the rest of my life having let him go. Is there a way to do both simultaneously? That may be the fine art of widowhood.

A relationship review would constitute such a strange full-stop. We do not look back and review something that's still in progress. This is just a new phase, the part where he's not here. This is not a marriage ended. Again, C. S. Lewis knew: ". . . for all pairs of lovers without exception, bereavement is a universal and integral part of our experience of love. It follows marriage as normally as marriage follows courtship or as autumn follows summer. It is not a truncation of the process but one of its phases; not the interruption of the dance, but the next figure."

No relationship review for me. We are still dancing, Laurence and I. Together.

I commit to a number of sessions with this grief coach, appreciating her conviction that if I do "the work," I can speed the process. A few sessions in, I am still resisting her exercises. I inform her that we are going to begin pretending instead. This is what we are going to pretend: that I would be coming to her at this point in my life for a tune-up even if my husband had not died, that I am here to create a new life plan. I know this is not true. No way. No how. Not me. But it is the best I can do—making believe I am here in order to come up with new, improved ways to keep in motion. I pretend I am sitting in her oversized leather chair, sculpting a sort of business plan out of this new amorphous blob of life.

Laurence hovers over our discussions, but I keep him at bay. We talk about goals instead—one-year, three years, five years out. Busywork, but helpful in a way. It reinforces the idea that I will be here in one year, three years, five years.

There are moments when I am especially sleep-deprived that I wonder if I ever related to the real him. I fear that I am transforming him into a sort of Platonic ideal of himself. Like everyone, Laurence was flawed. He drove me crazy. Yet, like Mary Poppins, he is suddenly "practically perfect in every way." I have to work to remember those times when he infuriated me. When I do, I wish I could have reacted less, been less hotheaded. Or at the very least, simply live those moments again, exactly as they were, like Emily in "Our Town." I experience my dead husband as at once acutely real and something of a fiction. I so readily relate to this figment—he is still so much with me—that I can no longer distinguish between the real him and what feels like the imaginary friend as constantly with me as any three-year-old's. Even the slightest business of daily life becomes less real, because nothing is real if I can't tell him about it. So I tell him about it.

In an exercise of admitted masochism, I picture him walking through the door, just to experience what that thrill would feel like. It's strange to imagine how absolute that thrill would be, after all the entrances made through all the doors in all the years. You know theoretically that you should be thrilled every single time, but when you're living your life, that's not how it works. Not until they pave paradise and put up that parking lot.

Now, if the phone rings when I am lying in bed watching television at night, I fill the seconds before I say "hello" with pretending it's Laurence calling to say he is on his way home from band practice. Part reflex, part intention, part invention. I make-believe those moments just to feel the synapses fire.

I circle his absence, trying to conjure him. Morning e-mails continue to drip with irony. One suggests "Laurence, check life coverage." Another—from godaddy.com—threatens that his domain registration is about to expire. A third is urging him to resubscribe to a magazine: "Laurence, we want you back."

I log onto our amazon.com file. "Hello, Laurence Starkman, we have recommendations for you." They are so wide and varied, it boggles my mind. *Iran in a Nutshell. Radar Men from the Moon. The Modern Art of Chinese Cooking.* Modern living is such that we leave these technological echoes behind.

I rummage through his pockets, pulling out half-filled packets of gum and narrow tins of Grether's black currant pastilles, now artifacts. I open the medicine chest over his sink and breathe deeply the smell of cheap Mennen Skin Bracer (he was never a fan of cologne). Three or four backup bottles line one side of the top shelf. The aroma mixes with the smell of the foam encrusted on the nozzle of a can of shave cream. The bristles of his old-fashioned shaving brush are still soft and slightly damp. And there sits his nose-hair trimmer.

When Cami was in the second grade, Laurence and I arrived for the first of the semiannual teacher conferences. As we sat in the mini chairs, her teacher smiled and said, "I thought you might like to see this." She handed us Cami's most recent literary effort: the fully illustrated "Attack of the Nose-Hair Clipper." Pictures of Daddy, a prominently errant nose hair prickling from one nostril, filled the top half of the pages; Cami's bulbous printing told the story across the bottom, guided by solid line, dotted line, solid line. Now the trimmer—along with everything else in his medicine chest, in his pockets, in the glove compartment of his car—is a relic. As the days pass, these things—just things—become objets d'art, like mementos picked up while traveling, reminding me not of a place I have once visited but of a receding life.

I fold open his wallet as though it were a treasure chest and pull out an old picture of the three of us—Cami, Laurence, and me—smiling into the camera as though the future could not possibly hold anything but more of the same. There it is: the card issued to him when we made our pilgrimage to the Norris Cancer Center. It is dated 12/14. What would I have done, what would I have said, if the receptionist had passed it through the open glass to us and announced, "Five more weeks"? I remember the fear that day. I remember Laurence's pain. His desperation to get at the drugs. But I also remember the tears of joy as we drove home. The guru had a plan, so many courses to try. Surely one of them would work. It still seemed impossible that one of them would not, could not work. And then I pull from the wallet a credit card, its expiration date years in the future. How could this piece of plastic have outlived my husband?

Sometimes late at night, I Google his name, as though I were a stalker or a crazed fan. Who will the cyberworld tell me he was? One entry tells me I can "Compare Prices for Laurence Starkman." Another helpful listing offers, "Laurence Starkman—Death—Send to Friend." I can track his political contributions, download a list of his awards, read his filmography, and surrealistically, "Find upcoming TV appearances." If only.

Even when the information, such as it is, makes a modicum of sense, does that person, in all his professional incarnations, bear any resemblance to the person who smiles at me from the gathering of pictures on the bulletin board to the side of our desk? A picture of Laurence, Cami, and me at an event at Cami's high school. Of the three of us, flanking the Penny Lane sign in Liverpool. Of Laurence and me meeting Grace Slick at an exhibit opening of her artwork. Of Cami and Laurence at a family dinner when he was nearing the end of his first round of chemo. He is relaxed, smiling, arm around his baby girl, believing he has come out the other side.

SNAPSHOT

A pad of vellum tracing paper lay on the kitchen counter along with Laurence's tools of the trade: X-Acto knife, non-photo blue pencil, T-square. He often said that had his father not been an architect, he probably would have grown up to be one himself. Architectural projects merged so many of his talents with so many of his personality traits. Focus on detail, excruciating precision, and a spectacular sense of design. When he trained these qualities on a project, it was likely to turn out as perfect as it could be. In truth, Laurence harbored a perfectionism that his easygoing, relaxed demeanor belied.

This kind of project brought that perfectionism bubbling to the surface until it reached a rolling boil. He measured. He folded. He made a mock-up. Then he laid the vellum on top of different-colored sheets of sturdy but translucent plastic and began slicing. These plastic sheets—yellow, pink, green—still bear his notations:

X2 = ROOF.
NOTE: Cut window for back!
And, on a tiny rectangle: X2 Porch Roof.

The cutouts within the sheets vary in shape and size. A cameo-sized oval suggesting one window. An elegant half-circle suggests another. The perimeters of the sheets themselves outline the overall look of a stately Georgian mansion with a peaked roof.

And then, scattered about the kitchen counter, there were the trees. A dozen or so cutouts of fir trees of varying height and dimension.

Laurence had built up to this project over the years, each Christmas developing a new template—larger, increasingly complex and detailed.

Finally, Carmi and I were called in to help. It was time to make the dough and the golden spun sugar for the windows, which, when inserted into the perfectly crafted window openings, glistened as though illuminated from the inside.

Another year. Another Christmas. Another gingerbread house.

CHAPTER EIGHTEEN

I change the outgoing message on our answering machine, debating which will be the more difficult for our friends: hearing the message that includes Laurence's name, or hearing this new one without it. I listen one last time. "If you need to reach Laurence immediately, his cell phone number is . . ." If I leave the message as is, how many people will battle the urge to call that number? I consider the possibility myself. If he's not here, maybe he exists in some ether realm with good reception.

I am constantly trying to figure out where he is. It is impossible that he has simply evaporated. In my dreams, I am wandering through a house I sense I am familiar with, but I cannot find the room I am looking for, as though I am trapped in a funhouse. I go up and down several staircases, but the particular room I am seeking is never at the top or bottom of any of them.

Even my little niece, now four years old, grapples with what my own subconscious relegates to sleep. She tells her mother, "I want to go visit Uncle Zippy in the hospital again." She knows he has died, but I can't help but wonder if she secretly worries about having been fearful when she visited him there, even though her disquiet was so bravely camouflaged. Maybe not. Maybe she just wants to see him again, like we all do. Her mother explains again: Uncle Zippy has died.

Little Mila offers another suggestion. "Maybe he's in another room in the hospital."

I understand exactly how she feels. Surely he has just been misplaced.

— —

The night before Cami and I leave for Europe, I dream that I am remodeling our house. I have added on a new bathroom. When I examine it, I discover it is all wrong. Strange paneling, striped in different woods, lines the walls. Odd flower-shaped pulls stud the drawer fronts. It is hideous. I say to no one in particular, "Go wake up Laurence. Go get him. This will wake him up. He won't be able to stand it; he'll have to fix it."

I awake with a start, disoriented and agitated as though on the verge of breaking a stubborn fever. I get out of bed and finish packing. I wish we weren't going on the trip at all, the way that you wish you hadn't ordered theater tickets months in advance when the night arrives and you are slogging through a head cold. Though I am lacking in enthusiasm for the trip, I lack travel anxiety as well. None of my usual mental lists. No fretting over maneuvering between terminals or making connecting flights. No game plan. There is no anxiety left over for the navigation of international travel—it has all been spent at home.

Similarly, once in London, I amble onto the Millennium Wheel, that *uber* Ferris wheel known as the London Eye that revolves to 450 feet high. Previously, it embodied many of my phobias soldered into one enormous Tinkertoy. Not this year. Confine me in a glass capsule. Add more bodies packed in like sardines. Spin me up so high that I get Peter Pan's perspective over Big Ben. No sweaty palms, no shortness of breath, no problem. No nothing.

"Paris will be there next year." That's what we said when we were forced to pull the plug on our travel plans when Laurence was first diagnosed. And indeed it is. It is Laurence who is no longer here.

April in Paris. Despite the song, the weather can be dodgy. April in London. Almost always dodgy. Not this year. We encounter weather which is astounding the locals in both places. Picture-postcard blue skies. Perfect walking weather. And that is what we do. We hit the streets of Paris, where Cami has never been, and we walk for a solid week.

Laurence and I had never been to Paris together. That is a blessing and a curse. There are no memories here . . . and, there are no memories here. There is none of the "Remember when . . ." that we encounter in London. It hardly makes a difference. Everywhere, we are tormented by "If only . . ." and "Daddy would love this . . ." Worst of all, there is regret. Why didn't we do more traveling? How did we let life get in the way? What were we waiting for? And then I remember—we were waiting for this very stage of our lives.

Cami and I manage to have a good time. That is what I will say when we return home. "We managed to have a good time." And it's true. We are in constant motion—walking, walking, walking—as you do in Europe but cannot in L.A. The walking helps, tricking your body into feeling like you are outrunning your grief. I wonder if we Angelenos protract our grieving, stuck in grief gridlock, stuck in our cars.

Everywhere we go, Cami and I exchange glances. We share a secret: there is someone else here with us, someone unseen but so present. At other moments, his absence crashes down around us.

Cami becomes nearly hysterical as we tour the Musée Cinémathèque. My French, unused for decades, allows me to ask directions, provide a taxi driver with an address, or order an omelette. What I cannot do is translate the explanations printed beneath early zoetropes and other paraphernalia of the flickers era. But Daddy would know these things. He would know how they all worked, or could figure them out just by looking. And his fascination would be so contagious that our own would double.

Every time we are handed a menu, Cami and I exchange that look. Daddy would order this. Daddy would order that. Our last night in Paris, I stare at a *mille-feuille* placed in front of me and marvel at how some puff pastry and whipped cream can carry such emotional weight. The first bite leads me to declare this, *sans doute*, the world's best Napoleon. It is such perfection that I cannot eat it. Laurence's name may as well be piped across the top in chocolate.

Three months to the day after Laurence died, Cami and I spend the day at Giverny. We tour Monet's house—the yellow dining room, the blue-tiled kitchen, the smile suggested by its blush stucco exterior burst into full-blown laughter with its kelly-green shutters. And then the gardens. Our timing is beyond serendipitous. An early spring has swept through the countryside. Lace-edged tulips stand proud over mauve and golden ground cover, not to mention expanses of green, shades of green so alive there is no wonder why Monet felt compelled to stay in Giverny and to paint what surrounded him there.

We wander the gardens with the other tourists, but it doesn't matter that so many strangers are strolling with us. We are communing with Claude himself. And, as always, with Laurence. We can hear his comments about the special quality of the light. We can feel his enthusiasm for the place. And then, when we climb the Japanese bridge over the lily pond, finding ourselves right there inside the paintings, overlooking the lily pads, we know that this is where Laurence would want us to be on this day, this three-month anniversary. I feel his delight so palpably, I say, as I do so many times a day, "Daddy would love this so much." More than that, I feel one of the many hatches that have shut tight in my heart squeak open a crack and let in some of Monet's Giverny light.

Our last night in Paris, Cami and I return to our hotel and pause in the lobby to ask a few questions of the concierge. We turn from the desk, and there's Bob Dylan crossing the lobby. Momentous enough. But there is more. There's backstory.

It was de rigueur at Cami's high school for the parents of graduating seniors to sponsor a page in the yearbook as a send-off for their child. For weeks, Laurence and I deliberated over precisely how to fashion Cami's page. We didn't want a cheesy headshot or a collage of her life thus far. We wanted something that said who she was and that resonated of her life at this school that she had loved for thirteen years. Finally, it came to us. We would use a photo of her from the third grade—Halloween. She had dressed as a hippie. Eight years old, wearing a tie-dyed T-shirt and fringed suede vest, peering over a pair of tinted granny glasses, and flashing a peace sign.

Now, for the text. We debated that long and hard as well, try-ing various song lyrics, one after the other. And then it came to us: "Yes, to dance beneath the diamond sky with one hand wav-ing free . . ." When in doubt, Bob Dylan.

When I sat down at our desk to write Laurence's obituary the day after he died—my partner's empty chair across from me—I muddled through the first paragraph, declining to name the disease that killed him. Then the second paragraph with its pro forma listing of survived by's, spousal parentheses and all. Then came the paragraph that was supposed to say who he was. An impossible task, of course. A life in a paragraph. But when I got to the end of the paragraph, my fingers typed what my mind had not even formulated: "Yes, to dance beneath the diamond sky with one hand waving free . . ."

So there is Bob Dylan crossing the lobby of our hotel in Paris, small and weathered, but huge and forever young. Cami and I look at him, then look at each other, eyes widened in that cat-that-ate-the-canary way, struggling to maintain some semblance of cool. And then he is out the door. Cami and I each raise a hand and wave in the very particular way that Daddy always did when he heard Bobby sing that line.

"Yes, to dance beneath the diamond sky with one hand wav-ing free . . ."

We look for signs.

When you are fourteen and lovesick, you look for signs. He loves me; he loves me not.

When your husband has died and is so gone, you look for signs. He is still here, he is still with me. Bob Dylan in the lobby of a Paris hotel.

CARLA MALDEN

A cricket in the den. Three days after Laurence died, I was sitting in our den talking with Larry and Cami. Suddenly, a cricket began to chirp. Loudly. At first, we couldn't figure out where it was coming from, but after a while, we decided it might be emanating from a high bookshelf. Every time I stood on the coffee table to try to see, it stopped. Only to start up as soon as I returned to the couch and we started talking again. This was a cricket who wanted to add his two cents. We have lived in our home for twenty-two years and we have never before been paid a visit by a cricket.

Crickets are considered good luck for Chinese New Year.

We had said it so many times. "All we have to do is get to Chinese New Year and then, energy—up, up, up."

We look for signs.

I read my horoscope in the paper. One morning, it advises me to "give up the ghost." It is a challenge I am not up to. Not yet.

I read physics and philosophy, frantic for an explanation of why we have had so many power failures in our home since Laurence's death, or why, two days before he died, I felt his essence, healthy and strong and whole, wash over me. No—through me, throughout me, cell by cell—as manifestly as any other physical sensation I have ever felt, like a handshake or a kiss. Physics suggests that energy does not just vanish. Is there some scientific (or para-scientific) explanation for these phenomena? Are these phenomena even real, or just the results of hyperawareness? Why does the phone ring so often now with no one on the line, as it did that first early morning after Laurence died, like a hotel wake-up call? This happens so frequently that one night, I can no longer hold it in and I whisper to the static, "Laurence?" I whisper almost inaudibly, in case there is someone there, on the other end of the line, poised to have me carted off, but I say it nonetheless.

Philosopher John Locke pondered the concept of the sameness of consciousness. He proposed that if two people share enough memory, they merge identities. It works for me. Something to explain the signs and permit me to believe I see them. Because maybe they really are there, not only because I am looking so hard. Something to fill the space between what I believe and what I long to believe, the space other people fill with faith.

Is it peculiar to our generation to find signs in music? It will be so much more difficult for my daughter's generation because they are always in control. Laptops and iPods and BlackBerries. CDs in the car. Downloads. No more radio gods causing you to gasp when a particular song comes on at just that particular moment.

Cami and I are riding in the back of a hired car from London to Stratford and the countryside beyond when the driver grows chatty. "Where are you from?"

"California."

"I was there once, many years ago. When I was young. Great music."

I agree, and we swap memories about the music of the good old days.

"You'll like this then," he offers, and slides in a CD. The Byrds singing Dylan.

> Crimson flames tied through my ears
> Rollin' high and mighty traps,
> Ah, but I was so much older then,
> I'm younger than that now.

"My Back Pages." The soundtrack for the video Cami made for Laurence's memorial.

So, weeping in the backseat, we wend through the English countryside, wrestling with the difference between coincidence and sign—wondering if there is any difference at all. Whatever gets you through the night or, in this case, the Cotswolds.

Cami and I stop in the storybook village of Chipping Campden for a stroll along its High Street. We wander into a gallery where an artist is helping the owner hang for a new exhibition. We visit with the artist, complimenting him on several pieces. We are both quite taken with the work and with the gallery, a charming converted cottage. The downstairs is to be hung with oils on canvas, mostly in sherbet tones. Cami and I make our way upstairs into a small room already hung with a few graphite works on paper. We are in the middle of the English countryside when we find ourselves in front of a sketch of a palm tree, the Los Angeles icon that Laurence most often doodled or sketched or painted.

"We have to buy it, Mommy," Cami says.

I already know that.

We have been buying all over Europe. In fact, the shopping thing borders on out of control. I run my brain through the pop psychology meat grinder and am fully aware that the impulse (or lack of impulse control) reflects all the same dynamics that led me to shop when Laurence was sick—to combat the powerlessness.

We are making our way through Harrods when I turn to Cami. Suddenly, I lose the past fourteen months as totally as an amnesiac. I say, "What time are we supposed to meet Daddy?"

Then it really hits me. All that shopping. It makes sense. Daddy should be everywhere else. Across the desk from me. At my sister's for dinner. In the gardens at the foot of the Eiffel Tower.

But not here in the women's wear department, not in ladies' shoes, not in cosmetics. While I would be there, he would be off browsing in the men's furnishings or playing in electronics. Yes, it is the power in the transaction, the satisfaction of credit-card cause and effect, the promise of life accompanying a new T-shirt or this spring's lip gloss. But here in Europe, just as at home, these are the only places—this literal no man's land—where it feels natural that Laurence should not be there. So I gravitate to these places. And we come home with an extra suitcase.

When we have settled into our seats for the flight home, I turn to Cami. "We should be proud of ourselves." She nods.

And then I look across the aisle and spot a television actress whom I know passingly as a parent from Cami's school. She is settling in for a transatlantic nap, but first cuddles into her husband and kisses him. Jealousy tightens my chest. Why does this woman who apparently has everything else get to have her husband as well?

Since Laurence died, the world has turned into Noah's Ark, but I have been especially bombarded by coupledom while in Europe. Couples travel. Husbands doing the business of being husbands are everywhere. Husbands hefting luggage off of airport carousels; husbands ordering in dimly lit restaurants; husbands holding open elevator doors.

Jet lag combines with exhaustion combines with grief to make the next few weeks every bit as unbearable as the months preceding the trip, maybe more so. I don't know what I expected might change at home while we were away. Of course, nothing has.

A friend remarks, "The trip was a good punctuation mark."

And I think, *What kind of punctuation mark? Certainly not a period. No full-stop on this grief. A comma? An exclamation point? Perhaps, at best, an ellipsis.* Nothing has changed; even the fight-or-flight reflex remains in full force. One morning I happen to tune into a radio talk show while driving and catch the guest discussing holistic medicine, one remedy in particular. I think, *Shit, we didn't try that one. Do-over, please.* How do you press the UNDO button and wipe out all that just happened?

I read an article about supplements purported to ease the neuropathy that Laurence had suffered. I am compelled to Google them. I type in "calcium gluconate" and "magnesium sulfate," panting with anticipation as to what will pop up. I end up in a chat room for the first time in my life, unable to stop researching, casting about for magic. I rage at myself for not discovering these supplements when they might have done some good. So many people are writing in, three years out of stage 3 colon cancer. I don't understand why that isn't us. If I had found this chat room nine months earlier, would I now be sharing our happy ending like these confident chatters? Not likely, I know. Possibly delusional, in fact. But I am so angry that reason knows no reason.

After five months, I come across an oversized envelope on our desk. Laurence's side, beneath a few folders. I pull out a copy of the fifty-page medical history Laurence had compiled to send to Sloan-Kettering. My heart races. I speed-read through the pages like I'm cramming for an exam, half expecting to find new information, something we hadn't uncovered, something that could have changed the outcome—crazily, something that can still change the outcome. The blood work, the meds, the scans. Those scans with their "shadows"—something real, or just the illusory afterimage of the pariah that had taken up residence there for who-knows-how-long? Cancer, after all, turned out to be the master manipulator of illusion versus reality, awesomely adept at its insidious sleight of hand. The information is horribly familiar, like the details of a recurrent and vivid bad dream. All I uncover is a typo.

> "... *restaging, r/o recurrent colon caner* ..." [sic]
> "   *abundant cytoplasm* ..."
> "... *infiltrate through the connective tissue* ..."
> "... *positive in signet ring type cells* ..."
> "... *a new focal hypermetabolic lesion at the left superior manubrium* ..."
> "*Thus the findings are consistent with a metastatic colonic adenocarcinoma.*"

All these months later, how do these words—so clinical and reductive—make my heart do its pancake flip? Why do they still frighten me so? Where do they still get their power? As I leaf through the stack, I cannot focus to read more than a few phrases at a time, never a full page. They are more than confirmation; they are the verbal manifestation of the disease which ravaged my husband. When they were first written, one report after another, week after week, they held a horrible prediction. Reading them now, I wonder if I always knew the prediction would come true.

On Wednesdays the *Los Angeles Times* includes its "Health" section. One Wednesday morning, the newspaper contains a first-person account of colon cancer written by a professor. It leaves me shaking. I have forgotten all the side effects of treatment: the cracked and burning fingers and feet which force this man to walk with a cane. The tingling and numbness of the neuropathy.

The fatigue. The miseries of the treatment have receded like the pain of childbirth. I remember only that my husband is dead.

But I am compelled to read on, reflexively searching for the list of treatments that are keeping this man alive. And then, when I discover his list is no different from ours, I am outraged. Grossly ashamed, I half-hope for a coda at the end of the piece informing us that this gentleman died a few days after submitting the article. I begrudge him his success that much, no matter how tenuous it may be. The seeds of bitterness take hold, pernicious and disgraceful. A perversion of "Why me?" It begs for reassurance that we were not cherry-picked by fate. It seems I am still scrounging for fairness where I know full well there is none.

I am deeply happy for a friend undergoing cancer surgery when the word comes back that his lymph nodes are clean and that his surgical cure requires no follow-up treatment. He nabbed the fucker in time. I am so deeply happy . . . and so deeply envious that I can feel the bile rise in my throat at the good news. Followed by shame, equally deep and bilious.

I return to the manila envelope on our desk to compare its contents to the news from our friend. I flip to later pages, the ones that concern the second go-round. I cannot read the reports without feeling as though I am going to vomit, but I read them anyway.

> *"The atypical cells show almost similar morphology when compared to the colon excision."*
>
> *"Positive for metastatic adenocarcinoma, morphologically compatible with the clinical history of colonic signet cell adenocarcinoma."*

"Regions of hypermetabolic activity within the abdomen consistent with neoplastic disease likely representing early peritoneal carcinomatosis."

None of this tells me what I want to know. Where was the moment when it all could have been reversed? Or did that moment come only prior to the dictation of all these reports by various doctors at the end of their long days? Before my husband lay on the table having a colonoscopy a few years overdue? Did such a moment ever exist at all?

And then, there's that number. The number of lymph nodes. "Serosa contains metastatic carcinoma in approximately nine out of thirty-nine lymph nodes, plus extranodal soft tissue invasion plus multiple serosal and possibly omental tumor nodules."

Nine lymph nodes. Nine would not have sounded that bad. Not even double digits. Less than 25 percent of the nodes they tested. So manageable. I so could have handled nine.

All those months of being fixated on a number I didn't know . . . when the more ominous information fell in the latter half of that sentence. "Soft tissue invasion . . . multiple nodules . . ."

I am forced to the dictionary where I learn that *serosa* refers to the thin membrane lining the closed cavities of the body, like the peritoneum. Once that was "invaded" (there you have it—even the medical personnel adopt warfare imagery), perhaps numbers of lymph nodes were already irrelevant.

I open the Commando Cody notebook beneath the envelope. There it is. All of it. The drug brochures. The printed diets. Pages of Xeroxed business cards, twelve to a page, doctor after doctor, specialist after specialist. The Grand Master's qi dong exercises. Copies of meditations offered by acquaintances. Scraps of paper with the phone numbers of friends of friends who have lived through the cancer saga, now at the ready with support and advice. Another paper with the names and phone numbers of all the alternative-treatment personnel—scribbled to one side, a reminder: appointment with the USC Guru, January 22nd, 10:30. The appointment we never made it to. The appointment on *that* date. The date now in bronze under my husband's name in a graveyard.

And tucked behind the appointment reminder, a full-color catalog from Fiorella's Jack Stack Barbecue, promising free shipping with any seventy-five-dollar order.

SNAPSHOT

In early March of Cami's senior year of high school, Laurence and I attended a meeting entitled "Parent Separation." The evening was run by the two school psychologists and the head of the human development program. We had sat in parent circles like these for twelve years, ever since Cami was in kindergarten. She was what her school calls a "lifer"—a K-through-12 kid. Our school (because it was "our school," not just hers) called these meetings "counsels."

By senior year, we knew the drill. At some point a candle would be lit. We would pass something, some object, known as "the talking object." These were the rules. You must truly listen to the person speaking, the person holding the talking object; you must be in the moment; and you must not plan ahead for what you will say when it is your turn to speak. When it is your turn, you must speak from the heart.

Over the years, I experienced particular difficulty with the part about not planning ahead. It must be the curse of the public-speaking-phobic. I just couldn't stop thinking about what I was going to say when the crystal or the rain stick, or in the case of this spring evening, the Koosh ball, landed in my sweaty palms.

So that was what I was doing as the Koosh ball made its way around the circle. I was formulating what I was going to say about the topic of the night: what was it like for you when you left home? Most people seemed eager to finally have the opportunity to air their grievances about how their own parents handled this event some thirty or even forty years earlier. We heard about the withholding mother who couldn't bring herself to admit that she missed her daughter. We heard about the parents who did not drive their daughter to college, but sent her off with her older brother at the wheel. And the son who couldn't wait to get out of the house to escape his parents' fighting, only to discover that they were waiting for him to leave so they could get a divorce.

I was sitting there, thinking about what I was going to say, when I found that Laurence, seated next to me, suddenly had the Koosh ball in hand.

"It doesn't really matter what it was like for me," he said. "I'm just so excited for Cami. I'm just so excited for her." And he was. Nothing else mattered to him one bit. Not how his own parents dealt with his college career or, as he occasionally commented during that time when our own household was abuzz with college talk, how they did nothing in preparation for him. Not even how Cami was beginning, as most kids do, to push the envelope in preparation for her departure. Laurence was the person in the circle who held the Koosh ball and, in essence, said, "This is our children's time."

He passed me the Koosh ball, the "talking object," but there was really nothing more to say.

CHAPTER NINETEEN

I scribble down the names of books recommended, hoping (if not believing) that one will contain a paragraph or two that might lessen my pain. I am reminded of when Cami was a baby and I found myself at a children's book and music store. I felt equipped to select books competently enough, but I was unfamiliar with children's music. I asked a saleslady for suggestions. My insecurity as a new mother made me an easy mark, and this woman had very definite ideas. I snatched up all the recommended audiotapes. If I didn't, would my daughter miss a crucial opportunity for added IQ points, or be lacking in interpersonal skills, or not have the backbone to just say no when she was offered drugs?

I feel that kind of desperation and pressure now. I must not miss a trick. If even one sentence can help me, I must find it. I must read it. I order book after book, hope after hope, and tear open the boxes when they arrive.

Friends give me books as well. Multiple copies of *When Bad Things Happen to Good People* and several others that contain the word "power" in their titles. I can only presume the use of the word to be ironic. Powerful is far too ambitious an aspiration. I am struggling for *present*, grateful for *functional*.

One friend presents me with a book of poetry written by Mary Oliver after the death of her lifelong partner. I relegate all the other books to a shelf, with gratitude to the well-wishers who sent them, but this book's title moves me to open the thin volume. It is called *Thirst*. The poet understands what the self-help pop psychologist may not. Yearning, not peace. Dissolution, not self-reinvention. Thirst, not power. I dog-ear one page and read that poem over and over until I know it by heart. Literally.

> *From the complications of loving you*
> *I think there is no end or return.*
> *No answer, no coming out of it.*
>
> *Which is the only way to love, isn't it?*
> *This isn't a playground, this is*
> *earth, our heaven, for a while.*
>
> *Therefore I have given precedence*
> *to all my sudden, sullen, dark moods*
> *that hold you in the center of my world.*
>
> *And I say to my body: grow thinner still.*
> *And I say to my fingers, type me a pretty song.*
> *And I say to my heart: rave on.*

It is no revelation to me that Laurence knew what the poet reminds us; he was grateful for "this green earth . . . I know where heaven is." Disappointed, despondent—undoubtedly.

Brokenhearted—to be sure. Betrayed by the inaccessibility of a cure, he lay in his hospital bed and said that one late night, "I guess we've just been unlucky." He was entitled to say that, to be dismayed, but that was not how other people saw him. Unluckiness was not the sum of his life.

On the contrary.

In the guest book friends signed at the memorial, one colleague cited a line of dialogue from a movie: "'Sometimes you're walking around lucky and you don't even know it.'" He added, "Laurence always walked around lucky—and unlike most of us, he knew it. And he was thankful for it."

Many friends referred to the light inside him. One wrote, "This quality—that he knew precisely who he was, a joy that he had easy access to, a sense of wonder that was both childlike but also grounded. He was a source of light, and others gravitated to him because of it, but he also made them feel that all was right with the world, or could be right or would be right again."

Lucky or unlucky, it hardly matters in the long run. Luck runs out. A "source of light" does not. That is what I tell myself when the longing, the yearning, the thirst, overtake me.

Thirst, first thing in the morning, when I open our e-mail and see some promotional slug line: "Laurence, last call."

Thirst, in the evening when the phone rings and I hear, "Laurence Starkman, please."

"Who's calling?" I ask, knowing it must be a solicitor of some sort. USC Alumni Association, the Democratic Party, the Sierra Club.

"Please take him off your list. He's deceased." I learn to say it with such ease, so dispassionately, as though the clinical "deceased" means something different from dead. He may be deceased, but he is not dead. That is the reality in this house, a reality which dangles me over the gulf between the two.

So tenuous is this existence that I become a different person, someone whose ability to hold anything in my brain, let alone concentrate, remains just out of reach. The grief is so huge, so impossible to maneuver around, that it leaves no room for making mental lists of any kind.

I spend my days running from room to room, taking care of any little thing that needs to be done the very second I think of it. I spend hours repeating a singsong list in my head: Q-Tips and toothpaste, Q-Tips and toothpaste, in an effort to remember why I have gone to the drugstore. I have no short-term memory. My memory is filled to capacity with memories.

I set a goal of accomplishing one thing a day. Just something. Like a patient recovering from a devastating injury striving for a single step. Pay one bill. Walk around the block. Read one chapter in a novel—a task that takes an inordinate amount of time because I seem to have developed dyslexia. Like a shut-in old maid, I use photos as bookmarks, pictures of the babies in our family. One sticks out her tongue, mocking her father, the photographer. Another smiles at me through strained carrots. Seeing their faces yanks me back to the present as I open my book. Then, after a few minutes' effort, the words jumble on the page. I slide the photo back between the pages so that when I next pick up the book, these faces can tell me where I am.

I go through a phase in which I am drawn to the wistful poetry and music of my early adolescence. Judy Collins, Joni Mitchell, Leonard Cohen. "Suzanne takes you down to her place by the river . . ." I rifle through old vinyl—mine, his, ours all commingled—feeling all the more disconnected from, disgruntled with the world around me. I am downright curmudgeonly. I don't belong here anymore. Without the person who shared my history, shared my memory—my partner in irony—how can I maneuver a civilization so deteriorated, from "Ladies of the Canyon" to "My Hump, My Hump, My Lovely Lady Lump"?

— —

People don't go around asking you if you are married, yet I become convinced that the question hangs in the air everywhere I go, like a pop quiz. I formulate answers so that I will be prepared when someone actually hauls off and asks.

I'll be ready in the grocery store. "Paper or plastic, and are you married?"

I'll be ready at Starbucks. "Whole or two percent, and are you married?"

I'll be ready at Bloomingdales. "Do you need that in another size, and are you married?"

Most writers harbor a gnawing suspicion that someday their bluff will be called. "Exactly who do you think you are, arranging words for a living?" This new in-between state makes me feel similarly fraudulent. "You may be wearing that ring, but we know you're not really married."

So I ready an answer. And finally the day comes when I have to take it out for a test drive. I am sitting alone in a movie theater waiting for a screening to begin. A couple inquires about the empty seats next to me, and I tell them the seats are free. They sit down. The man starts chatting with me. After a few minutes, he says it.

"Are you married?"

"I was recently widowed." That's what comes out of my mouth. It sounds arch and odd. Dialogue that looks serviceable on paper, but doesn't play. How would I know? Laurence wasn't here to try it out loud with me. It was the answer I'd rehearsed in my head, explanatory, yet skirting the yes/no dilemma.

The man to my left shrinks back ever so slightly, shakes his head in sympathy. Apparently, I do not match his idea of a widow any more than I do my own.

I don't say it again anytime soon. I keep to myself that I now inhabit a purgatory where I am neither married nor single, unable to expiate whatever sins assigned me there. The truth is, I'd rather stay there, in limbo, than move farther away from Laurence.

Strangely, so many household mishaps continue to occur, many years' worth in a matter of months. Appliances give up. Plumbing rebels. Lighting goes kaput. I rarely called on professionals for any of these things in the past. Laurence was good at that stuff. (Upon discovering the vast organizational wonderland of Laurence's tool closet—complete with dozens of clear plastic boxes bearing labels such as BATTERIES, CABLE ADAPTORS, and PICTURE-HANGING KIT—my brother-in-law chuckled that he would have given Laurence a much harder time had he known about this compulsive side of him.) Laurence enjoyed being Mr. Fix-It. I enjoyed his enjoying it.

"You're so handy," I'd say. Again, one of those long-married routines.

To which he'd reply, a nod to James Taylor, "If only I could fix broken hearts."

If only he were here, he would do just that, along with fixing the blinds, the garbage disposal, the timer on the outdoor lights. Now, these things require a constant parade of repairmen.

The electrician discovers a half-dozen fixtures on the verge of blowing and asks if he should replace them all, adding, "You don't need to hire an electrician to do this."

I don't say, "I'm a widow." I just say, "I can't do it." Let him think he's doing a good deed for a feeble divorcee.

— ⁓

Cami designs for herself a patchwork summer consisting of two part-time internships and a job as an editorial assistant for a documentary film she can cut at home on her daddy's computer. I hear her working at his desk into the night, and once again, the sound is familiar, reassuring.

We are back from Europe only a few months—just the summer—when I am antsy again, ready for a change of scene. Cami and I decide to spend a few days in San Francisco before she goes back to school for the fall semester.

The night before we leave, I dream I am there, in San Francisco. I know—in that way that you know things in dreams—that a killer is terrorizing the city, sticking a shotgun into random windows and shooting. I look out and see him—faceless, menacing, evil—on the fire escape. We dash off, Cami and I, each lugging a single suitcase up and down the hills, unable to move with any speed, trying to escape a madman.

Versions on this theme begin to haunt my dreams. Faceless gunmen spraying bullets wherever I go. Running from them through unfamiliar streets, knowing that I have been separated from someone in the mayhem.

I have survived, but my dreams tell me otherwise. My life of ease and assurance did not survive. They call it survivor's guilt.

As desperately as I wonder, "Why him?" I also wonder "Why not me?" Is it just because I won the genetic coin toss? If so, not good enough.

These days, the answers to so many questions are not good enough. Though weeks dissolve into months and months into seasons, bunching into whole hunks of a year, I continue to wonder, *Where is he? Where did he go? How can someone who was so here just disappear?*

Cami is wondering the same things. Sometimes, we ask each other these questions—urgent non sequiturs that we simply cannot contain.

And then there are the questions that friends ask. "How are you doing?"

"I'm doing."

I adopt perpetual motion as my modus operandi. I strive to become a whirling dervish, exhausted and numb. Instead, I feel like a tetherball whipping around a pole that is not secured to the ground. I accept every invitation that comes my way, though what I really want to do is stay in bed . . . until I try staying in bed and discover I want to run away. It continues to be excruciating to read friends' faces across the table. To them, I am half. But evening after evening, I bop from restaurant to restaurant. I keep moving because I am unable to just be.

And yes, I shop.

Another word about the shopping. I tsk-tsked with the rest of the country a few years ago when articles appeared denouncing the frivolous spending of some of the 9/11 widows. How dare they squander government aid on designer jeans and swimming pools and top-of-the-line kitchen appliances? I get it now. The dynamic is complex, but like any other self-soother, anxiety-reducer, or would-be addiction, shopping attempts to fill a hole. When that hole is so deep that you cannot see the bottom, you just keep tossing things in. *If I cannot have my husband, I will have this jacket.* I continue to try to convince myself: there is a life out there that requires black patent wedges. I cannot envision it, but I will be in style if it comes.

I begin buying stuff for our house as well. New flatware, though I cannot conceive of ever entertaining again. Artwork, which we traditionally bought to celebrate our anniversary. Even a duvet. A new bedspread is something I actually do need. Our old one is stained by the lotion I rubbed into Laurence's cracked and prickling feet night after night. Over the years, Laurence and I had an ongoing debate about the virtues of duvet versus comforter. He lobbied for a duvet, but I always won, preferring the weight of blankets and a quilt. Now, suddenly, I buy a duvet. I rationalize that it goes with the decor of the bedroom better than anything else I can find, but I wonder if I am really making a peace offering. *Okay, you win. You can come back now.*

The believing that he is gone does not get easier. Nearly five months after Laurence's death, a letter arrives in the mail bearing a law firm's letterhead. At first, I wonder if I am being sued for some reason I cannot guess. But as I read on, I discover that it is a letter inquiring if we might be interested in revisiting the film project whose option we had lost. After breaking our hearts two years ago, they want to do business again.

"Laurence!" I call out loud, "You won't believe this!"

I've said it before I realize I've said it. I wonder if I will do that for the rest of my life. I might hope I do.

Though I feel frozen in time, time, of course, pays me no mind. Winter and spring turn into summer as they do, even when your husband has died.

I make it through Mother's Day in May, for which Cami gives me a beautiful gold disc on a chain. The disc is inscribed with a lotus. "It means rising from the ashes," she tells me. I take to wearing it all the time.

We stumble through Father's Day in June, half pretending it's just an ordinary day, half pretending we didn't go all out in years past with gifts to welcome summer: a deluxe barbecue, swimming trunks, a cool Hawaiian shirt to add to the collection.

I stay in on the Fourth of July, hearing the kaboom of fireworks as I lie in bed. Laurence, an avid fireworks fan, would have dashed to our porch for a peek.

My birthday means phone calls from friends. I debate about answering the phone and sometimes do not. When I give in, so many people say, "Are you okay?"

It is a meaningless question, less than rhetorical, steeped in doublespeak. They know that I am not okay, but they need for me to tell them I am. It is too much for them to handle if I say, "No. I can't bear this day." It is too much for them if I reflect their own worst fears of what being alone looks like.

Only one friend calls and says, "Happy birthday. I'm so sorry."

"Thank you," I say. "Thank you for that."

Worse than the special days—Mother's Day, Father's Day, my birthday—are the ones that blindside me. I am admonished to stay away from Jane Anderson's new play, *The Quality of Life*, a treatise on life and death and grief and, specifically, dying from cancer. I understand friends' impulse to protect me, and I do as I am told. I may be a glutton for punishment in the privacy of my own home—watching over and over again home movies and the memorial video, listening to favorite music, wallowing and wailing when no one can hear. But far be it from me to order a public meltdown. However, as the run of the play goes on, a few people tell me that seeing the play might do me some good. Reviewers and friends alike rave about the piece. Besides, good art about a painful subject is preferable to bad art about a benign subject. One friend in particular makes a case for seeing the play, so I acquiesce. We go to a matinee.

I am, astoundingly, fine. I listen to the well-crafted arguments for and against facilitating the death of the husband suffering from cancer. I listen to the arguments for and against his wife taking her own life along with his. And then my chest constricts in the dark theater. Not because of these arguments for and against, but when the husband appears wearing khaki cargo pants, Laurence's everyday wear of choice. I listen to the words and I manage to stay largely in my head and out of my gut. I tear up at the end, but so does everyone else. No spectacle, I. Just another theatergoer, not a woman who lived the ordeal just condensed into two hours on the stage. Perhaps it is more difficult for everyone around me, everyone projected for two hours into that life out of their own, everyone imagining the sorrow. For me, fiction still cannot touch the truth.

My friend and I meet other friends for dinner and then join them for an improv show at The Groundlings Theater. Comedy for dessert after the entree of heavy drama. We take our seats directly behind the three-piece combo. I eye the drum set. My breath catches. We dismantled Laurence's drum kit to make more space for the memorial, and it has remained packed up ever since. I didn't realize how much I miss it in the corner of our study until this moment. I didn't even realize how much I miss Laurence at the drums.

Laurence would close the door to the study where the drums lived in order to muffle their noise. But sometimes the pounding would get to me even so. I would open the door and find him, headphones on, wailing on his kit.

"That's enough!" I'd shout, trying to be heard over the noise. "Enough!"

He'd perform one last flourish—snare, bass, cymbal.

Make all the noise you like, I want to say. *If you come back, you can play the drums all night.*

I look away from the drums in the darkened club, and return my attention to my companions' conversation. Just before the show starts, the lights go down and the musicians take their places. The drummer looks nothing like my husband, but when he picks up his sticks and starts to play, I might need to scream.

Such is grief. Sometimes it pounces from deep within the unexpected, even the absurd, because it is always there—waiting for when you let down your guard. The play's intellectual discourse, no matter how poignant or artfully constructed, could not pack the visceral wallop of a man picking up a pair of drumsticks and pounding out a beat in the dark.

I spend the rest of the show looking anywhere but directly in front of me, at the drummer punctuating the evening's silliness with a flourish—snare, bass, cymbal.

CHAPTER TWENTY

Cami returns to school in the fall. Moving her into an apartment becomes an exercise in biting our tongues about how badly we need Daddy. Between her computer, its accoutrements, and the cable TV, we struggle to do all the things Daddy would have done—that he did just last year, riding high at the supposed finish of the chemo. This year we hire people for certain tasks and attempt others ourselves. By the time everything is up and running, we are at once bleary and proud. And sad.

It is right that Cami should be living on her own again. When Laurence first died, I wondered if his job here was to be Cami's daddy, and that now she must be fully baked if he could leave. She is not. And yet she is. She is at an in-between age. Had she been younger and in need of everyday care—bathing, feeding, dressing—my days would take shape around her. Were she a bona fide adult, that, too, would provide its own structure. But now both our lives are similarly poised. We are both on the cusp of we-don't-know-what.

I leave my daughter in her new apartment and return home.

I have been steeled against the empty house for months. Laurence and I had just become acclimated to Cami's being away when he was diagnosed. I have gone from three to one in a heartbeat. I run the dishwasher only when I am out of teaspoons and mugs. When I walk into a room, it is exactly as I left it. There is no motor humming happily in the house anymore. Laurence was the motor. I am a ghost in my own home. Worse, I become cranky if anything disrupts my routine. I am becoming someone who lives alone.

When Laurence first died, the nights were the most difficult. Sundowners—that's what they call the syndrome that torments the old coots who roam the halls at dusk in veterans' hospitals and other such institutions. After some months, however, the mornings become the hardest. There seems no bigger challenge than getting out of bed. I lie there listening for the predawn thud of the newspaper hitting the driveway and wonder if it marks a day ended or a day beginning, uncertain as to which is the more treacherous. When I make it downstairs to the kitchen, I stare at the blank Sudoku in that morning paper and cannot remember how to solve it.

Weeks before I leave Cami at school, I realize that a plan is required. I need something to get me out of the house, something that obliges me to be at a certain place at a certain time. I know that the void will seep into any schedule I devise. I do not pretend otherwise. But I devise one nonetheless. I take a job— barely even part-time—in the writing lab of a local college. There I attempt to teach basic grammar to students who, for a variety of reasons, have reached college age without being able to identify a subject, verb, or prepositional phrase. I carve out as my particular challenge demonstrating grammar's relevance in their lives.

On Mondays and Wednesdays, the alarm goes off at six-thirty, and when I arrive home at two o'clock, I am so fatigued, I often fall asleep. Who knew the exertion required to explain comma placement would be such a blessing? I am grateful for sleep when I can catch it, but still spend most nights channel-surfing. To prove it, I am the proud owner of that wonder chopper/blender/party-with-a-rotating-blade known as the Magic Bullet.

I had believed that physically being in a place where Laurence had never been would mitigate the sensation that he should be there. I was wrong. One day in the writing lab at the college, I look up from where I am crouched next to a student, attempting to help him identify a topic sentence, and I swear Laurence is about to walk through the door. It just feels like he has been gone long enough. This room with the flickering overhead lighting, the institutional blue chairs, and the wood-grained laminate tables is as good a place as any for him to make his return appearance.

I go to this job for three months and never mention to any of my fellow "instructional assistants" that I am a widow. At first, this is not a conscious decision, but gradually it becomes one. Keeping this secret is at once liberating and oppressive. On the one hand, I am a normal person to my colleagues. On the other, I must constantly remind myself how to navigate conversations as though I were that normal person. When one woman mentions her husband, how do I respond? What tense do I use if I mention mine? I settle into, "My husband used to . . . ," implying a past that does not preclude his still existing in the present.

Inevitably, one day it comes out. My allusion to something my husband "used to do" requires further explanation. I don't want to, I don't intend to, but before I know it, I have said, "My husband died in January."

There it is.

One of the other women with whom I work says, "Wow, you'd never know it." This is meant as a compliment, but it leaves a strange taste. Once again, I feel like a fraud. Once again, I dive into the gulf between how I seem and how I feel. Once again, I stumble, tripping over who I am now.

My antennae stab the air to sense if suddenly, shrouded in widowhood, I have transmogrified into something else. I have now declared myself one of the walking wounded. Even casual acquaintances—these women I work with and others—begin to confide in me the most personal of anecdotes as though we are automatic compatriots in pain, members of a secret society whose initiation is fortune's slash to the heart. I keep friends' secrets, always have, but I realize now that I used to assume there was a tacit caveat: tell no one—but Laurence, of course. Now, other people's secrets are just so much baggage, added to the constant stream of thoughts that find no outlet. With no escape valve, surely an explosion must be imminent.

∽ ∼

You'd think you'd run out of tears, but you don't. After a while, crying just becomes something that you do every day. In the beginning, I had so lost my equilibrium that it seemed crucial to discern whether life was normal with an overlay of abnormal, or utterly abnormal masquerading as normal. It doesn't matter anymore. There will never be normal again. I blasted off from normal long ago, and it is now just a distant planet, alien and nearly forgotten. There will always be something wrong. There will always be someone missing. People say, "You will create a new normal. You will have a different life." Of course that will, by definition, be true, but it will never match the life I still live in my heart.

Friends seek to give me a gentle nudge into this new life, if not a hefty boot. Some gingerly suggest I move. Others simply assume a move will be forthcoming. The concern that my house holds "too many memories" is their oxymoronic refrain. Not so. There could not be too many memories. Memories are what I subsist on. Why would I leave this house, this treasure chest that holds them so snugly?

Nor could I move anyplace gloomy and overcast. Usually content with cozying up on gray days, I become hypersensitive to the weather. Not so much the weather as the light. Suddenly I require sunlight. I add to the alphabet soup of self-diagnosed disorders: seasonal affective disorder. SAD. Of course it is actually "season of life" affective disorder explained as a need for blue skies.

The truth is, it is easier to open the shades in the morning if the sun is shining. Laurence always used to do that—open the shades. It never used to occur to me. I don't mind that nesting dimness. But he was crazy for light. Both times we remodeled our home, he insisted that there could never be enough electrical outlets in a room. But mostly, he liked natural light. So he was the one who opened the shades. Now, I forget to some mornings. Others, I just don't feel like it. But many mornings, especially if the sun is shining, I open the shades and let the light in.

—   —

When I purchased the cemetery plots on the first of November, the lady in the black suit informed me the area would not be ready until April. I had told her that would not be a problem. We wouldn't need them for decades . . . years at least. I have lived through remodels before, so I was not surprised when April came and went and the new area was still under construction. Cami and I traveled to Europe and Laurence remained in Westminster.

Then it was May.

Then it was June.

There was talk of July. And then August.

We went to San Francisco and Laurence remained in Westminster.

"If anyone would want his place perfect, it would be Laurence." My standard line is not funny anymore. He would also be screaming at the contractor by now. So that's what I begin to do. The mortuary's chorus becomes, "Two more weeks."

They promise October. Early in the month, my sister, Mila, phones me one afternoon. She is furious. Her friend's mother has just died and the family had gone to "our" cemetery where they were informed that "our" area, as my sister definitively determined, would not be ready for at least another four to six months. Mila has already called the mortuary to yell. I make a follow-up call and add tears to the tirade.

They assure me they have no idea who provided that incorrect information. The contractors are making progress. It will be soon.

"When?"

"Soon."

Not good enough, I insist. I need satisfaction. I need an apology. I need a date.

I am fairly conflict-averse. I don't honk the horn that much. I never send back food in a restaurant. If it means avoiding a shouting match, I'll lose an argument even if I know I'm right. Especially in the past eighteen months, I have learned about whether or not to sweat the small stuff. (Don't.) Besides, I harbor no illusion that moving Laurence will afford me any peace.

Even so, I am moved to action. I send a threatening letter that includes words like "attorney" and phrases like "Better Business Bureau." I follow up with more phone calls. I become a nag, indignant and sarcastic. I invoke my daughter's trauma. I play both bad cop and good cop, appealing to their empathy. "I'm sure you understand." I say, "You must understand what this is like for us."

Within two weeks, there is a message on my machine informing me I can select a date. The area has been completed.

No sigh of relief. No satisfaction. No—the most vacant word—closure. Now that the date is set, there is no more process. Moving my husband to his final resting place will be . . . well, final.

I choose the Saturday after Thanksgiving so that my nieces will be in town. Only the very immediate family will be attending. No more speeches, please.

We celebrate Thanksgiving at my sister's as we have for twenty years. There is comfort in tradition—in turkey and wild rice dressing and far too many pies. Most thankfully, the three little ones in the family preoccupy us all. Cami had told me weeks before that she wanted to have everyone around the table say something about her father, but when the time comes, it doesn't feel necessary. We know that everyone around the table is thinking some version of the same thing. We are all thinking of Laurence.

Our niece, Emily, newly pregnant and a tad queasy, finds the Thanksgiving bread stuffing appealing. She heartily finishes a second helping. Then she smiles at me across the table and says, "I dedicate this performance to my Uncle Zippy."

The next day, Friday, I phone the cemetery mid-afternoon to double-check that everything is all-systems-go. They assure me and reassure me.

The phone rings at seven o'clock that evening.

"Just listen to me before you start screaming," says one of the black-suit ladies.

Again, I fall victim to Too Many Movies Syndrome. A montage of black comedy unspools in my mind's eye. My first reaction is that they have lost my husband. I picture a pileup on the 405, hearse door flying open, coffin sliding across the freeway into a ravine. All manner of funereal farce.

No. They know where he is. The woman is calling to inform me of a disaster movie of a different sort. Apparently, they had begun preparing the site and, upon removing the cover of the crypt—you cannot believe you are having a true-life conversation involving the word "crypt," let alone for your husband, you simply cannot believe it—they discovered that the hole in the ground, this hole we have so long been waiting for, was flooded. They have been pumping out the water for hours, but the hole keeps refilling as fast as the pump can pump, and the women in the black suits cannot figure out the source. "It could be from a swimming pool down the block for all we know."

Since the new construction included what they enticingly referred to as a "water feature" (a fountain), it seems unlikely that a neighbor's swimming pool is the culprit. Perhaps, I suggest, they should consider the water feature. For reasons that do not fully register, it has already been ruled out.

Cami and I jump in the car and drive to the cemetery, gearing up for a tantrum in stereo. And we deliver. Outrage in full tilt.

We are led by flashlight through the graveyard grounds to the infamous "area," though the flashlight is hardly needed. We can follow the sound of the pump. It reminds me of the sound of the pump attached to the hose that snaked down Laurence's gullet—rhythmic, mechanical, unsettling. The fountain has indeed been turned off and the water is indeed still gushing in. Neither Cami nor I had been particularly pleased with the aesthetics of how this long-touted water feature had turned out. The small, newly refurbished area is supposed to be highly desirable, with its granite markers and secluded setting, but I look across at the old part of the cemetery. It is simpler, more park-like. More Grover's Corners. I begin to wonder: even if they manage to straighten this matter out (or, more precisely, dry this matter out), there still might be a phone call in my future—in a month or six months or five years—informing me that the site is flooding again.

In short, I don't like this spot anymore. Take it back. I don't want it.

I stop shrieking long enough to ask if there is anything else available, as if I have arrived to pick up a new car and decided at the last minute that I want to check out a different model. Surprisingly, the ladies in black lead us to the older, original area of the small cemetery. They have recently discovered that one particular plot might be available. Ascertaining if this is actually the case will involve digging and probing and excavating. It will take a few days. (These ladies represent the management company that took over the cemetery just a few years ago; it seems that since the place dates back over a hundred years, apparently some areas are less . . . What? . . . Claimed?)

Although it's nighttime, Cami and I cross to this other area. It is situated under a massive moonlit tree. Two tall slender palms are visible farther off. Laurence and his palm trees. Both Cami and I know instantly that this is the spot.

I recall my first visit to the cemetery exactly one year earlier.

"This is what's going to happen," I had said. "I'm going to bring my husband here in three years, and he's going to scream at me for picking the wrong spot."

It didn't take three years, but he found a way to let me know, and, fittingly, for me to do all the screaming.

We go back the next morning and check out the new spot by daylight. I wander the surrounding area, studying the markers—some old and worn, others shiny and new. I do a lot of subtraction—year of birth from year of death—intent on discovering how long these people lived. Many lived into their seventies, eighties, even nineties. Others died in middle age, and some, tragically young. How naive I have been, assuming we are guaranteed old age.

There is no doubt. We prefer the new spot. We don't want the other one anymore. Let it flood.

We await word of this new spot's availability.

It comes a few days later. Yes, it is available. It is ours.

I ask one of the black-suit ladies what kind of tree it is that marks the spot. It is a camphor tree. Indigenous to China. Used medicinally, as in camphor oil. But also used in the original manufacture of celluloid. It's a film tree.

We look for signs.

And we reschedule.

It is too bizarre to explain. When friends ask if I have plans for the upcoming weekend, I cannot bring myself to say, "We are burying Laurence tomorrow morning, and then I might go to the movies on Sunday." But that's the way it is. On a bitterly cold December morning, more than ten months after he died, I bury my husband.

I was not an easy young child. In today's euphemisms, I would have been called challenging or strong-willed. I wanted my own way no matter what. There is a story told in my family of an incident when I was two years old. Someone had given me a stick of gum. I wanted to chew it at bedtime, but was told I had to wait until the next day. My mother and I went several rounds of "Now"/"Not now." I unwrapped the thing and stuffed it in my mouth. My mother reached into my mouth and grabbed it out, then flushed it down the toilet. I stood there, ready for bed in my footed pajamas. Regardless, I stepped into the toilet and flushed repeatedly, declaring, "I'm going down after it."

A lifetime later, we bring our boom box to the cemetery and Warren Zevon sings, imploring us (not long before his own death), "Keep me in your heart for a while."

My sister watches me watching my husband lowered into the earth and whispers to me, "I'm going down after it."

— —

I dread the holidays for months ahead of time. I decide that what Cami and I will need to do is make Christmas, like so many other traditions, the-same-but-different/different-but-the-same, though I am unsure exactly how. We begin debating tree/no-tree well before Thanksgiving. I know that I don't have the energy required to deck the halls, let alone the heart, but at the last minute, Cami insists that Christmas morning will be even more desolate without a tree. We compromise and decide to buy a scaled-down tree that will require just a couple of boxes of ornaments—that the rest of the house will remain undecked. Cami is, however, adamant about digging out all the bell ornaments. She doesn't have to say what she is thinking, this child who has celluloid in her blood.

"Teacher says, 'Every time a bell rings, an angel gets his wings.'"

As usual, my daughter's instinct proves more reliable than my own. The small tree in the corner where a bigger tree usually stands makes it feel a bit like Christmas.

In striving for the-same-but-different, Cami decides, too, that we will forego a gingerbread house and make gingerbread cookies instead. It must sound like Ozzie and Harriet live next door, but to us, Christmas includes the smell of cinnamon. We normally bake with Christmas music playing—Frank and Dean and Tony and the gang, but this year I draw the line at getting down from its high shelf the blue box covered with gold angels in which we keep our Christmas CDs. Embarrassingly, Andy Williams singing "O, Holy Night" moves me, an admitted heathen, to tears every year. I can only imagine what would happen this year.

So we play non-holiday fare on the stereo and break out the cookie cutters. Gingerbread men, bells, stars, the usual. And then Cami decides she wants to make wreaths. She improvises, using a plain round cookie cutter to make the initial cut and a spice bottle top to cut out the center. I put my cookie cutter down and watch as she takes a sharp paring knife and cuts a scrap of excess dough, then slices that long strand into two triangles and two shorter pieces, ends cut on the diagonal, to fashion a bow for the top of the wreath. We smile at each other over the sheet of unbaked cookies, knowing that is precisely how Daddy would have done it.

When Cami was three weeks old, she was hospitalized with what the doctor thought might be meningitis but turned out to be a mercifully minor infection. I swaddled her in a fringed blanket, already a favorite. When the pediatrician entered the room and looked at the tiny person in the vast hospital crib, he said, "She's got her blanket so she'll know who she is." I may not be able to listen to the usual Christmas music, but we decorate a tree. And we bake. And we tie ribbons around gifts. This year, especially this year, we wrap ourselves in our rituals so that we know who we are.

I go overboard shopping for presents for Cami, but have to circumnavigate men's departments all over town. I cannot bear crossing through them. I am nonetheless unable to stop myself from scanning the Sunday supplement with its book and DVD gift-giving suggestions. There are so many gift DVD sets I would have been buying, should have been buying: *The Man From U.N.C.L.E.* boxed set; the Coen Brothers boxed set; Ray Harryhausen, Special Effects Wizard; and more books than I can count.

On Christmas Eve, I usher Cami up to bed so that I can play Santa. In a quirk of heavy-handed imagery one would dare not invent were it not true, we are experiencing yet another of the many power failures we have had since Laurence died. The one on Christmas Eve lasts nine hours. I tuck a flashlight under my arm to light my way back and forth between the present closet and the tree. I scribble last-minute gift tags and stick on bows by candlelight. Suddenly I am haunted by an image of Laurence lying in his hospital bed, saying to Oncology Man with all assurance—but now, in hindsight, also with a tinge of desperation, "You're going to fix me up, right?"

As I feared, I am losing my foothold this Christmas Eve. Laurence's birthday.

Just as I had done one year ago, I nibble the cookies Cami left on the hearth. But last year, adrenaline coursed. We were still on a mission in our household. I was frantic and terrified, but not alone. This year, there is nothing left to fight. This year, the downsized tree is burdened with ornaments, and beneath it lie, in a stunning demonstration of overcompensating, more piles of packages than ever before. But also this year, the house is without heat and pitch dark.

SNAPSHOT

Laurence loved to cook. First of all, he loved to eat. But while his love of cooking centered around making wonderful food, it went beyond that. As with most great chefs, it had to do with giving. It had to do with presentation. It had to do with inventing. A sprinkle of fresh parsley, a dusting of toasted sesame seeds, the fan of an exquisite lemon. All these things graced our dinners even when it was just the three of us eating at the kitchen table on a school night.

It was our nightly refrain: "Daddy, you should open a restaurant."

Like most of what Laurence did, his cooking had to do with style. It had to do with creating.

When we were young, Laurence fell in love with cooking Chinese food. There was something so theatrical about it. All that prep—the shopping, the cubing, the marinating—the preproduction, if you will, before the main event; firing up multiple woks to blazing hot; stir-frying Day-Glo peppers with gleaming long-handled spatulas.

Even cleaning the woks afterward with boiling water and a bamboo brush whose bristles spread like an exotic blossom. Laurence found something satisfying to the soul in cooking Chinese food.

As the years passed, the business of everyday life interfered with devoting so many hours to chopping and dicing. Though the occasional Chinese dish ended up on our table, Laurence—our chef in residence—offered up dishes from other countries, or, more frequently, from his own imagination.

One day we discovered that a friend of Cami's lived in Danny Kaye's old house. Danny Kaye had been a renowned Chinese chef, having gone to the extent of building a second kitchen in his home—a Chinese kitchen. Laurence told Cami's friend that he would love to cook in that kitchen sometime. And then years went by.

Laurence had almost finished his chemo (what was destined to be the first round of chemo). He was feeling a bit ass-kicked, but all in all, pretty good—good enough to say yes when the invitation came to cook in Danny Kaye's Chinese kitchen.

If he gave any thought to planning the menu, he didn't mention it. The menu seemed to spring fully developed, as though it had been simmering on the back burner of his brain for a long time. It probably had. It featured his childhood favorites, dishes steaming under chrome domes when they were brought to the table at old L.A. favorites, Wan-Q or Ah Fong's.

Moo Goo Gai Pan. Sweet and Sour Shrimp. Beef Soo Chow. Laurence could remember a scene from a movie, shot for shot, or drum the backbeat of a song he'd heard only once. Similarly, he could cook something he had tasted only once with the same kind of sensorial expertise. He had eaten Beef Soo Chow, a signature dish from Ah Fong's, a thousand times. That one he had re-created with remarkably little experimentation years and years before. For

*the Danny Kaye kitchen extravaganza, he planned Cantonese clas-
sics that recalled simpler culinary times, before the advent of the
Szechwan craze, or the more-recent trend toward the precious chic
of unlikely fusions. Asia de Cuba, anyone?*

*Prepping at home, Laurence shopped and chopped. He mixed
and marinated. He sliced and slurried. He had to ask for our help,
Cami's and mine, because the neuropathy prohibited him from
touching anything cold. So he instructed Cami how to slice the
semi-frozen flank steak just so, wafer thin, at a slight angle to the
grain of the meat. I fetched items from the refrigerator as needed,
reprimanding him every time he forgot and reached for something
chilled.*

*He packed the car with shopping bags heaped with Ziplocs and
Tupperware, each ingredient in its own individual baggie, each
elegant garnish in its own little container. A box held special utensils: a wide metal spatula, a long-handled mesh strainer, a bamboo
brush for quick-scouring the wok.*

*It was a great day when Laurence took over Danny Kaye's
kitchen. Restaurant-quality flames shot from beneath the enormous woks. These were no home appliances; you could bathe a
toddler in one of these things. Laurence stirred together sauces and
fried the shrimp until they were golden crisp. He turned pieces of
chicken into perfectly tender morsels. And as for that Soo Chow—
he tossed a handful of rice noodles into hot oil and they promptly
puffed into crackling ribbons. Then he laid them on an enormous
platter and placed the beef—mahogany-glazed and glistening—on
top.*

*As our host stood by, watching in amazement, he mentioned
that he no longer ate beef, though he remembered Beef Soo Chow
fondly from his own childhood. He was an L.A. native just like*

Laurence, and his family had frequented Ah Fong's just as had Laurence's (and mine, too, for that matter).

By the time we all sat down in the dining room, our host couldn't resist. He decided to taste the special beef. With one bite, he was transported back to his childhood. We each served ourselves a spoonful or two of the beef, along with the other dishes. But our host, the non-meat eater, ended up sliding the giant platter in front of his plate so that he could polish it off, serving after serving. Laurence had delivered the Beef Soo Chow of his past. Exactly.

Laurence was drenched in sweat from manning the flames. He was tired from hours on his feet, prepping in our kitchen all morning and afternoon, and then cooking over those shooting flames into the evening. But he was thrilled. He had reveled in every moment. He had made the best Chinese food any of us had ever tasted.

And he had made it in Danny Kaye's famous Chinese kitchen.

CHAPTER TWENTY-ONE

There will come a day when Cami tells her husband about the daddy he never got to meet. And then her children after that. She will say, "I wish you could have known my daddy. You would have loved him so much, and he would have loved you so much." There is nothing we can do about that. My job is to stay as whole as possible so that she does not also have to say, "I wish you could have known my mother before—before something tore in her that could never be patched." There is a tear, of course, so deep and wide, thorough and profound, that it never will be patched.

But, as Anne Lamott reminds me:

If you haven't already, you will lose someone you can't live without, and your heart will be badly broken, and you never completely get over the loss of a deeply beloved person. But this is also good news. The person lives forever, in your broken heart that doesn't seal back up. And you come through, and you learn to dance with the banged-up heart.

I am not dancing yet. I cannot imagine dancing ever again, dancing without my partner, without his backbeat. But finally, there are moments, even occasional hours, when I am no longer drowning, either.

A few friends have shared snippets of conversations they had with Laurence at particularly vulnerable moments, when doubt overwhelmed him. He knew that Cami would be fine. He wasn't so sure about me. But he must have known, too, that I would do anything for our daughter, even if that meant keeping on keeping on when I didn't want to. We do things like that for our children. We live even when we don't want to, and they save us in that way. In my recurring nightmares of crazed gunmen exploding into whatever strange environment the dream has dropped me, I am often carrying a baby. I must protect this baby above all else. It is as though I suddenly find myself in a long-distance relationship. Very long-distance. My daughter keeps me anchored on this coast when the lure of the faraway one might otherwise tug irresistibly.

You get up in the morning because there is no other choice. You struggle to tap into that tiny itch in your brain, the itch that is just curious enough about what may happen next to keep you going. As a wise friend pointed out, "The difference between the past and the future is that you can be relatively sure of what happened in the past."

You learn that all the supposed either/or's can actually coexist, do coexist. Dividing lines blur, even dissolve before your eyes, within your very heart. Not now *or* never, but now *and* never. Hope *and* resignation. Faith *and* betrayal. Severed *and* inseparable. Life *and* death.

When Laurence was first diagnosed, we were assured that there would come a time when we would not think of the cancer every minute, every hour, even every day. That time never came for us. I have spent much of the past months wondering if there will ever come a time when I do not miss my husband so palpably every minute, every hour, every day. I cannot imagine such a time. I can only strive to believe that just as I had a momentary epiphany that I was not sick, a similar moment awaits that will remind me that I am alive, not straddling life and memory. Until then, my challenge has become to live anyway, without waiting for that moment to arrive.

Friends insist that one day I will realize I have "come out the other side." When I inform them I am no longer waiting, they say they know the time will come whether or not I am keeping watch. I entrust them with custody of that belief. I don't want it. It carries too heavy a burden. Waiting for normal preoccupied me for too long. I, such a novice, wondered how I could possibly live with the anxiety accompanying biannual scans, waiting for something to go that never gets *gone*. I lowered the bar for normal, then lowered it again and again—diagnosis, pathology report, recurrence, the pain worsening, worsening, worsening. Then I stopped lowering the bar, hung on for dear life, and plunged into a full-out free fall.

My secret is that I am not sure I want to land on the other side. I grapple with the wisdom of allowing the void to define me. But still, I bristle at the notion that it will all become easier. Why would I want it to? *Don't take this away from me. It is all that I have left.*

So there will be no more waiting. No more feeling that if I can just get through this day, then another day, this week, the next month, life will change; the pain will ease. This is not a phase. Each day brings me closer only to the next day, identical and equally without.

It is strangely liberating—abandoning the waiting. No longer on the lookout for the anguish to subside, for the yearning to slacken, for the thirst to abate, I must relax and ride the waves, however they crash.

All I can do is what I whispered to Laurence as he lay dying. Keep swimming.

SNAPSHOT

Sometimes I sit in the black sling chair that often cradled my husband's savaged body in the last few months of his life. It's a cheap collapsible canvas piece. I have no idea where it came from. But Laurence found it comfortable—something about the way it nestled the curve of his lower back. He sat there, often with a heating pad wedged just so, usually listening to music, but sometimes alone with his thoughts and his pain, staring at the bulletin board on the opposite wall of his home office.

An acquaintance had suggested Laurence print out a picture of Buddha, the healing Buddha to be exact, and Laurence did so, tacking a headshot-sized copy onto that bulletin board. Appropriately serene and sporting a topknot, he is the deep blue of lapis lazuli. He sits cross-legged, Buddha-style predictably, his left hand palm up, holding a bowl of miraculous healing nectar. His right hand is poised on his knee, palm outward, holding a magic plant which cures all diseases. In theory.

Laurence did his best to meditate on this azure fellow, to subjugate entreaties for his own health to the health and well-being of others, to generate such deep positive intention that he could cure himself from the inside out. Why not? The outside-in approach was not working.

I'm sure that my husband was better at meditating than I could ever be. He did not find the task of concentrating on his own breathing as burdensome as do I, nor did he have the same internal tick-tick-ticking that I do. But even so, meditating was not really his thing. I imagine that his eyes and mind frequently wandered to the rest of the bulletin-board landscape. Now mine do, too. That is what draws me to this chair—all the tidbits of years past, randomly tacked to a rectangle of cork.

Among them:

On the lower-left corner, a postcard Laurence designed as an invitation to a reading of one of our scripts. I remember thinking that he was taking too much time perfecting something that would end up in most people's trash cans. But there it is, a masterpiece of design, capturing the entire script in a series of images.

Above that, a photograph of the Pan-Pacific Auditorium, an icon of Streamline Moderne architecture and so quintessentially L.A.

A black-and-white doodle from who-knows-when that covers an entire piece of paper, done with a Rapidograph, I believe. Tiny, intricate squiggles undulating around and back in on themselves. It hearkens back to the kind of art produced by speed freaks in the '60s.

There's an original ticket to Woodstock given to us as a gift.

Three postcard-sized gouache abstracts Laurence painted many years ago.

A Christmas card from Cami, an intricately snipped origami snowflake.

The envelope that had held another card from her, from longer ago, on which "Daddy" is printed in silver glitter.

A flyer he designed for a gig by his band, The Lower Companions. "Get out yer rockin' shoes."

A picture of King Kong on top of the Empire State Building. When Laurence was a film major in college, he was required to take one acting class. While other budding auteurs performed monologues from Shakespeare and Arthur Miller, Laurence offered a speech from the movie, King Kong, *forever after quoting his favorite line: "The public . . . bless 'em."*

A drawing in crayon of three palm trees. Freehand, casual, sketchy, nearly a scribble, but strangely capturing the light hitting the trees.

A flyer for a drum teacher.

A friendship bracelet Cami wove at camp one year. Chevron stripes of yellow, orange, and green, capturing the sunshine and the grass for her daddy.

Articles torn from the newspaper and trade papers. Out-of-the-ordinary sights in London. How to best book travel plans online. New production companies or the results of the latest round of movie-biz musical chairs.

A favorite photo of Cami, age five, that Laurence took in the vacant lot that used to stand across the street from our house. Our own private park. Cami climbed trees there with her daddy poised below in case of a misstep. We erected a badminton net there summer after summer. In this picture, Cami is staring directly into her father's lens, her face partially obscured by tree branches.

Pictures of Cami and me. One in Hawaii. At the Mauna Lani on the Big Island, there sits a bench on your way to the Canoe House restaurant. It has been our tradition to take a picture on that bench during each visit. In this one, Cami is fourteen—the first of the bench pictures where she and I are the same size.

There is a postcard from Philippe's, the downtown L.A. home of the French dip sandwich. It was sent by our friend Elisha, though the card is so battered, its message is too smudged to read. It is addressed to Laurence at the apartment he lived in before we lived together. It is so old that under the street address is written, simply, "Beverly Hills, California." No zip code.

There is also a business card from Art's Deli, where "Every Sandwich is a Work of Art." On the front is a corned-beef sandwich, piled inches high, dripping with mustard. Once or twice during the months when Laurence was ill, I'd walk into his office and find him sitting there, supposedly communing with the healing Buddha, but more likely communing with the corned-beef sandwich. "We'll go for one of those when you're all better," I'd say. That would be a great day.

There is a stack of pages ripped from a steno pad on which Cami drew pictures for her daddy when he was in the hospital. I don't remember pinning them to his bulletin board, but I must have as I unpacked the belongings from his hospital bag in the days following his death. A hula girl. Fish puckering up for a smooch under the sea. A huge palm tree reaching high above Los Angeles, with a heart floating between the tree and the skyline.

And, in the upper-right-hand corner of the bulletin board, a Native American dream catcher. A circular web of straw-colored thread punctuated, off center, with a single malachite bead, and an amber feather dangling from the woven frame. An old colleague of Laurence's brought it to the memorial. He had, the card informed me, intended to deliver it to Laurence in the months preceding, but never got around to it.

That I do remember removing from its gift box and pinning to the bulletin board, hoping that somehow it was never too late to catch a dream.

EPILOGUE

As for life after death, there just might be. Cami's for sure. Mine, maybe. So much of me died with Laurence that maybe that much of him—at least that much of him—stayed alive in me. Sometimes it takes too much effort to remember that, and I give up. Other times, nothing seems more self-evidently true.

Time heals nothing. Time passes. That is what time does. Patterns change. Rhythms change. Habits erode and new ones, gradually, are formed. The pain does not diminish. The pain does not change. It becomes woven into the new patterns, the new rhythms, the new habits. In the beginning, you think you cannot live in this much pain. And still the pain does not go away. Time does not take away the pain. But somehow you are still alive. So what you learn is that you *can* live in this much pain, you *do* live in this much pain. You just do. That is what time does. It allows you to accumulate numbers of days lived in pain, one after the other—days that you would have believed would have killed you, but have not.

The accumulation of those days occasionally bolsters you. Sometimes, it brings only weariness. But that fatigue, that sheer exhaustion, can offer its own gift: the quieting of the brain chatter.

And that, occasionally, makes accumulating more days a bit less terrifying, and the patina of survival encrusts around your heart.

In the end, grief—like love—is simple. It is all-consuming and profoundly uncomplicated.

I had been fortunate. I was someone remarkably untouched by loss, now plunged into the deep end of grief. Carl Jung said, "You meet your destiny on the road you take to avoid it." I don't believe this was my destiny any more than I believe an early death was my husband's; yet, by definition, these were the fates we met. John Lennon said it more aptly: "Life is what happens to you while you're busy making other plans."

The night Laurence died, our daughter wailed, "How will we ever listen to music again? How will we ever eat food again?" In short, how will we ever know joy? We do those things now. We do them for him. We do them while we miss him, as we miss him, even because we miss him. And I begin to learn that my own joy has to be enough.

Sometimes, I try to avoid thinking about the things I miss. I know, rationally, that it does me no good to keep a mental list of these things, to dwell on the empty spaces. But the list is precious because it reminds me of what I had, and, in many ways, will always have—of how those spaces would not echo with such emptiness if they had not once been so full.

I was known. I was understood. Someone else in the world peered into the darkest corners of my soul and stuck around. He witnessed my meanest, my most vindictive, my most venomous—sometimes directed at him—and he chose to believe that there was a force inside me good and powerful enough to tip the scales in my favor. He knew what I thought, what I believed, where I failed, and he loved me with the in-spite-of and because-of all mixed up. Always coming up love. That is what I miss. Certainly, the being loved. But equally, the being known. Having someone whose very existence confirmed, "I know who you are. You are you."

I miss seeing myself reflected through the prism of someone who knew me and chose to love me. After all, if he loved me, I had to be worth something even at my worst, and we all need to be reminded of that more often than we are willing to admit.

I miss being part of something beyond myself, being part of an entity that was more than me. That Laurence-and-Carla, that synergism, in which I felt more myself than I do alone. This is not fodder for feminist attack. This was not a phenomenon that involved a dissolving of the self, but rather an enrichment of the self. This was no "You complete me." It was a question of being comfortable with myself—more comfortable with him than with anyone else, of course—but also more comfortable, more the inhabitant of my own skin, with him than when I am alone.

I miss having a reason to scream when I see a spider.

I miss having a partner in parenting. In the challenging times, I am alone at the wheel. Worse, in the exuberant times, I am also alone. My pride in the person our daughter has become—even though her father is so present, so alive in her—is left only to me.

I miss watching Laurence's face when our daughter walked into the room. She couldn't pass within ten feet of him without his saying, "I'll take a hug." And he knew how lucky he was that no matter how old she got, she was always happy to oblige.

I miss looking at a face I know as well as my own.

I miss my best friend. Being something of a misanthrope (I can hear Laurence now: "*Something* of a misanthrope? There's no something about it!"), I married the person I liked best.

I miss my writing partner who never settled for good enough, who always made my work better.

I miss feeling taken care of, looked out for, protected, part of a team. Being a solo act is exhausting and nowhere near as much fun. Especially when you are still doing two-part harmony in your head.

I miss being held together. Held up. Just held.

I miss the love of my life. During the first several years of Cami's life, when both Laurence and I were in the throes of falling in love with her, new and fresh every day, I had decided that maybe the big revelation—the marvelous surprise—is that you give birth to the love of your life. This child was the love of our life, of our life together. The instant Laurence was gone, I knew that wasn't true, not singly true. I had indeed married the love of my life, as reticent as I had been for so long to confess it. Apparently, everyone around us saw this is as a given—*You two led a charmed life*, they say—but we had woven the fabric of our life so tightly knit that I couldn't see it anymore, particularly once our daughter came along and lit up everything so brightly. Maybe this phenomenon, this wild and intense focus, is unique to families with only children. I don't know. Maybe it doesn't matter. Maybe being a family—with however many loves of your life that may bring—is all that matters. Counting love makes no sense.

I miss sharing a history.

I miss looking forward to a shared future.

I miss assuming there is all the time in the world.

I miss believing the best is always yet to come. The caterpillar cocoons and then dissolves away, so that the butterfly can be born from the merest traces of what that creature used to be. I try to shove myself into that metaphor, but cannot make it fit. I am no longer waiting for gossamer flight. If and when I struggle free of this cocoon, I will be content to inch along the ground.

I miss making dinner with my husband and suddenly finding ourselves dancing in the kitchen to the Beatles, to Michael Franks, to Frank Sinatra singing "Our Love Is Here To Stay."

I miss knowing exactly what Laurence would say.

I miss his saying something unexpected. And making me laugh.

I miss his not having to say anything at all to know precisely what he was thinking.

What I am grateful for is having a husband who said exactly what I expected, who said something surprising and made me laugh, and who never had to say anything at all.

Whatever richness I have known in my life comes from having been able to share it so completely. It may be the kind of quote adolescent girls write in their diaries, but what Tolstoy said is true: *All, everything that I understand, I understand only because I love.*

There are moments when you know this so completely, so fully, and with such peace, that you think you could never possibly forget this simple truth. Sometimes—usually—those moments come when you least expect them, where you least expect them: as you turn onto your neighborhood cul-de-sac, waiting in line at an amusement park, in the courtyard of a ramshackle school between classes. These moments, this love, this Earth. As Laurence said—that is where heaven is.

ACKNOWLEDGMENTS

My family's support for this book has been surpassed only by their support for me. They have cried with me—and, I know—without me. They have reminded me how to laugh as well. I thank: my mother, Mona; my brother-in-law, Tom; Alison and Simon; Emily and Boz; the spectacular Mila, Stella, Charlie, and Thomas Karl; and most especially, my sister, Mila, who is quite simply, the best sister imaginable.

I am only just beginning to understand the depth and breadth of what my father taught me, but this I know. He taught me to work hard on everything you care about and to care passionately about everything you work on. I am grateful he got to read this book. He was my safe harbor and I miss him every day.

I thank my Starkman family for keeping my daughter and me in their fold.

Thanks to my agents, Ellen Pepus of Signature Literary Agency and Ken Sherman of Ken Sherman Associates. When others were afraid of a "cancer book," Ellen knew this was a love story. And Ken was there from the start. I also thank my editor, Mary Norris, who received this project with sensitivity and kindness.

I thank Rod Maxwell for making picture-taking as painless as possible.

I thank Bess Petlak for helping me secure the clearances that allowed me to cite more than my share of other people's words.

Several early readers offered more than encouragement, both professional and personal. They were never afraid to let me know how much they, too, miss Laurence, because they knew having partners in the missing is the one thing that makes it easier. They continue to hold my hand for the long haul. I am indebted to them all: Deborah Maxwell Dion, Stephen Farber, Judith Fuller, Cathy Heiliger, Lesley Karsten, Richard Saul, Carol Schneider, Andrea Sobel.

In particular:

I thank Leslie Jacobs, dearest friend of my youth, for always being a phone call away during that last pass.

I thank Jim and Dana House who hawked my manuscript to reading groups up and down the coast of California. Their persistent enthusiasm buoyed me time and again, and Jim's assurances that Laurence would be proud of this book mean more than I could ever say.

I thank Norman Beil who provided legal expertise and technical support, and, more important, repeatedly argued that this was a book, no matter if it was a stack of pages in a FedEx box. (And for having the patience to piece together that jigsaw puzzle when the writing was done.)

I thank Blair Richwood whose support for this book took

too may forms to enumerate. Her indignation at moments of disappointment and her celebration at moments of promise were not just on my behalf; they were shared with me . . . because, let's face it, though we dragged ourselves there reluctantly, we crossed into the land of friendship.

As for my daughter, Cami—you remind me every day that life is still big. You and I know there will always be three of us.

And to Laurence who informs every moment. Still.

PERMISSIONS

Dear Mr. Fantasy
Words and Music by James Capaldi, Chris Wood and Steve Winwood.
Copyright ©1968 Universal/Island Music Ltd. and F.S. Music Ltd.
Copyright Renewed.
All Rights for Universal/Island Music Ltd. Controlled and
Administered in the United States and Canada by Universal-Songs of
Polygram International, Inc.
All Rights for F.S. Music Ltd. Controlled and Administered by
Warner-Tamerlane Publishing Corp.
All Rights Reserved. Used by Permission.
Reprinted by Permission of Hal Leonard Corporation.

Volare
Music by Domenico Modugno English Lyric by Mitchell Parish.
Original Italian Text by Domenico Modugno and Francesco Migliacci
© 1958 (renewed) Edizioni Curzi, Milan, Italy.
Rights in the U.S. and Canada Administered by EMI Robbins Catalog,
Inc. (Publishing) and Alfred Publishing Co., Inc. (Print).
All Rights Reserved.
Used by Permission of Alfred Music Publishing Co., Inc.

ABOUT THE AUTHOR

CARLA MALDEN graduated magna cum laude from UCLA with a Bachelor of Arts in English and was inducted into the Phi Beta Kappa Society for her academic achievement.

Malden has been a screenwriter and published author for more than twenty years. She began her career as the assistant to renowned director Elia Kazan on his last film and went on to work extensively in motion picture production and development. With her husband and screenwriting partner, Laurence Starkman, she co-wrote many screenplays and produced and wrote several short films that won awards at festivals throughout the country.

Along with her father, Academy Award–winning actor Karl Malden, she co-authored his critically acclaimed memoir, *When Do I Start?*, which was hailed as "a joy to read, written with passionate intensity" and "the best of the bunch." Booklist remarked, "Carla Malden tells [this] story engagingly and literately."

Carla Malden lives in Brentwood, California, where she is completing her first novel. She is also working on a children's book with her daughter, Cami Starkman, who currently attends the American Film Institute.